Ninya Mikhaila and Jane Malcolm-Davies

THE TUDOR TAILOR

Reconstructing 16th-century dress

with additional research by Caroline Johnson and illustrations by Michael Perry

Costume and Fashion Press
an imprint of
Quite Specific Media Group, Ltd
Hollywood

First published 2006
Reprinted 2008, 2012, 2014

Printed and bound by 1010 Printing International Ltd, China
for the publisher
Batsford
10 Southcombe Street,
London, W14 0RA
www.anovabooks.com

First published in the United States of America
by Costume & Fashion Press/Quite Specific Media
an imprint of
Silman-James Press, Inc
email: info@silmanjamespress.com

(323) 661-9922 voice, (323) 661-9933 fax

ISBN-13: 9780896762558

Other Quite Specific Media Group Ltd. imprints:
Drama Publishers
By Design Press
EntertainmentPro
Jade Rabbit

Design by Lee-May Lim
Additional research by Caroline Johnson
Illustrations by Michael Perry
Photography by Henrietta Clare
Pattern digitizing by Complan Technology

CONTENTS

Acknowledgements

All reliable research stands upon the shoulders of previous giants. The inspirational work of Janet Arnold and F G Emmison has provided many of the puzzle pieces with which we have worked to produce our picture of 16th-century dress.

Our grateful thanks go to the team of costumed interpreters at Hampton Court Palace (1992–2004), who wore our early experiments in reproduction clothing, reported on their usefulness and then agreed to try the next prototypes. Daily wear and discussion with the visiting public have been key ingredients in the process of demystifying clothes of the Tudor era.

We would also like to thank the following people who have provided encouragement, tested patterns, been photographed in reproduction costume or commented on the text for this book (and in some cases all four):

Sarah Augbaya, Holly Bailey, the curators at Bayerisches Nationalmuseum in Munich, Lucy Capito, Bess Chilver, Suzi Clarke, Valerie Cumming, Alexandra de-la-Haye, Colin Dixon, David Hicks, Caroline Johnson, Rita Kelly, Emily Knapp, Drea Leed, Jessica Laslett, Constance Mackenzie, Pam Macmillan, Susan North, Michael Perry, Roy Porter, Luke Purser, Laura Rushton, John Sherlock, Matthew Tyler-Jones, Louise Wheeler and Catherine Weiss.

Any remaining errors are our own. Please visit www.tudortailor.com to tell us about them.

We began our careers in costumed interpretation as volunteers at Kentwell Hall's annual re-creation of Tudor life in Suffolk, England, where we were inspired by the power of dress to communicate ideas about the past. We hope that our book will encourage others to discover more about 16th-century people and their world.

Jane Malcolm-Davies, Godalming
Ninya Mikhaila, Nottingham

FOREWORD

It is fitting that I write this foreword on 31 October 2005, Hallowe'en being one of the prime dressing-up occasions in contemporary western society. Dressing up has evolved dramatically in the past 40 years. From entertainment, both amateur and professional in a wide variety of media, costume has taken on an important educational purpose. Historical reenactment is now both hobby and industry – an imaginative recreational pursuit as well as a key interpretive activity in tourism and historic sites around the world. Increasing knowledge of the past drives an ever-growing demand for accuracy in re-enactment. In turn, historical interpretation voraciously seeks new information from current research in archaeology, art, social and dress history.

The Tudor Tailor is a superb compilation of new and current research on 16th-century dress, with the prime purpose of encouraging accurate reproduction dress. The combined talents of the authors in dress history and clothing construction offer a well-researched and extremely practical approach to the subject. New visual sources and studies of 16th-century documents provide valuable factual evidence. Drawing on a wide range of recent secondary sources that include economic history, climate change, archaeology and the history of medicine, the authors examine in detail the physical characteristics and social importance of dress at all levels of Tudor society. Based on in-depth study and long experience of making and wearing reproduction dress, the patterns provide complete ensembles for both men and women.

This book has much to offer a range of readers. The principles of reconstruction and re-enactment clearly defined in the first chapter are useful guidelines applicable to the dressing of any period of history. Teachers and students dressing a school play or pursuing a history project will find straightforward and useful information and instructions. For costumiers of the stage and film, the advice on fabrics, accessories and construction will ensure a convincing result. Students and scholars of dress history will find excellent information on 16th-century clothing in the first four chapters, with carefully assessed evaluations of appropriate visual and documentary sources and how they can be employed in research. Re-enactors, historical interpreters and those running such programmes in cultural institutions will find this book an excellent guide to planning and executing visually exciting and sartorially accurate activities.

Properly researched, accurately made reproduction historical costume has an important role beyond the stage or historic site. It operates as a form of empirical research or laboratory experiment for dress history. Clothing has a functional as well as decorative purpose; each garment must work as an article of attire encasing the body yet able to accommodate regular movement. The proof is in the wearing. It is impossible to use surviving historical dress to discover whether details actually work: whether the wearer can walk, sit down, ascend and descend stairs in a particular style of garment. In addition, reproduction dress re-creates the dynamic splendour of clothing of the past. Movement can be considered the fourth dimension of dress – one that portraiture and museum display can never capture. The sweep of a cloak, the flow of a train and the ripple of a veil, which might otherwise be forever lost to us, come alive in the carefully studied, skilfully made re-creation of historical dress.

The Tudor Tailor is an excellent guide to understanding and re-creating the splendour of 16th-century dress.

Susan North
Curator of 17th- and 18th-century fashion
Victoria and Albert Museum

1. Pinked silk doublet, 1610–1625 (inventory no. T4094)
Bayerisches Nationalmuseum in Munich, Germany.

1. MAKING A START

**Know first who you are; and then adorn
yourself accordingly**
Epictetus (55–135AD)

Fragments of 16th-century clothing are scattered all over the world (fig 1): shoes
in a monastery in Germany, the frame of a headdress in London, a trunk full of
murder victims' clothes in Sweden, a silk jerkin in Los Angeles and an
embroidered bodice in Tokyo. These are some of the frustratingly small clues that
hint at the hidden world of historical clothes. The demanding detective work
required to reconstruct the dress of a long-gone 16th-century person is daunting,
and yet, as with any good mystery, the discoveries along the way promise to be as
exciting as the solution.

Four main sources of evidence are available for scrutiny. Each has its strengths
and weaknesses. Together, they provide a richer insight into the clothes of the past
than would any single source. There is a natural tendency to give pictorial
references premier position over the other three, which are written documents of
the period, the archaeological record and research by reputable costume historians.
Only this last resource deliberately sets out to provide a clear record of what was
being worn, by whom and for what, at a specific date. When studying the other
sources, the motivation of their originators and the processes that resulted in their
preservation are important considerations.

The most detailed visual references are portraits, which provide not only
form but both colour and a treatment of texture that can be of great use in
understanding fabrics. However, compared with later centuries, Tudor portraits are
relatively rare. They are formal, and until the 1530s show only the upper body
from the front. Paintings and drawings can be more helpful: for example, *The
field of the cloth of gold* shows a gentleman's gown from behind (fig 7), and
Holbein offers a rare and crucial look at the back of a 1540s lady (fig 2) plus the
detail of a shoe (fig 3). Illustrative prints in books and representations of the dead
on church monuments (fig 4) have their own limitations, especially where
questions of date are concerned. Whatever the medium, all representations require
careful interpretation. Often, discussions of a painting as a work of art, including
its symbolism and social significance, are of more relevance than works dealing
specifically with costume. However, there is no substitute for looking (at length
and often, if possible) at original paintings.

As with pictures, when it comes to written matter from the 16th century the
relative value of different sources has to be assessed. The vivid word pictures of
Stubbes' *Anatomie of Abuses*, for example, are coloured by his moralizing.

2. (top) *Two views of a woman wearing an English hood* by Hans
Holbein, c. 1528–30 (© The Trustees of the British Museum,
London). 3. (bottom) *A lady walking* by Hans Holbein, c. 1540
(© Ashmolean Museum, Oxford).

4. A weeper wearing contemporary dress in a monument to Sir George Vernon and his two wives, Margaret and Matilda, 1567 at All Saints' Church in Bakewell, Derbyshire (© Ninya Mikhaila and Jane Malcolm-Davies).

For John Basset – he hath never a good gown but one of camlet … very ill fashioned, but it is now a'mending. His damask gown is nothing worth, but if it be possible it shall make him a jacket, because his coat of velvet was broken to guard his camlet gown.
1535, The Lisle Letters, 826

Similarly, playwrights exaggerate for dramatic effect and court gossips to increase their own importance or according to their political prejudices. Documentary evidence is riddled with bias – what one observer regards as outlandish may be commonplace to another – and is rarely provided by a trained eye. Most historical commentators (ambassadors, playwrights, essayists and the like) are not garment makers. They are ignorant as to how their own clothes are constructed, let alone those of others. This is a problem exacerbated by cultural and language differences, since observers noting their comments are often visitors from other regions or countries.[1]

Some of the most detailed and reliable information is to be gleaned from the most mundane of sources, such as personal letters from the country commissioning purchases in town, or routine household accounts. Records covering a number of years can permit tentative generalizations about the size of a person's wardrobe or the proportion of their clothing that was made of silk. Two sets of records can allow a comparison between two different ranks in society.

When it comes to archaeological remains, there is very little surviving 16th-century clothing. It is not that textiles do not survive four centuries – there are tapestries of the same period still going strong – but that clothing textiles were just too valuable to leave in the wardrobe or pack away in the attic once the garments were outgrown or outdated. When Lady Lisle's daughters went to court, they required new gowns, but each had two kirtles made out of the fabric of old gowns that were no longer fit to wear.[2]

What does exist is fragmentary and rarely representative of more than one person at a particular place and time. The items of male dress from the excavation of the *Mary Rose* (an English ship which sank in 1546) are invaluable in providing a mass of individual accoutrements. However, there are major styles, fashionable for decades, of which there are no extant examples. Most of the garments in existence are very fragile and available for examination only with an appointment. Access to some of these items is provided by one of Janet Arnold's invaluable books, *Patterns of fashion: the cut and construction of clothes for men and women c. 1560–1620*. This provides highly detailed scale drawings of garments, diagrams of the pattern pieces required, together with photographs and drawings of details, to demonstrate tailoring techniques, fastenings and linings.

Arnold's introduction is a scholarly essay on tailoring, textiles, fashion and the obtaining and wearing of clothes, copiously illustrated with photographs of garments and reproductions of lesser-known contemporary pictures. Sadly, the book cannot be comprehensive because so many styles and types of garments common in the 16th century have not survived to enter museum collections. The majority of the items discussed may be of limited relevance to cultural contexts other than their place of origin (for example, Sweden or Italy). As with paintings, there is no substitute for examining the items themselves. There are many of the surviving examples which are yet to be treated to exhaustive scrutiny.[3]

It is useful to consider another book which distils a lifetime's experience: Jean Hunnisett's *Period costume for stage and screen: patterns for women's dress 1500–1800*. Only the early part of the book refers to the 16th century, and men's clothes are not discussed. However, compared with Janet Arnold's book, this one approaches the matter from the other end of the process in that it starts with the need to reproduce wearable costume rather than the details of existing garments. This said, the book is based on an excellent knowledge of fashion history and period cutting.

Most secondary sources rely on pictorial evidence rather than the study of actual garments or contemporary documents. It is important to recognize that secondary sources frequently disagree and the date of an author's work is highly pertinent – the confident assertions of earlier costume scholars have been reassessed as research has become more rigorous. Some historians have been misled by changes in terminology over time; for example, 'cotton' denotes two different fabrics in the 16th and 19th centuries. Secondary sources often include drawings from primary sources that betray the artist's ignorance of construction techniques.

Once all four sources have been thoroughly exhausted, attention turns to the body on which the costume is to be worn. It is often thought that people are bigger today than they were in the past, and that this makes accurate reconstruction of historical dress impossible. This is not true. Research into the sizes of skeletons reveals that height and limb length fluctuates through time (see table 1). Work at the Museum of London has shown that residents of the city grew near enough to today's average height from the Roman era: 'There were tall and small people in all periods of London's history, although in the 18th and 19th centuries the average height of the inhabitants was at its lowest.'[5]

Specific evidence from the 16th century is provided by the skeletal remains of the men drowned on the *Mary Rose*. Their left femurs were used to calculate heights, which ranged from 5ft 3in (1.6m) to 5ft 11in (1.8m). The average height was 5ft 7in (1.7m). Careful comparisons with records of military conscription in subsequent centuries suggests that the ship's crew were 'not as tall as the tallest modern Dutchmen or Scandinavian men, [but] they were no shorter than their modern counterparts.'[6]

5. The Tudor tailor was overwhelmed by a bewildering choice, according to Borde: 'And naked I stand here' from *The first boke of the introduction of knowledge*, 1542.[4]

Table 1: London body heights

Period	Male Feet & Inches	Male Centimetres	Female Feet & Inches	Female Centimetres
Prehistory	5ft 7in	170	5ft 2¼in	158
Roman	5ft 6¾in	169	5ft 2¼in	158
Saxon	5ft 8in	173	5ft 4¼in	163
Medieval	5ft 7½in	172	5ft 3in	160
Tudor	5ft 7½in	172	5ft 2¼in	158
Georgian	5ft 7¼in	171	5ft 1¾in	157
Victorian	5ft 5½in	166	5ft 1¼in	156
1998	5ft 9in	175	5ft 3¾in	162

There is also incredulity nowadays about the quantity of clothes worn in the past. Studies of climate history suggest that 16th-century people needed more garments than we do. Although the first half of the 16th century was genial (in comparison to the heat of the Middle Ages) and there were warm springs and summers from 1520 to 1560, there were three very cold years, from 1527 to 1529, when the Thames froze. From around 1560, temperatures dropped significantly. The weather became stormier and one of the coldest eras of 'Little Ice Age' began, albeit with some years less severe than others. The summers of the 1570s were very cold, although the 1590s was the coldest decade. Climate data suggests that the temperature in Europe was between 0.5 and 2.0°C cooler than it was from 1901 to 1960 (equivalent to a change of between 0.9 and 3.6°F), and the latter period was cooler than it is today by at least 1.0°C (1.8°F).[7]

On average, the 16th century was colder than today by at least two degrees celsius. This may not sound much, but it takes a drop of only five degrees for

… deliver yearly to Mary Russell, being at our finding, asmuche damaske as will make her a gowne and velvet to garde the same, with lyning, making, lace & silke for the same, asmuche yelow damaske as will make her a french kirtell with edging lyning and making, asmuche grosgrain chamlett as will make her gowne and velvet to garde the same with making lyning lace & silke for the same …

1554, Mary Tudor's accounts

6. A portrait of an unknown woman, 1568 (© Ninya Mikhaila).

7. Detail from *The field of the cloth of gold,* artist unknown (The Royal Collection © 2005 Her Majesty Queen Elizabeth II)

glaciation to occur. The people of the 16th century needed to wrap up more warmly than we do (fig 6), especially in homes with earth floors and even in palaces, where tapestries and rush matting could not keep the chill wind at bay. On warmer days, the populace were not in the habit of throwing off their clothes as we do. Contemporary depictions of bare heads, disordered dress or nakedness signalled distraction, madness or poverty.[8] The way reconstructions are worn is crucial to their success as communication tools. Standing up straight, keeping still, walking as though God is ever watching, and respectfully reverencing one's betters with a bow or curtsy were all necessary to avoid drawing critical attention to oneself in the 16th century.[9] Reconstructions are best worn with the same mindset.

It is wise to have decided the aim of a costume project before it begins. There is an identifiable hierarchy of activities: replication, reconstruction and re-creation. The first is an attempt to duplicate an extant item exactly; the second involves some justifiable speculation; and the third uses guesswork and imagination. This book is primarily concerned with reconstruction.[10]

The aim of the project will also determine the integrity with which the costume is used once it is made. It is better to be clear that an item is the product of a creative process rather than an investigative one for the benefit of the end user – the visiting public, the audience or the student. A key issue in this regard is the notion of 'authenticity'. The word has moved beyond its original meaning, which is 'genuine', according to the *Oxford English Dictionary*. 'Is it authentic?' is the old-fashioned (and grammatically correct) way of posing the question, and this requires a yes or a no answer. If a garment is an original, it is authentic. If it is a replica, a reconstruction or a re-creation, it is not authentic. The often-asked question 'How authentic is it?' demonstrates that the word now represents a scale on which to measure costume. 'Accuracy' better reflects what is under discussion. The more accurate a reproduction costume is, the more valuable it will be as an educational tool.[11]

What constitutes an accurate costume is rarely defined. One commentator contrasts 'totally stylistic' costume with 'historically accurate' costume, the former being inspired by historical sources rather than true to them in every detail.[12] Accuracy relates to both materials and construction method. In the 16th century, clothes moulded the body, rather than the other way around. The paper pattern had not yet appeared and the modern use of darts to eliminate wrinkles was unknown. Tailors often sewed certain kinds of garments only. They worked with a team of specialists, including professional hosiers, cappers, farthingale makers and embroiderers. It is a tall order for one person in the 21st century to reproduce an outfit that was the work of an army of experts in the 16th century. An accurate costume requires considerably higher investment (in terms of research, materials, specialist labour and time) than a stylized costume. However, this higher investment pays off in terms of its educational value.[13]

Whatever specific purpose a costume has (for a play, an interpreter or as a study piece), it serves as a form of communication, which means there is a great deal more than the garment itself to consider. Successful interpreters and educators use their clothes as entrées to topics as diverse as politics, economics, trade, conquest and culture. Each garment has a cultural biography, courtesy of the society that made it. A reconstruction takes shape as a biography is built for it.[14]

The cultural biography of a garment is linked to that of its wearer. In the 16th century, dress played a conventional role as shorthand for the wearer's financial and spiritual worth. Plato, the Bible, Erasmus and Shakespeare all agree that clothes demonstrated a person's inner self through exterior display.[15] Clothes demanded a higher proportion of people's incomes than is the case today. The cost of a suit of clothes was equal to a year's salary for many Tudor people. In 1533, a man with an annual income of £4 might spend up to 6s 8d a yard on his gown fabric, by law. The yardage required would cost one third of his £4 a year. The Earl of Leicester paid more for one item of clothing than Shakespeare paid for a house in Stratford-upon-Avon.[16] Decisions as to what to wear were on a par with setting up home. Clothes were accumulated over time and gradually constructed an individual's public self. They displayed gender, age, marital status, position in the family and social status. Clothing was an index to income, household, occupation and the type of work undertaken by the wearer. At a broader level, dress was influenced by geographical location, religion, and the availability of labour and materials. In any society where there are few possessions, clothes unite symbolism, aesthetics, utility and financial investment.[17]

Many of these aspects of an individual's clothes are defined by reference to others in society. They are not clearly identified as opposites, such as old/young or rich/poor, but as gradations along an imprecise spectrum. Tudor society comprised four 'sorts', according to a contemporary commentator: gentlemen (including the nobility), citizens or burgesses, yeomen artificers and labourers.[18] There were approximately 50 noble families, 350 knightly families, and 10,000 esquires or gentlemen in a population that rose from two and a half million in 1500 to four million in 1600.[19]

Styles of dress, colours and fabrics were conventionally assigned to the various ranks of society, but it is difficult to ascertain with certainty which belonged where. Social mobility, sumptuary laws, local custom and convention all played a part in determining what people wore. A contemporary crowd scene (figs 8 and 9) is invaluable in providing a range of social types who can be compared and contrasted to exemplify similarities and differences in dress. Reproductions also acquire meaning in comparison with others within, for example, a team of interpreters, the cast of a play, or participants in a re-enactment.

To know who you are in Tudor society was less about understanding yourself and more about knowing your place. Clothes did not broadcast the wearer's individuality but rather where s/he fitted into society. A long look at the individuals represented in *Study for a family portrait of Thomas More* (fig 10) reveals a range of people, each of whom knew their place and adorned themselves accordingly.

8 and 9. Details from *The Fête at Bermondsey* by Joris Hoefnagel, c. 1570 (courtesy of the Marquess of Salisbury).

10. *Study for a family portrait of Thomas More* by Hans Holbein, c. 1527 (© Kunstmuseum Basel, Kupferstichkabinett).

Ordinary people's clothing

A1 Farm worker c. 1500

A2 Farm worker c. 1500

A3 Gentlewoman 1511

A4 Gentleman 1511

A5 Soldier 1513

A6 Miner c. 1550

A7 Tradesman 1547

A8 Villager 1559

A9 Farm worker 1565

A10 Gentlewoman 1568

A11 Citizen 1563

A12 Countrywoman 1570

A13 Soldier 1572

A14 Doctor 1562

A15 Townswoman (undressed) 1572

A16 Countryman before 1588

A17 Musician 1588

A18 Gentlewoman 1604

A19 Servant c. 1600

A20 Nightwatchman c. 1600

A21 Pudding seller c. 1600

A22 Mat seller c. 1600

Clothing of the elite

B1 1500s

B2 1510s

B3 1520s

B4 1530s

B5 1540s

B6 1550s

B7 1560s

B8 1570s

B9 1580s

B10 1590s

C1 1500s

C2 1510s

C3 1520s

C4 1530s

C5 1540s

C6 1550s

C7 1560s

C8 1570s

C9 1580s

C10 1590s

For further details, see Footnotes, page 158

2. CLOTHING THE PEOPLE

Two fayre new kirtles to her backe
The one was blue the other black …
She had three smockes, she had no lesse
Thomas Churchyard, 1575

Histories of 16th-century dress usually chart chronological changes through the clothes of the top three to five percent of people. They concentrate on what was fashionable rather than what was ubiquitous. This chapter discusses the main garments worn by the majority of people in Tudor England from birth to the grave.

The range of clothes available to men and women was distinct to each sex with few exceptions and changed little in basic form throughout the 16th century. Gender roles were reinforced by notions of propriety in dress. Equally influential were the conventions appropriate to rank and status. A person's place in society was identifiable by the quality of their clothes and the number of garments available for them to wear. These conventions remained remarkably static despite the 16th century's dynamism in terms of trade, exploration and the arts.

Clues to ordinary people's dress have been gleaned for this book from a variety of sources, including an extensive survey of Elizabethan wills from Essex. Ten volumes contain 10,630 documents with 2,230 references to clothing. Although wills were rarely made by the very poor, and the majority of the testators are described as husbandman or yeoman, there are also a good number written by labourers, sailors, servants and the lower sorts of craftsmen and tradesmen, such as carpenters, blacksmiths, bakers and butchers. Women, unfortunately, are described only as widows or single women (wives having no property of their own to bequeath). However, they are likely to be of the same social levels as the men represented.

Nearly everyone began and ended their life wrapped in linen of some kind. A baby was swaddled in linen bands for most of his or her first year. A nursing manual published in 1612 advises that children be completely swaddled for the first month. Thereafter, their arms were free, until eight or nine months, when swaddling was abandoned.[1] A shoemaker's wife lists what was necessary for a baby in its early years: 'Beds, shirts, biggins, wastecoats, head-bands, swadlebands, crosse clothes, bibs, tailclouts, mantles, hose, shooes, coates, petticoat.'[2] The bed was a cloth which lay under the body and was folded up over the feet and pinned at the breast. Tailclouts were nappies or diapers, also known as doubleclouts because they were folded in two for use. Stockings, shoes, coats and petticoats would not be required until the child had been unswaddled.[3]

After swaddling and within the first year of life, children graduated from long wrappings to short coats (petticoats) and emerged from babyhood to be dressed in smaller versions of adult clothes, but with some notable concessions. The main

2. Detail from *The embarkation at Dover*, artist unknown (The Royal Collection © 2005 Her Majesty Queen Elizabeth II).

1. (opposite) *William, 3rd Lord Vaux of Harrowden*, Franco-Flemish School, c. 1575, wears a slashed jerkin over a slashed and pinked doublet. There is a pocket in his hose (© Weiss Gallery).

3. A thread-covered toggle and eyelet form the wrist fastening on an embroidered shirt (inventory no. 28.84), c. 1580 (© Museum of London).

4. A bundle of 20 laces of plaited gold and silver threads with points of gilded brass (inventory no. 3361–19840), c. 1600–1603 (© The Royal Armoury, Stockholm, photo Göran Schmidt).

identifiable differences between adult and children's dress, seen in paintings and hinted at in other sources, are shorter skirts than are necessarily fashionable, back-lacing gowns, protective aprons, sensible shoes, simple headwear and, towards the end of the century, leading strings. Lady Anne Clifford makes reference to her daughter's leading reins in May 1617: 'Upon the first I cut the child's strings off from her coats and made her use the togs [coats] alone, so she has two or three falls at first but no hurt with them.'[4] Little boys were dressed in skirts, though the trappings of gender were reinforced even at this young age: boys in portraits carry swords and wear manly hats and doublets (fig 8, page 11). Little girls have simpler versions of the finery worn by their older sisters and mothers. The younger the girl, the simpler her coiffure and jewellery, neckwear and foundation garments, and the more likely she is to be wearing an apron.

The next transition took place at the age when a boy was deemed old enough to put aside his skirts and wear breeches. Some accounts suggest this happened at seven years, some say five years or even younger. Prince Edward was breeched at the latest by six years two months.[5] After breeching, a boy wore some or all of the typical garments of the day: hose, doublet, coat, jerkin and gown (fig 2). His underwear, like that of adult men, was a long shirt, the hem reaching to at least mid-thigh. The side seams were left partly open so that the shirt could be tucked between the legs.[6] A shirt worn in this way, put on clean every day, would make drawers unnecessary. However, there is evidence that some men owned them and it may be that the late medieval style, called braies, continued to be worn, at least for the first half of the 16th century. Braies were short and close fitting and were pouched at the front by a drawstring at the waist.[7]

The fact that shirts and smocks were intended to survive regular washing is evident in the construction of extant examples. The stitches are very regular and tiny, often so small as to be almost invisible to the naked eye. The strength of the selvedges was exploited in the long seams down the sides, which were butted together. Seams made along a cut edge have the raw part carefully folded under and enclosed with another row of stitching (fig 6). The basic shapes of shirts and smocks remained unchanged throughout the century. They were made of a series of rectangles, squares and triangles (squares folded or cut in half). The width of the garment was determined by the width of the cloth. If a larger than average shirt or smock was needed, wider linen was used. The rest of the pattern pieces fitted neatly alongside each other. With no curved lines, there was very little waste when the pieces were cut out. The variations in style were mainly at the neckline and collar, which changed according to the fashion of the outer garments. Shirts and high-necked smocks were usually fastened with cord ties at neck and cuffs (fig 5). Pictorial evidence suggests that lower-class shirt sleeves were sometimes simply hemmed, without being gathered into a cuff, and could be rolled up out of the way. Those that had cuffs may have been fastened with ties or a cloth or thread button (fig 3).

All men, throughout the century, wore hose on their legs. Early hose were made with each leg cut as one piece from waist to foot. A woven fabric was cut on the bias to give the necessary elasticity for the hose to hug the leg. These were made with or without integral feet. The common method of construction is revealed by careful observation of the work by artists such as Memling and Breughel who depict hose with a seam running all the way up the back of the leg, over the buttock and up to the waist (A9, page 12). The only other seam joins the two legs at the centre back and crotch. The lack of any other seams indicates that each leg was cut in one piece with all the shaping along the centre back. This is borne out by a pair of hose, found at Alpirsbach in Germany, which has been carbon dated to between 1490 and 1529 (fig 7).[8]

5. Embroidered linen shirt c. 1580–1590 and embroidered linen smock c. 1610 (© Museum of Costume, Bath & North East Somerset Council).

6. Handstitched seam in a 16th-century shirt at Platt Hall, Manchester (© Manchester Art Gallery).

7. Linen hose found at Kloster Alpirsbach, Germany (inventory no. K-12-8-23), c. 1490–1529 (© Vermögen und Bau Baden-Württemberg, Staatliche Schlösser und Gärten; photo Adi Bachinger, Karlsruhe)

8. Knitted silk breeches of the Elector Augustus of Saxony, interlined with silk taffeta and lined with leather (inventory no. I 57), c. 1552–1555 (© Rüstkammer, Staatliche Kunstsammlungen, Dresden).

9. Detail from *The Embarkation at Dover*, artist unknown (The Royal Collection © 2005 Her Majesty Queen Elizabeth II).

The front of the hose has a long slit opening, which is partly covered by a triangular flap with eyelets for laces at its top edges. This flap was a modest affair in the medieval era but sprouted into a mock penis as the 16th century began. This became a beribboned and otherwise decorated display by the middle of the era. The codpiece was a symbol of male sexual prowess throughout Europe. Its name in other languages makes this all too clear: *braguette*, *bragueta* or *braga* to name but three. The Alpirsbach codpiece is made of two pieces of stiff material which are seamed to create a three-dimensional effect. It is not padded, although plenty of examples were. That the codpiece was a source of sexual humour is confirmed by contemporary jokes and allusions, such as the codpiece named 'Desyr' worn by Sir Thomas Knyvet as *Vaillant Desyr* in the 1511 Westminster pageant.[9]

The one-piece pattern for fitted hose continued to be used even after it separated into upper and lower (nether) parts, as demonstrated by the leather lining of an extant pair of knitted hose (fig 8). As late as 1596, a miser was described by Thomas Lodge in *Wit's Miserie* as having his 'breeches and stockings … of one piece.'[10] A typically Irish example of legwear called trews used an alternative, more economical method of construction. An extant example has a top section cut on the straight with a drawstring at the waist. The leg sections are made of many pieces of fabric cut on the bias.[11]

Later styles of hose, with gathered fabric at the waist, were venetians (A13, A17, A22, page 12) and trunkhose, or 'round hose' as they were usually called in the Essex wills (A20, page 12). The latter tended to be shorter than venetians, which were knee-length. Both styles were worn with separate nether hose. Trunkhose could be extended with tight-fitting canions, which covered the leg between the bottom of the gathered section and the knee (B9 and B10, page 13). They could also be decorated with vertical strips of fabric known as panes (B7, B9 and B10, page 13). The foundation required padding with 'bombast'. Extant garments and literary references suggest cotton, wool, rags, flax, horsehair and even bran were used for this. Very full versions of venetians, known as gaskins or galligaskins, required extra padding (B8, page 13). One Essex man owned 'gaskins and moldes to the same' in the 1570s.[12]

At the other end of the scale, some trunkhose were so short that they barely covered the genitalia. However, these extremes of width and miniaturization were typical of the elite, not the Essex man. Another style of hose had loose, straight legs cut to the ankle (A16, page 12). These are not very evident in the visual sources but appear to have been worn by rural working men throughout the period. The style became synonymous with sailors but was not worn by the fashionable for another 300 years.[13]

It was the job of the doublet to keep up the hose as well as to provide a covering for the torso. When doublet and hose were made of the same fabric, they were referred to as 'a suit of apparel'. The doublet was a fitted, usually sleeved, garment worn over the shirt. Etymology suggests the essential feature was that it was made double, that is, with a lining. In its simplest form it had no collar or skirts. Collars could be 'grown on', the shoulder seam being extended to curve up the neck (A7, page 12). Alternatively, the collar could be cut separately (A16, page 12). When skirts were added, they were usually short. Eyelets were worked around the waist, either directly through the doublet (A13, page 12) or in a concealed lacing strip under the skirts (fig 7, page 40). Short laces, known as points, were threaded through these eyelets, and those worked in the hose, to hold the two together (fig 4). Points were made from strips of leather or textile cords with metal ends, called aiglets or tags. The petticoat (*petit cote* or little coat) or waistcoat was a sleeveless garment worn beneath the doublet for extra warmth.

As the codpiece declined in popularity and size, a feature of the doublet took over responsibility for projecting the wearer's prowess. The peascod belly appears in portraiture in the late 1550s as a slightly padded area, starting above the waistline, which was rounded and extended down a little lower than the natural waist. By the 1570s, the waistline had risen back up to the natural level at the sides and dipped down to a point at the front. The peascod became more sculptured to fit with this new shape and the doublet was fitted tightly to the body to accentuate the waist. By the 1590s, the peascod was displayed in its most extreme form, with some versions overhanging the girdle, or belt, and curving down beyond the bottom of the doublet skirts (B10, page 13).

Over his doublet, a man might wear a jacket, coat or jerkin – all of which could be made with or without sleeves (fig 9). It is difficult to put exact descriptions to each term as they seem to be interchangeable in contemporary records. Henry VIII's accounts list both coats and jackets. Jackets in these royal accounts are always of rich materials and none of the servants are given them. It is likely that in this case the term refers to the full-skirted garment worn over the doublet and under the gown. In the 1537 accounts of Henry Fitzroy, Duke of Richmond, there are no jackets, only doublets, coats and gowns, suggesting that the term coat is used for the same garment. Both jackets and coats were interlined.[14]

By the end of Henry VIII's reign, the term jerkin replaces jacket in fashionable circles and coat generally describes an outer garment worn over both doublet and jerkin (fig 12). Jerkins are mentioned in the accounts of ordinary countrymen earlier than in those of the court, and they are frequently made of leather. It is estimated that parts of at least 46 leather jerkins were found on the *Mary Rose*. They show great variety in style and detail. Many have waist seams and deep skirts; some have integral wings and pinked decoration, and one has a pocket on the inside of the front skirt. Fastenings include front closing with buttons, front closing with eyelet holes and side fastening with eyelet holes.

The simplest form of button used for fastening doublets, jerkins and coats was the ball button made from the same cloth as the garment it was sewn to. Thread buttons were also popular and inexpensive. These were worked over wooden bases in a variety of shapes, sometimes with very complex and intricate designs. Examples found on the *Mary Rose* include some with pear-shaped bases as well as the simple round ones. Buttons of gold and silver were worn by the fashionable. In 1588, an Essex man left 'a white fustian doublet with silver buttons' and a glazier left his 'white canvas doublet with the silver buttons'.[15] Although buttons were mainly used for male garments, Queen Elizabeth owned some particularly impressive sets, including some shaped as stars, tortoises set with pearls and 'Xij buttons faces enamelled.'[16] An alternative method of fastening was with the use of hooks and eyes. Extant examples are made in brass and steel and look almost identical to modern ones. They were bought in great quantities for the royal wardrobe. Queen Elizabeth's tailor ordered them by the pound.[17]

An optional top layer for men, if they could afford it, was a gown (fig 11). Long gowns were associated with the learned professions, such as doctors (A14, page 12), and with older men, and were worn by the fashionable middle to upper ranks. Acts of apparel issued throughout the period restricted the permitted yardage in ordinary men's gowns. Men exaggerated the width of their shoulders with large puffed gown sleeves in the first half of the century and wore them closer fitting towards the end.[18]

Outer garments also included cassocks and cloaks. Cassocks were loose-fitting and reached to the top of the thigh (A17, page 12). They appear frequently in Elizabethan wills of both men and women. Cloaks were very varied. They could

10 and 11. Details from *The field of the cloth of gold*, artist unknown (The Royal Collection © 2005, Her Majesty Queen Elizabeth II).

12. Detail from *The field of the cloth of gold*, artist unknown (The Royal Collection © 2005, Her Majesty Queen Elizabeth II).

13. French gown with a trained kirtle beneath represented in a monument to Thomas Manners, Earl of Rutland in St Mary's Church, Bottesford, Leicestershire, 1543 (© Ninya Mikhaila and Jane Malcolm-Davies).

have collars, hoods and sleeves. Many of the pictorial sources show little evidence of fastening, the cloaks appearing to hang effortlessly from one or both shoulders. It may be that some of these cloaks were held in position with cords that passed under the arms and were tied at the back. However, study of extant cloaks reveals that most appear never to have had any ties long enough to serve this purpose. The evidence suggests that the majority of rich fashionable cloaks had no fastenings. These cloaks are often semi-circular in shape, and mainly serve a decorative function. Although cloaks in general provide extra warmth and protection from the elements, they need to be at least three-quarters of a circle to serve any practical purpose.

The practicalities of working in all seasons demanded that the dress of the labouring man be flexible. Breughel's painting of *Summer* in the Museum of Fine Arts, Budapest, shows men working in shirt and hose only. Harvest time was one of the few occasions when a lack of doublet or jerkin was acceptable. Two of the men are depicted wearing short hose and sleeveless garments, which could be petticoats. The points that would normally secure the two together are left unfastened to allow for ease of movement. The Essex wills contain references to short hose and, in one case, two pairs of 'hosen cut off at the knees'.[19] A garment that is notably absent in the wills of sailors is the doublet. However, several of the sailors own a number of petticoats. That numerous loose outer garments such as coats and cassocks are also listed suggests that they were worn directly over petticoats to protect the body from severe cold and damp, while still allowing easy movement of the limbs.

Apart from her linen smock, the 16th-century woman had nothing between her honour and the rest of the world. There is no evidence that women wore drawers in 16th-century England. The contemporary effigy of Queen Elizabeth in Westminster Abbey has a pair in fustian but it seems unlikely that the queen herself ever wore them. There are no references to drawers in Elizabeth's accounts, unless some of the items listed as linen hose are drawers rather than stockings. The maker's bill for the effigy specifically uses the term drawers. If the queen actually owned any during her lifetime, it would be surprising not to find them recorded.[20] In these circumstances, there was no need to wrestle with lacings and layers for any bodily functions. Lift a woman's skirts and her honour might be satisfied – or taken by force.

A woman's outer clothes consisted of various combinations of petticoat, kirtle, gown and jacket. Which of these she wore, and how many of them at one time, depended upon her rank, the weather, the occasion and the gradual evolution of fashion through the century. The petticoat, if worn, was the first to be put on, followed by the kirtle, if any, and a gown or jacket formed the top layer. Both petticoats and kirtles were commonly made of two fabrics (because they were usually only partly visible) – a rich one for the areas on show and a cheaper one for the hidden portions. In 1570, a yeoman bequeathed 'a worsted kirtle the upperbody and sleeves of branched damask'.[21] An extant kirtle dated 1570–1580 in the Germanisches Nationalmuseum in Nurnberg is similar, being plain ivory silk mounted on linen, with silver and ivory embroidered silk for the front section and matching sleeves.[22]

Contemporary documents reveal that many petticoats and kirtles had bodices, and most had sleeves as well, which were often pinned or laced to the rest of the garment (fig 10). Petticoat and kirtle bodies were fastened either by being laced through eyelets with a single lace knotted at one end, or with hooks and eyes (A15, page 12). Front fastening was usual, although side and back closures were used when the front of the bodice was to be displayed under a gown. Skirt openings did not have plackets like modern skirts; instead there was a simple hemmed slit. Since the openings in the different layers rarely coincided, there was no danger of indecent exposure, as all that was visible through the opening was the underlying garment.

Wearing a single layer on top of her smock in public was not the habit of a respectable woman. To be properly dressed required a gown too, although many women might wear this for best on Sundays and holidays. There were several versions of the gown, but all were full-length garments, with long or short sleeves. The French gown had a tightly fitted bodice (fig 13), whereas loose gowns could be semi-fitted, belted or left to flow freely (fig 14). Middling people and the lower sort used the word 'frock' in their wills to describe these loose gowns (fig 16). 'A round gown' had a level hem all the way round, whereas a train was a feature of the 'French gown'.[23] In the late 1530s, in Edinburgh, Sir David Lindsay commented on the merchants' wives who looked ridiculous with trailing gowns dragging in the mud.

A typically English arrangement seems to have been that observed by the Venetian ambassador in 1554. He commented that Queen Mary's gowns were of two sorts: one is clearly a French gown, while the other is 'a gown such as men wear but fitting very close, with an under petticoat which has a very long train; and this is her ordinary costume, being also that of gentlewomen of England.'[24]

Variations on these basic shapes for gowns were also worn, the main differences being in the sleeves or half-sleeves (fig 16). Larger sleeves have always been the preserve of gentlefolk, since anyone who has to do manual labour would find them impractical. In the Henrician period, ladies wore enormous turnback sleeves to their French gowns (C3, C4, C5 and C6, page 13). In the late Elizabethan period, trunk sleeves or verthingale sleeves were so big that they required extra support from rolls of fabric or bones. Any woman aspiring to dress well might spend what she could afford on a fancy pair of sleeves to smarten her everyday dress for special occasions.[25]

The area displayed by open-fronted gowns and bodices could be filled with a separate, decorative stomacher. The wardrobe accounts of Queen Elizabeth describe many of these made in rich fabrics, often embellished with embroidery. However, only two are mentioned in the Essex wills, and these both date from the last five years of the century. It would appear that the stomacher was the preserve of the elite woman.[26]

Another outer garment worn by women was a waistcoat. This was a short jacket, fitted to the waist and shaped over the hips. Waistcoats were worn informally by the upper classes at the end of the century, when they were often made of linen and embroidered. They may have been worn by ordinary women from as early as the 1550s, and possibly earlier.[27] They were certainly typical by the end of the century. Many of the women depicted in the 16th-century *Cries of London* woodcuts wear them over their petticoats (A21, page 12).[28]

The shape of women's skirts changed throughout the century. One crucial item of dress to influence this was the farthingale, a hooped petticoat designed to hold the skirts away from the body. Catherine of Aragon and her Spanish attendants wore farthingales when they arrived in England in 1501 but they soon abandoned them in favour of the flowing skirts of their adopted country. More than 50 years passed before the Spanish farthingale held sway in England (fig 15). The future Queen Elizabeth wore the first recorded English farthingale in 1545.[29] Just two years afterwards, Bess Cavendish (later Bess of Hardwick) purchased a farthingale for her nine-year-old stepdaughter.[30]

All the early farthingales that were made for Queen Elizabeth were stiffened with ropes. The queen's tailor, Walter Fyshe, used seven and a half yards of kersey 'for the ropes' of a farthingale in 1560. Ropes could also be made from plaited or bound

14. A loose gown or 'frock' worn over a kirtle represented in a monument to Sir George Vernon and his two wives, Margaret and Matilda, 1567 at All Saints' Church in Bakewell, Derbyshire (© Ninya Mikhaila and Jane Malcolm-Davies).

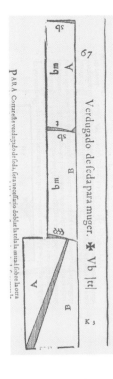

15. A farthingale pattern (inventory no. T.171.486-1903) from Alcega, J (1589) *Geometria, pratica, ey traca*, Madrid (© V & A Images/Victoria & Albert Museum, London)

16. Detail of a country woman feeding chickens with her red petticoat visible at the hem, from an embroidered panel of a rustic scene (inventory no. 29/121), early 17th century, in the Burrell Collection, Glasgow (© Glasgow City Council/Museums).

17. A red petticoat worn under a small farthingale represented in a monument to Sir Fulke Greville and Elizabeth his wife, in St Nicholas's Church, Alcester, Warwickshire, 1559 (© Ninya Mikhaila & Jane Malcolm-Davies).

18. A pair of silk bodies (inventory no. T4111), 1598 (© Bayerisches Nationalmuseum, Munich, Germany).

lengths of bents, which were dried grass stems.[31] From the 1560s, French farthingales – or bum rolls – make their first appearance. These were worn on top of the Spanish farthingale and gave the skirt a bell shape. This roll grew bigger and more substantial until it superseded the Spanish farthingale and was worn on its own.[32]

A French farthingale worn alone gave the skirt a drum-like appearance (A18, page 12). This shape was further enhanced toward the end of the century by pinning the skirt into a ruffled frill around the widest part of the roll. The final incarnation of the farthingale, in the 1590s, took the drum shape to greater extremes with the skirts standing straight out at waist level (C10, page 13). Most farthingales seem to have been of a modest size (fig 17). However, there is no evidence that working women wore either style. Alternative methods of holding out the skirts included lining petticoats with substantial woollen fabrics, such as kersey or cotton and adding extra bands of fabric to the hem, called welts. An Essex widow owned a 'red petticoat welted about beneath' in 1581.[33]

The fitted bodice of the kirtle or petticoat formed the foundation of most styles of Tudor dress for women. In the early 16th century, the fashion was moving away from the soft, curvy lines of the medieval period. Bodices began to be fitted closely to the torso, with the bust held in a high position and an increasing emphasis on a small waist. At first, the shape of the bosom was still fairly natural, with its curves visible beneath the bodice. The hips were enhanced by the soft voluminous folds of long skirts. After the first two decades of the century, the clothes depicted in contemporary sources appear to be stiffer and the curves less evident (fig 12, page 11; C4, page 13). It is clear that by this time, the bodice of the gown, or another beneath it, was interlined with some form of stiffening.

Interlinings of canvas and buckram provide sufficient stiffening for these early bodices. Buckram is frequently mentioned in association with women's clothing. It was often stiffened with paste or glue. The 'paste wyfe' could also supply wire, which became necessary as the waist changed from a natural line to a point in the 1540s. References to boning proper appear in household accounts after the middle of the 16th century, but the first mention of whalebone in the wardrobe accounts of Queen Elizabeth is not until 1580.[34]

A 'pair of bodies' is the 16th-century phrase for stays (later called a corset), although 'bodies' often refer to the upper part of a full-length garment, hence 'bodice'. Household accounts (from the royals down the social hierarchy) show that bodies were made to go with petticoats, kirtles and farthingales. Some were stiffened and boned; some were not. These bodies were sometimes sewn on or attached by means of points, and served the dual function of moulding the body and holding the weight of the skirts.[35]

The earliest surviving pair of boned bodies is in the Bayerisches Museum in Munich and dates from the 1590s.[36] The bodies are made in ivory silk and have closely worked rows of stitching which once contained bents or whalebone, but these have all rotted away (fig 18). The bodies lace up at the back through eyelets worked over metal rings. Another pair of surviving bodies was made for an effigy of Queen Elizabeth after her death (fig 21). This pair is made from two layers of white fustian. They are stiffened with whalebone and are front-lacing. An interesting detail of both the Munich bodies and those made for the effigy is that the bones in the channels stop short of the top edge of the neckline.

From the 1570s, the centre front of bodices was sometimes given extra stiffening in the form of a busk.[37] The materials from which the earliest extant examples are made include wood, bone and ivory. The Munich bodies have a channel down the centre front to house the busk. By the end of the century, the extreme, final form of the farthingale mentioned above required a busk at the front in order to achieve the fashionable tilt – up at the back and down at the front. As the woman dressed, the relatively flexible pointed waist of the bodies was pulled over the top of the farthingale. The busk was then inserted into its channel in the bodies and tied in place with a busk point (laced through eyelets in the bodies) to hold the front of the farthingale down.[38]

Only four pairs of bodies are mentioned in the Essex wills. They appear to belong almost exclusively to the upper classes, appearing in their accounts in the last quarter of the century. The mass of the female population wore kirtle, petticoat and/or gown bodices with various forms of stiffening, such as buckram and quilting, which could be combined with cords or bents. How the various layers of early Tudor women's dress were combined remains something of a conundrum. Women in portraits and drawings of the 1520s to 1540s wear garments that appear to be sprayed on their bodies. There are no obvious fastenings at either front or back. However, in her portrait by Holbein, Jane Seymour's gown (fig 13, page 43) is fastened by 13 gold pins. Jane Small has a similar row of vertical pins (fig 1, page 26). Pins were used extensively in the wardrobe of the Tudor woman and were purchased in astonishing quantities. In 1539, the Great Wardrobe account for Mary Tudor includes a typical entry, 'for ten thousand pins price the thousand 20d.'[39]

There are a number of other references in contemporary sources that suggest how this tight-fitting look was achieved. Mary Tudor's French gowns all had 'fore bodyes' in a different fabric from the gown and its lining, usually satin. Placards and stomachers of rich fabric also appear in the accounts (both separately and as part of garments) and these were intended for display.[40] Hunnisett's modern pattern recreates this arrangement by using panels at each side of the front (the forebodies), which are laced together and hidden by a wide panel (the placard) that is secured across the body with pins, as in the portraits.[41]

Further clues to the construction of bodices are provided by the portrait of Catherine Parr (fig 20), formerly thought to be of Jane Grey. Tiny hairs of fur lining in the gown can be seen along the bottom edge of the jewelled neckline (the square). This indicates that the top of the gown stops short of the square, which must be mounted on the kirtle rather than the gown (fig 21). As in other portraits, there is a faint depression discernible between the breasts and there is no break in the square at the neckline to allow for a centre front opening. These details suggest

19: A French gown worn by Catherine Parr attributed to Master John (NPG 4451), c. 1545 (© National Portrait Gallery, London).

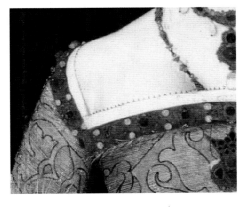

20. Tiny hairs of the fur lining of the gown are visible in a detail from NPG 4451 (as above).

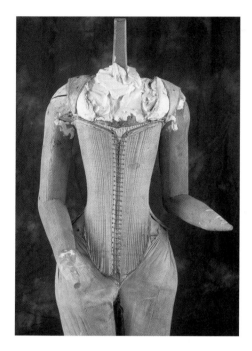

21. A pair of fustian 'straight' bodies stiffened with whalebones and bound with suede from Queen Elizabeth's funeral effigy at Westminster Abbey. They were probably made by her tailor in 1603 (© Dean and Chapter of Westminster).

1 frizado petticoat which I did use to wear to market – 1588

my workingday russet petticoat lacking sleeves – 1586

my buffin gown which I use to wear in the summer – 1591

To my sister Margaret my last wife's wedding gown and her petticoat – 1595

Essex women's wills

that the kirtle is laced at the side or back. The overlying gown neckline butts up to the bottom edge of the decoration, minimizing its chunkiness and concealing its own thickness. The minimal petticoat bodice underneath adds very little to the bulk of the layers.

Tudor women wore up to five layers of clothing on their torsos. They often wore three over their smocks: a petticoat covered by a kirtle with a gown on top, and possibly a separate pair of bodies as well. It is not clear which and how many of these layers were stiffened. However, a series of experiments which stiffened each of these layers in turn revealed two features which help achieve the contemporary look. First, boning must not rise over the bust (as in the extant pairs of bodies) in order to retain the softness which is evident in the portraits. Secondly, the fastening for the stiffened layer must be at the back or sides and, for the fuller figure, be laced from top to bottom. This draws the bust down and avoids cleavage.[42]

Changes in the provision of kirtles, petticoats and gowns marked transitional stages in the lives of three girls whose expenses are detailed in the probate account of their father, a gentleman. Millicent Crayforde received her first kirtle (as opposed to the petticoats with upper bodies she wore previously) when she was around 15 to 17 years old. A second kirtle coincided with her 18th birthday.[43] Though girls had no equivalent change in dress to boys' breeching, they underwent a dramatic alteration in their bodies at puberty. Euphemisms for menstruation abound. After her marriage, Elisabeth de Valois's ladies-in-waiting promised that they would write to her mother the moment her 'besongnes' or 'needs' arrived. More frequently recorded terms are 'little secrets', 'the courses', 'the months' or 'menses' and 'the flowers'. This last is thought to be a corruption of the French 'fluor' meaning 'a flowing'.[44]

There is almost complete silence in the archival record on the practical business of coping with menstruation. That menstruous cloths were used is mentioned in 16th-century translations of *The Bible* (*Isaiah*, chapter 3, verse 22).[45] There are a few clues in, for example, Queen Elizabeth's household accounts, where long and short 'vallopes all of fine hollande clothe' are listed by the dozen with other plain linen items. With the frequent transposition of v and w in English, this is probably a reference to 'wallops', a term for fluttering rags, which may have been used as sanitary towels or rolled as tampons.[46] Queen Elizabeth also had three 'gyrdelles of blak Jeane silk made on the fingers garnished with buckelles hookes & eyes whipped over with silke' which may have provided the necessary sanitary belt for use with the vallopes.[47] There was certainly no taboo on inserting objects into the vagina (with a string for removal). Medicinal pessaries of shorn wool, fine linen or silk bags containing herbs are mentioned in surviving 17th-century editions of earlier medical manuals.[48]

In the eyes of Tudor society, a woman achieved her proper place when she found herself a husband. Weddings were opportunities for families to show off their wealth. Silver and gold seem to have been appropriate if the bride's family could afford it. Silver did not refer to the colour of the fabric but rather to the raw material for the fabric or trimming. In 1538, poor Frances Plantagenet was criticized for failing to wear sufficient tinsel (silver or gold) in her sleeves or a silver kirtle at her wedding.[49] Often the guests as well as the bride wore white. A waiting gentlewoman at Lady Gertrude Manners' wedding on 25 April 1539 was delivered 12 yards of white damask among other items to clothe herself appropriately for the occasion.[50] A lower-ranking woman would aspire to wear her best clothes – if not her newest – on her wedding day. In the Essex wills, wedding clothes are bequeathed by men and women which suggests that, long after they had married, these were still valuable outfits.[51]

Becoming a mother was the most dramatic of changes in a woman's life. The extent to which women had to cope with their expanding torso has been exaggerated. On average, in the early modern period, a woman had six or seven pregnancies in her lifetime – some of which might not run to full term.[52] The arrangement of loosened and later abandoned bodies, with a pinned placard or stomacher to ease garments was a very flexible one. Both Anne Boleyn and Jane Seymour were observed using these solutions. The French ambassador reported Anne 'unlaced with a placard, having put in a piece to enlarge her gown, as ladies do when in the family way' in May 1533.[53] Jane was 'great with child, and shall be open-laced with stomacher by Corpus Christi Day at the farthest' says John Husee in a letter to his master Lord Lisle in Calais on 23 May 1537. He predicts Jane's change in dress will happen about 20 weeks into her pregnancy.[54] Lady Honor Lisle herself received half a yard of fabric that served the same purpose. She was given 'a stomacher cloth of cloth-of-gold … I pray Jesu if it be his pleasure it may cover a young Lord Plantagenet.'[55] Pregnancy portraits show that placards were adaptations to existing clothes (fig 19, page 46). Lower down the social scale, the same arrangements were possible with meaner fabrics and the 'judicious arrangement of aprons and skirts' to hide burgeoning gaps in usually tight-fitting garments.[56]

For mourning the end of life, black clothes were the norm in the 16th century. The cut of these could differ from ordinary wear, as illustrated by the will of a gentleman's wife in 1588 in which she described 'my black gown made of my mourning gown'.[57]

There was specific garb for the chief mourners at funerals throughout the era: a coat with a train and a mourning hood, although the latter was worn around the neck rather than on the head towards the end of the century. The bodies of the dead were wrapped in linen shrouds. These were about 12 inches longer and three times wider than the body. The shroud was gathered at each end and pinned or sewn down the middle. The knots at top and bottom were secured with a twisted strip of fabric.[58]

So it was that the great and the good, the lowly and the humble were levelled by death. Whatever change there was in high fashion or in individuals' lives, linen was what brought them into the world and linen was what took them out of it.

22. Open-laced gown represented in a detail from *Study for a family portrait of Thomas More by Hans Holbein*, c. 1527 (© Kunstmuseum Basel, Kupferstichkabinett).

…and Anne winstandley to have my workedaye clothes which I shall heppen at my Decease to weare 1584, will of a St Helens woman, Lancashire

ANNO ETATIS SVAE 23

3. LOOKING THE PART

Four rayles and eke five kerchers fayre
Of hose and shoes she had a payre …
She would go bare-foot for to save
Her shoes and hose for they were deere
Thomas Churchyard, 1575

The proper appearance of linen, the quality of headgear, and the stoutness of shoes were more than functional requirements in the 16th century. These bespoke a Tudor's person station in life as eloquently as their garments. Hats served more than the purpose of keeping people's heads covered. They were an important part of social life, demonstrating status and deference. For men, doffing or touching the hat was an indication of respect and an appropriate acknowledgement in return was an obligation of rank:

> 'Any cap, whate'er it be
> Is still the sign of some degree.'[1]

For men, flat bonnets predominated during the first half of the century. They consisted of a soft circular crown with a brim which was sometimes stiffened (fig 2). Women also wore bonnets over coifs, although not as frequently as other forms of headgear (fig 3). An analysis of Henry VIII's caps recorded in his 1547–50 inventory show that his most usual headwear was black

2. (above) Bonnet worn by Richard Martin by Steven van Herwijck, 1562 (© The Trustees of the British Museum).

3. (left) Detail from *The field of the cloth of gold*, artist unknown (The Royal Collection © 2005 Her Majesty Queen Elizabeth II).

1. (opposite) Jane Small wears a white neckerchief over a black partlet in a miniature by Hans Holbein, 1540 (© V&A Images/Victoria & Albert Museum, London). A row of pins is visible down the side of her bodice.

4. A hat represented on a monument to Thomas, Lord Scrope in St Andrew's Church, Langar, Nottinghamshire, 1609 (© Ninya Mikhaila and Jane Malcolm-Davies).

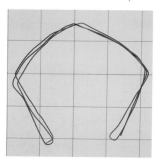

5. Wire stiffener for a 16th-century woman's headdress (inventory no. Z640*) from an unknown London site (© Museum of London).

6. A gable headdress with lappets and veils hanging over the shoulders, represented in a monument to Sir John Dawtrey and his wife in St Mary's Church, Petworth, West Sussex, 1542 (© Jane Malcolm-Davies and Ninya Mikhaila).

(85 per cent of 70 items). Most were made from velvet with silk linings, such as sarcenet and taffeta.[2]

Knitted caps were widely worn from Henry VIII's reign onwards and several survive today. The collection in the Museum of London includes one with a brim that has been cut in from the edges to form decorative slashes. The knitting is felted and the surface has been brushed to raise a fluffy nap that obscures the stitches.[3]

As the century progressed, bonnets became much smaller, and while low-crowned bonnets and caps remained popular, the 1560s saw the (literal) rise of the high-crowned hat (fig 4). Both men and women adopted these with enthusiasm. Those worn by the masses were made of felt and covered in silk, if the budget stretched to it. Very fine ones were made from beaver hair. Fashionable hats were frequently lined in materials that were just as exquisite as those covering the outside. Examples left in Essex wills include several with silk linings, such as velvet or taffeta.[4] Hat bands were always worn. These could be delicate and simple, such as the silk ribbon on a knitted cap on the *Mary Rose*, or much more showy, such as the impressive gold cable twist on Lord Vaux's hat (fig 1, page 14). Hat bands for the wealthy were often jewelled with pearls or buttons of goldsmith's work.

St Paul decreed that women's hair should be covered (1 *Corinthians*, chapter 11, verse 6), which was to have a profound effect on women's headwear in Christian communities through the centuries. Unbound hair was acceptable for unmarried girls, but signified a lack of discipline or dangerous intent in others. Depictions of women in grief, despair or beating their husbands have disordered hair as a sign that they have temporarily or permanently lost their wits.[5] The way hair was bound was crucial to the security of headdresses – whether simple or highly fashionable. Contemporary depictions suggest that hanks on either side of a centre parting were plaited with a long ribbon which ran from the nape of the neck to the bottom of each plait, with the extra length of the ribbon hanging beyond it. These plaits were crossed and secured on top of the head by tying the ribbon ends together. This provided the firm foundation to which all headrails and headdresses were fixed.[6]

For the fashionable woman, the primary form of headgear was the hood. This was not as simple a garment as the name suggests. It usually consisted of several separate elements. There was always a white linen cap, which formed the foundation and could be washed. This was partially or entirely covered by the other parts, such as the frontlet, billiments, lappets and veil. When pinned together, these components formed the full headdress. The early Tudor style has become known as the English or gable hood; the gable refers to the roof of a house, which the style resembles (fig 5). At first, the veil and embroidered decorative strips called lappets fell to or beyond the shoulders. By the 1530s, the lappets were folded back on themselves over the head and the veil became a rigid box-shaped cap with two long strips attached to it (fig 6). These strips hung down the wearer's back or were flipped up (together or singly) and pinned to create stiff, angular lines (fig 13, page 43). Early versions displayed a small section of centre-parted hair under the point of the gable. After about 1520, the front of the hood had retreated a little and two crossed hanks of hair bound with ribbon were visible. A further development was to conceal the hair in rolls of striped silk which were arranged in the same way: 'The heare of a woman that is layde over hir forehead, nowe gentlewomen do call them their rolles.'[7]

The French hood had a rounded top instead of the gable point. The under cap was set back on the head to display more hair than was visible with the English version. It fitted closely to the head, with a brim curving forward to cover the ears. The brim was sometimes edged with a pleated strip of gauzy silk. A decorative band, the upper billiment, was then pinned to the cap, at the point where the

7. (left) A French hood in black fabric overlaid with gold upper and nether billiments with a crescent-shaped billiment of white fabric, represented in a monument to Sir Fulke Greville and Elizabeth, his wife in St Nicholas's Church, Alcester, Warwickshire, 1559. The veil emerges from the top of the hood, where it is arranged in pleats. 8. (above) A range of coifs and hoods, some of which have integral bongraces flipped over the head, represented in a monument to Sir John Harper in St James's Church, Swarkestone, Derbyshire, before 1627.

underlying hair crossed over the head, adding height. This could be plain velvet, taffeta or satin, and might be jewelled or consist entirely of goldsmith's work. Frontlets and nether (lower) billiments could be worn in addition to the upper. These were pinned to the front of the cap, following the shape of the brim. The veil could take several forms and was attached in various ways (fig 7). It either hung down the back or was flipped up over the top of the head. When flipped up, the veil became known as a bongrace, and later as a shadow, since it protected the face from the sun (fig 8). The colours used for both styles of hoods did not vary very much. The under cap was always white, the veil always black, frontlets were usually black, and the lappets and billiments were limited to black, red, white or gold.

French hoods continued to be worn right through the Elizabethan period, though they tended to be smaller and set on the back of the head, where they were less visible once the hair began to be dressed over pads at the front. Evidence from effigies and brasses suggests that headwear often lagged behind or went before the prevailing style for other garments. Items of dress that became fashionable at different dates were combined, suggesting that crossover combinations were worn. A typical example is the effigy of Elizabeth Fielding in St Edith's Church, Monks Kirby, Warwickshire. She wears a gable headdress with a set of ruffs. Alternative headgear took the form of nets, creppins, cauls, carcanets and 'attires for the head' which only partially covered the dressed hair beneath (fig 9).

The headwear of the common woman throughout the period consisted of various arrangements of white linen. The women of Essex owned an enormous assortment of linen in the form of cross-cloths, quarters, kerchiefs, neckerchers, rails, partlets and aprons. The quantity of items owned by each woman suggests that 'small wearing linen' was intended to be changed regularly. Fine, clean linen was a source of pride. The presentation and cleanliness of linen head and neckwear has been an index of godliness throughout history.[8] Linen was inextricably linked to propriety and respectability for 16th-century people. Headrails and headkerchers usually consisted of a square yard of linen, folded in half and pinned to the hair or another band of linen beneath. The arrangement could be very simple, although many wearers transformed the flat piece of linen into complex

9. (above) Caul represented in a monument to John, 4th Earl of Rutland in St Mary's Church, Bottesford, Leicestershire, 1591. (All images © Ninya Mikhaila and Jane Malcolm-Davies).

10. Jewels worn by Frances, Lady Reynell in her portrait by Robert Peake, c. 1595 (© Weiss Gallery).

11. A purse represented on a monument to Sir Thomas Babington in All Saints' Church, Ashover, Derbyshire, 1511 (© Ninya Mikhaila and Jane Malcolm-Davies).

structures with skilful folding, tucking and pinning (fig 10, page 19; A15, page 12). While headdressess were worn throughout the period, structured coifs became increasingly popular as the century progressed (fig 8). One of the reasons for the rise of the coif was the fashion for shaped and wired brims. Triangular pieces of linen called cross-cloths or quarters (being a quarter of a square yard) were sometimes worn underneath coifs. The bias edge was laid just above the forehead, probably because of its elasticity, with the triangle point toward the back.

Close-fitting coifs, which tied under the chin, were worn throughout the period by old men, lawyers and doctors (A14, page 12). These were made in white linen or black silk, often under bonnets or hats. This style of linen coif – known as a biggin – was also worn by babies and young children (A7, page 12).

Covering the throat was another sign of propriety, particularly after marriage, for lower and middling women. Queen Elizabeth was described as having 'her bosum uncovered, as all the English ladies have it, till they marry.'[9] Partlets and neckerchiefs were worn both over and under the bodies to fill in the neckline (fig 1). A Coventry woman of 1558 owned 'rayllys, partlettys, with other lynyns'.[10] Some of these items may be the mysterious white bands which appear neatly folded and pinned to the shoulders of women in Henrician portraits and drawings, where they may serve to demonstrate the fineness of the linen.

The quintessential item of Elizabethan neckwear was the ruff. Beginning as the gathered frills on shirt collars and cuffs, they grew into separate, exaggerated, formal 'sewts' (neck and wrist ruffs). These were often made up separately and pinned or basted to the shirt or smock (fig 6, page 10). For collars and ruffs to be part of the shirt was a stigma. In 1570, a husbandman's lowly status was emphasized by his

'Shyrt of canvas hard and tough
Of which the band and ruffes, were both of one.'[11]

It was starch that set ruffs on their way to greatness in 1564 when a Dutch woman, Gwillam Boone, employed by a Flemish woman, set up a starching business. They trained English women in the mysteries of their art, much to the disgust of native commentators. Starching turned a food source into a frippery and was controversial for it, especially in times of dearth such as the poor harvests of the 1590s.[12] Extant ruffs reveal that, although there appear to have been many different and complex styles, they were all made on the same principle. They consisted of long strips of lightweight linen, gathered into cartridge pleats and attached to a neck band. The variation of style depended on the type and amount of material used and the way in which the laundress starched and set the pleats. Hot poking sticks were used to fix the sets, which were sometimes held in place with wax or pins. An original ruff survives with wax fixings in the Bayerisches Nationalmuseum in Munich. However, close examination of ruffs in paintings suggests they were not always caught together but might stay in place by starching alone.[13] The large ruffs of the 1580s and 1590s required additional support from underproppers, or supportasses (figs 14 and 15). Stubbes described them as 'stately arches of pride.' Ruffs such as these, he predicted, will collapse in the rain and lie on the wearer's shoulders 'like the dishclout of a slut.'[14]

Aprons were worn both as practical items, protecting the skirts from dirt and grease, and as fashionable accessories in fine fabrics. The majority of Elizabethan aprons mentioned in wills are black (57 percent of 67 items). For the ordinary

12. A selection of necklaces from the Cheapside Hoard, early 17th century (© Museum of London).

woman, unbleached blue and green linen were usual for working days, while white and black were reserved for best.

A favourite fabric for working aprons was durance, which, having a very close woollen weave, made it a safe choice when working over an open fire. Working aprons in wills include some made of russet, while fashionable versions were made in fine linens and silk. The greatest proportions are of worsted (33 percent) and lockram (30 percent of 106 items). Crisp creases can be observed in aprons in many contemporary paintings, showing that they were neatly folded for storage (fig 13).

For the wealthy, jewellery included rings, brooches ('ooches'), necklaces and bracelets. The wedding ring was worn on the third finger of the left hand as this was thought to be directly connected to the heart.[15] Without exception, it is women who own and leave wedding rings in the Essex wills, suggesting that men did not wear them. Necklaces were worn by men and women, as were bracelets. Francis I gave Henry VIII a 'bracelet of precyouse stone' at the Field of the Cloth of Gold in 1520.[16] In pre-reformation days, rosary beads were a common accessory. A Coventry draper's wife of 1544 owned five pairs, including beads of coral, jet guarded with silver, and amber guarded with silver.[17] When jewellery was set with stones, there was great variety, both precious and semiprecious. Shapes were simpler than today, usually pointed or tabled – the brilliant cut was unknown. Jewels were sometimes called 'flowers', although these were not necessarily flower-shaped (fig 10).[18] A yeoman in 1589 left a 'velvet cap with a flower in it' in his will. Enamelled jewels were also popular, and less costly. The Cheapside hoard contains dozens of beautiful examples (fig 12). The Elizabethan fascination with all things natural, so evident in the embroidery of the period, applied to jewels. Creatures, birds and flowers were a constant source of inspiration.

Some form of belt or girdle was always worn by both sexes. For men, leather belts with brass fittings were most common. They were typically very narrow (less than an inch wide) and dyed or decorated with stamped motifs. Fashionable Henrician men wore long girdles of silk, wrapped twice around the waist, from which a dagger or knife could be hung. Henry VIII's silk girdles were described as 'in bredith three nayles (six inches)'.[19] During the first half of the century, purses hanging from belts were indispensable accessories. They were made from leather or fabric sewn over a metal frame (fig 11). As the inclusion of integral pockets in

a black worsted apron
1596, an Essex widow's will

1 holland apron of green
1596, an Essex widow's will

a white linen apron
1585, an Essex will

13. Creased apron worn by a servant in *A family saying grace before a meal* by Anthonius Claessins, 1585 (© Weiss Gallery).

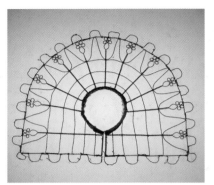

14 (above) Wire supportasse (inventory no. T4065), 1630–1640 (© Bayerisches Nationalmuseum in Munich, Germany).

15. A ribbon securing a lace-trimmed collar and supportasse to the collar of a gown with a decorative bow, represented in a monument to Sir Thomas Barnardiston in the Church of St Peter and St Paul, Kedington, Suffolk, c. 1610 (© Ninya Mikhaila and Jane Malcolm-Davies).

men's clothing became the norm, purses became less common. For women, girdles were usually textile rather than leather. They served a number of purposes, both decorative and functional. Plain and jewelled versions were worn over the gown and adorned with pendants of jewels, tassels, miniature books or perfume holders. Pomanders were often jewelled; tiny versions could also be worn strung together as necklaces or used as buttons.[20] Other girdles were worn beneath the skirts, with valuable objects such as drawstring purses or keys suspended from them. Many wills written by women leave pairs of silver hooks, which were probably used to keep skirts off the ground (fig 3, page 7). These are often amongst the few metal items, also including pins and silver rings, that ordinary women owned.[21]

Once men's leg wear had separated into two parts, nether hose were required to cover the bottom of the leg. These half-length hose were worn by women too. Most were made in the same way as full-length hose, cut on the bias. Knitted hose, made from wool, were probably worn by ordinary people earlier in the century than they were by the wealthy. Mary Tudor's fool, Jane, was provided with 'thirtene peire of blak knit hoose' in 1558, when Mary's own hose were made from cloth. The Petre girls had stockings knitted and dyed for them by local women in the 1550s, as did Ellin, a maid in rural Wales in the 1590s. She received thread stockings at 9d a pair and her sister charged 4d a pair for knitting another pair with wool from her master's flock. The first knitted stockings appear in Queen Elizabeth's wardrobe in 1561, and were made from silk.[22] Protective under hose were worn next to the skin. There are 12 pairs of hose and 30 pairs of 'base sockis' of fine linen listed in Henry VIII's accounts of 1534.[23] Nether hose were attached to the upper hose, possibly with temporary stitching, although a pair of trunkhose in the Museo Parmigianino, Reggio Emilia, have eyelet holes worked into a band at the bottom, which suggests the accompanying nether hose were to be tied to them.[24]

Garters were also used to hold up nether hose. These were usually plain, functional lengths of ribbon. Queen Mary's wardrobe was supplied with 'collen reband' (Cologne ribbon) for her garters, and Henry VIII ordered 'Toures Reabande … for our sockis'.[25] In the 1580s and 1590s, when men were wearing trunkhose with canions, it was usual to pull the top of the hose up over the canions and tie the garter, which often had fringed ends, over it (fig 16).

The standard shoe for country people was the startup. Worn by men and women, it was a sturdy high-fitting ankle boot (fig 17, below). These practical boots were worn for outdoor activities by higher-ranking people too. The Petre accounts list 'a payre of starups to hawke in' in 1569.[26] Long boots were restricted to outdoor use. They were used for riding and were worn by soldiers. A pair found on the *Mary Rose* had wool and straw padding in the sole.[27] Urban dwellers might wear more fashionable styles – low-cut and square-toed, fastening with a narrow strap and buckle in the Henrician period, almond-toed with latchet fastening in the Elizabethan era. Most people's shoes were made in leather, with single soles without heels. They were made as turn shoes: stitched inside out, soaked and then turned the right way round. This produced a shoe that looks like a modern slipper. Welted construction started to be used around the middle of the century and heels were coming in toward the end. Those who wore their shoes out quickly had them reinforced with extra soles. Henry VIII's footmen were all given 'duble soled shois' in 1509. Fashionable shoes might be covered in satin or velvet.[28]

For keeping the hands warm, both gloves and mittens were worn. Mittens were practical rather than fashionable items. A leather pair was found on the *Mary Rose* and the Museum of London has a knitted pair dating from the middle of the 16th century. These are of soft white wool with a contrasting band of black wool worked around the wrist.[29] Fashionable gloves were made in soft kidskin, often slit at the fingers to reveal rings beneath. These fine leathers were usually perfumed. Glove gauntlets became increasingly elaborate and many surviving examples from the late 16th century display beautiful embroidery. Gloves such as these were not necessarily worn, but were carried in the hands as a purely decorative accessory (fig 16). Gloves were important gifts because they extended the symbolic hand of friendship and pledged loyalty. New gloves were given to guests even at humble weddings and funerals. An Essex servant left money for gloves in 1592 in the hope that he was respectable enough to be worthy of remembrance: 'I will that special gloves be provided for my good master, good mistress, Mr Walter Myldmay, and my good friend Mr Pickering if it please them to wear gloves for my sake.'[30] Custom and convention governed clothing after death as it did through life.

16. Garter worn by *William, Lord Fitzwilliam of Milton and Gainspark (c. 1570–1643/4) and later 1st Baron Fitzwilliam of Lifford* by William Segar (circle of), c. 1595 (© Weiss Gallery).

17. Shoe for a young woman (inventory no. 4569 6.12.01) found in the River Thames, assembled 1975, c. 1580; fragment of a leather shoe (inventory no. 4571 6.11.31), England 1545–1550; probably a worker's shoe in leather (inventory no. 4560 6.11.06), England 1520–1530 (© DLM – Ledermuseum Offenbach).

4. CHOOSING THE MATERIALS

For now I wyll were thys, and now I wyll were that;
Now I wyll were I cannot tell what
Andrew Borde, 1542

The purchase of new clothes for people in the 16th century began with the choice of fabrics. There was a hierarchy for clothing as there was for people. From 1363, successive sumptuary laws attempted to enforce the notion that certain details of dress were appropriate to specific ranks of society. Restrictions were set not only as to the types of fabric permitted but also the amount that could be used in a single garment. In 1533, the use of velvet for gowns and coats was limited to those with £200 or more per year. In 1562, the 'greatness of hose' was a target. Tailors and hosiers were to use just one and a half yards of fabric per pair. In 1574, all women were brought within the terms of the acts of apparel for the first time since 1483.[1]

Despite regular repetition, sumptuary law was remarkably unsuccessful (there are few recorded prosecutions). It enshrined an ideal instead of reflecting reality. Social pressure was probably more effective than fines: Lord Clifford criticized his own son for clothing himself in cloth of gold 'more like a duke's son than a poor baron's son as he is' and Queen Elizabeth relieved her attendant Lady Mary Howard of a petticoat with the words: 'I am minded it shall never become thee, as being too fine.'[2]

People strove to wear the best they could afford. Essex wills show evidence of people aspiring to wear better quality cloth and silk in small details of their dress: for example, a coat 'which is lined with velvet in the collar' (1585) and 'a red silk purse' (1593).[3] It was the value of fabrics in relation to income that governed most people's textile purchases. Christmas expenses for the Lestrange family in 1519 serve to illustrate purchasing power at the beginning of the century. A day's wage for a labourer would buy a yard of the cheapest cloth (canvas at 4d a yard), while his wages for six months would barely buy a yard of the dearest (cloth of gold at 58s 8d a yard), and a fine cloak, at £20, would require more than three years' labour.[4]

The contemporary hierarchy of fabrics is outlined in table 2 (pages 36–37). Within each category, the fabrics are listed in approximate order of value, starting with the most expensive. The fabrics available to the 16th-century consumer were made only from natural animal and vegetable fibres – mainly wool, linen and silk – all of which were processed entirely by hand. Despite this apparent restriction, a staggering range of different types and qualities was produced by highly skilled professionals. Expertise within each specialized craft was honed to such a degree that the quality of some of these materials is hard to match today. Some Tudor fabrics are familiar (the equivalent of broadcloth for a winter coat or silk satin for a ball gown), but others, such as tufted mockadoes and tissued taffetas, are not so easy to visualize.

a peticoate of crymsen Satten lined with red kersie the bodies and placarde lined with fyne lennen cloth
1554, Mary Tudor's accounts

1. *The Tailor* by Giovanni Moroni, 1579
(© The National Gallery, London).

Table 2: Clothing fabrics in the 16th century

c16th name	Characteristics and use	Contemporary evidence	Note
LINEN			
Lawn	Often transparent, woven of gossamer-fine thread. Used by the wealthy for partlets, ruffs, collars, cuffs, aprons, kerchiefs	'2 doz lawnes for partlettes price the dox 60s … 2 doz lawnes for pastes price the doz 12s' for Lady Mary Tudor (1538); 'Two yardes of laune at 7s 4d then to make ruffes 14s 8d' (1592)	A
Cambric	Very high quality linen of a plain, even weave, very white. Used for the finest shirts, smocks, rails, kerchiefs, aprons	'Twenty elles of Camericke for Raills and other necessaries' for Lady Mary Tudor (1534); 'A cambric ruff' Widow (1590s)	B
Holland	Good to middling quality. Used for shirts, smocks, coifs, headrails, neckerchiefs, ruffs, aprons for upper and middling sort; linings, interlinings of fine garments	'Oon piece of holland cloth at 3s 4d thell for smokkes and kercheffs' for Lady Mary Tudor (1534); 'An holland apron gathered' Widow (1572); 'A holland neckercher with strings' Widow (1586)	C
Lockram	A coarse, loosely woven fabric of hemp or flax. Used for coifs, rails, shirts, smocks, aprons and kerchiefs for yeomen and husbandmen.	'3 new neckerchers (the ruffs are holland, the bands and bodies lockram' (1587)	D
Canvas and sackcloth	A hemp cloth available in several qualities; could be striped or tufted. Used for shirts and smocks for yeomen and husbandmen; heavier canvas for doublets, interlinings for doublets, upperbodies, breeches	'My white sack doublet' Husbandman (1567); 'Russet petticoat upperbodied with canvas' (1576); '1 pair of white canvas breeches' Sailor (1585)	E
Buckram	Weighty, fairly coarse; glued for paste buckram. Used for farthingales; lining, edging and interlining of coats, gowns; paste buckram for stiffening bodies, standing collars, hoods	'A Louse Gowne of Russett Taphata … the coller lined with past buckeram' for Queen Mary (1558); 'For making a verthingale of fine blak buckeram with ropes of bente and bottomed with kersey' for Queen Elizabeth (1571)	F
WOOL			
Scarlet	Broadcloth of the highest quality; dyed in kermes, usually red. Used for petticoats, waistcoats, hose, gowns, cloaks, linings	'A peyre of Scarlet hoses … two stomagers of Crymson Saten lyned with Scaarlet' for Henry VIII (1510); '3 yardes 1 quarter fyne skarlett for a Clooke … at 20s' for Catherine Parr (1546)	G
Broadcloth	Finest woollen cloth, 54 to 63 inches wide (hence the name), of plain weave, with a weft of good-quality carded short-staple wool, well-fulled, a nap raised on it and then sheared; for gowns, coats, cassocks	'4 brode yardes of wollen cloth … every yarde 10s' (1533); 'A black broadcloth cassock' Widow (1573); 'Black broadcloth coat' Husbandman (1592)	H
Stammel	Lesser quality than the above; always red. Used for petticoats for the middling and lower sorts	'My red petticoat of stammel colour' Woman (1583); 'Stammel at 14s 6d the yard' (1592)	I
Kersey	Cloth a yard wide with a fairly coarse twill weave, not as much fulled as broadcloth. Used for hose, petticoats, stockings, linings, cloaks	'9 yards of green kersey for 6 pair of hose at 3s 4d' for Henry VIII's yeoman and grooms of the longbows, crossbows and leash (1539)	J
Russet	Country russet, a coarse narrow wool, undyed and unfinished; broad russet, better quality, might be dyed; London russet, as wide and costly as broadcloth. Used for breeches, petticoats, kirtles, coats, gowns	'Two gownes … of Russett Furred with foxx and … of Tawney furred with blak bogie price of every yarde 5s' for Sir Edmond de la Pole (1511); '3 yardes brode russett at 2s 8d the yarde for a kyrtell' for Thomasine Petre (1555)	K
Frizado	Similar to but better quality than frieze (see below). Used for gowns, cloaks, petticoats, kirtles	'A spanysshe Clooke of freiseado' for Henry VIII's page, Culpepir (1534); 'Crimson freseadowe 5s 6d a yd' (1591)	L
Frieze	Very thick, heavy, plain weave, well-fulled cloth, with raised hairy surface on one or both sides. Made from cheaper fleeces unfit for finer cloth. Used for outer garments such as gowns and coats; linings and interlinings for the well-to-do with silk and worsted; and in natural, undyed colours for petticoats, kirtles, gowns, coats, jerkins, breeches, hose	'Oon coote of grene cloth lynyd with yrisshe frise' for the king's henchmen (1534); 'My black frize gown' (1567); 'Making your frese yerkyn … 16d … frese to it … 6s 8d' for Nathaniel Bacon (1590); 'My best frize gown faced with coney' Widow (1595)	M
Kendall	A narrow woollen fabric dyed green; often lightly napped. Used for coats, gowns	'40 yards of Kendall at 16d per yard to make them a coat each' for five grooms of Henry VIII's buckhounds (1539)	N
Cotton	Narrow wool, loosely woven and fairly lightweight; there was no cotton fibre in this fabric – raising the nap was known as 'cottoning'. Used for bum rolls; linings of coats, doublets, gowns, kirtles, stomachers	'Eight yardes of blak cotton for lynyng of the said Cotes price every yerde eight pens' for Henry VIII's yeomen of the leash (1534); 'Half yard of cotton to make a roll and a yard of lace 6d' for Mistress Bacon (1591)	O
Flannel	A lightweight cloth with a plain open weave, made of loosely spun wool, soft and spongy. Used for petticoats and waistcoats for ordinary folk; warm linings for the fashionable	'A payer of hose of blake cloth stokyde with cloth of silver and blake tynsent … & a yerde half of fyne skarlet flannon for lynyng of the same' for Henry VIII (1522)	P
Worsted (see also below)	A well-twisted yarn, spun from long fleece; and a smooth, strong, light, cool, fluid fabric woven from this yarn. Used for summer gowns, kirtles, doublets, aprons	'3 ells of blacke English worsted … at 13s the ell' for Thomasine Petre (1559); 'Worsted kirtle with two velvet guards' Widow (1588)	Q
Grogram and buffin	Ribbed worsteds, sometimes mixed with silk; buffin was more delicate than grogram. Used for gowns, cassocks, petticoats	'Five yardes of yellowe buffin to make mistress Win apetacote 1s 4d the yard' ?? (1592); 'My grogram cassock garded with velvet' Bricklayer (1602)	R
Russells	A luxury worsted with a satin weave, and sometimes a damasked pattern. Used for gowns, kirtles	'7 yardes of Russell worsted … for a gowne for mistris Kedall price the yarde 20d – 12s 11d' for Catherine Parr (1554/5); 'A kyrtle … of striped Russels lyned with cotton' for Jane, Queen Mary's fool (1558); 'A yarde of blacke russells for upperboding of a gowne 3s 8d' for Thomasine Petre (1559)	S

c16th name	Characteristics and use	Contemporary evidence	Note
Durance	Closely woven worsteds. Used for aprons	'My new green durance apron and the lace to make the same' (c1587–1599)	T
Say and serge	Lightweight, hardwearing twills. Some says had a silk warp; serges had a worsted warp and a woollen weft. Used for linings, everyday wear for the middling sort	'One yarde ½ tawny saye for a wastcote and an apron 2s 6d' ie 10d a yard for Thomasine Petre (1555); 'My say jacket' Mercer (1579)	U
Bay	Lightweight cloth of loose, plain weave; worsted warp and wool weft, with a napped surface. Used for petticoats, gowns, linings	'2 yardes of bayes for my mistress petecote – 5s … 3 yardes of taweney bayes 8s' (1591)	V
SILK			
Velvet	An expensive weave with two warps, one of which passed over metal rods in the loom to create loops which were left or cut to form a pile; the use of both in one fabric made a pattern. Velvet was restricted by sumptuary law. Used for gowns, kirtles, coats, jackets, jerkins, doublets, hose, partlets, shoes, headgear for the wealthy; also guarding garments of less costly or lighter-weight materials; purses, partlets, bonnets for lesser folk	'Black velvet for doublets at 13s 4d' for three viol players in Henry VIII's household (1531); 'None shall wear in his apparel any … velvet, crimson, scarlet or blue … except dukes, marquises, earls or their children, barons, and knights of the order [of the garter]' (1533); '1 of my coats which is lined with velvet in the collar' Widow (1585); 'A pair of venetians of buff leather with velvet guards' (1586); 'My kirtle of wrought velvet' Widow (1590)	W
Satin	A twill weave in which the weft threads are not seen on the surface and the vertical warp threads give a rich, glossy sheen; lighter than velvet. Used for gowns, kirtles, coats, jackets, jerkins, doublets; linings and unseen portions in velvet and cloth-of-gold garments	'60 yards of Satten for 20 doblettes for the saide Neweyeres giftes divers officers of the howsholde … at 3s 6d' from Catherine Parr (1544); 'My satin kirtle' Widow (1577); 'My best puke gown faced with satin and welted with velvet' Citizen and mercer of London (1584)	X
Damask	A smooth weave, often with a satin background, on which a design is created by bringing the weft threads to the surface. Used for summer gowns, kirtles, coats, jackets, jerkins, partlets	'A shorte stalking cote of white damaske' for Henry VIII (1512); 'Black damaske for a Gowne for mistress Kidall price of evrye yarde 7s' for Catherine Parr (1543); '1 red petticoat that hath a damask body' Widow (1576)	Y
Taffeta (see also below)	Plain weave silk with a stiff papery quality; could be a single colour or changeable (warp and weft of differing colours); tuft taffeta was woven with raised spots or stripes cut to produce a velvet pile of a different colour to the ground. Used for gowns, kirtles, coats, doublets, hose, petticoats, stomachers and garment linings or pullings out; hat linings	'17 yerdes of ell braude taffete at 8s the yerd' for Anne of Cleves (1540); 'A satin doublet sleeved with taffeta' Yeoman (1566); 'Tuft taffeta kirtle' Widow (1588); 'A white taffeta doublet and sleeves' Widow (1587–1599)	Z
Grosgrain	A type of taffeta, with wefts thicker than the warp to give a ribbed surface; sometimes 'tabbied' – given a moiré effect. Used for gowns, kirtles, jerkins	'My silk grogram doublet' Yeoman (1588); '4 yards ¼ of silke grogrinn to the alteringe of mistress Ann Bacons goune at 8s – 34s' (1592)	a
Sarcenet	A lightweight even-weave taffeta. Used for linings, pullings-out and small items	'Two hatbandes of sarcenet' Henry VIII's henchmen (1534); 'A Louse Gowne of Russett Taphata … The Sleves pulled owte with russet Taphata Sarceonet' for Queen Mary (1558)	b
MIXES			
Cloth of gold, cloth of silver and tinsel	Woven with a warp of silk and wefts of silk and/or bullion, these were all restricted by sumptuary law. Cloths of silver and gold were weighty and could be patterned by means of their differing wefts or with raised loops like an uncut velvet. Used for gowns, coats, jackets, doublets, stomachers, kirtles, partlets, shoes. Tinsel (tylsent) was cheaper and lighter, unpatterned, but displaying both the colour of the silk and the glitter of the bullion	'For making and lynyng of a dublet of cloth of gold of damaske' for Henry VIII (1510); 'A doublet of blewe tynsell…for Culpepir oure page' Henry VIII's accounts (1534); 'A cote…with a pair of sleeves of tinsel' for Prince Edward (1539); '16 yardes of Clothe of Silver playn for a French gowne for the Quenes grace price of everye yarde 28s,' for Catherine Parr (1544); '2 yardes ½ of Tinsell at 2s 4d yd' for the Bacon family (1591)	c
Chamlet	Lightweight material made from a mix of silk with hair and/or linen; could be watered or grosgrain; the most affordable silk; gowns limited to those with £40 a year. Used for doublets, coats, kirtles	'Oon dublet of chamlet … price every yarde thre shillinges and foure pens' for Henry VIII's children of the leash (1531); 'My red petticoat with the chamlet over body' Widow (1578)	d
Cyprus	Thin and transparent, usually a silk/linen mix, sometimes with a crepe weave. Used for linings, hat bands, especially black cypress for mourning	'Item an olde tawny gowne of damaske Lyned wythe satteny Cypres valewed at 10s' inventory of William Legh Esquire (1537)	e
Mockado	Sometimes called mock velvet but the pile was of wool not silk; the ground was any combination of wool, silk and linen; it might be plain striped or tufted, the pile being a different colour to the ground. Used for gowns, kirtles, coats, farthingales	'A verdingall of red mockado' for Lady Jane Seymour, Henry VIII's accounts (1558); 'Red petticoat with an upper body of red mockado' Widow (1576); 'A mockado half kirtle' Single woman (1588)	f
Fustian	The only common fabric at this time that might contain cotton thread; featured a linen or worsted warp (smooth and strong) and a cotton or wool weft (soft and fluffy); made in Lancashire and Genoa ('jean'), Ulm ('holmes'), Milan (at twice the price of the others) and Naples (with a dense velvety nap, this could be embroidered and perfumed). Prices ranged from 8d to 4s a yard. Used for doublets, kirtles, gowns, sleeves, linings for all these	'Satin for two doublets … fustian for lining the same … at 8d … fustian for two other doublets at 12d. … cotton for lining the same at 8d' for Henry VIII's serjeants of the buckhounds (1539); 'A gowne of red fustian enaples for Jane our foole' from Queen Mary (1558); 'Black fustian doublet' Husbandman (1572); 'A cotton waistcoat with a pair of fustian sleeves' Millwright (1585); 'A fustian doublet lined with silver lace' Gentleman (1590)	g
Satin de Bruges; bridges satin	A cheaper imitation of silk satin with close-packed warp threads hiding the linen weft threads. The warp could be silk or worsted. Used for unseen portions of garments by the wealthy and to replace satin by the less well off; it is possible that items listed as satin by the lower orders may have been satin de bruges not silk satin	'3 quarters of blacke bruges Satten for a gowne for mistris Kedall price the yarde 20d' for Catherine Parr (1543); '2 yards whyte bridge satten to pece the white satten kirtle at 2s 6d the yarde' for Thomasine Petre's wedding kirtle (1559)	h
Linsey-wolsey	Loosely woven cloth of linen warp and woollen weft. Used for gowns, coats, petticoats by the poorer sort	'A pair of linsey woolsey sleeves' Single woman (1582)	i

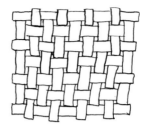

2. (left) Plain weave.

3. (left) Twill weave.

4. *Martin Frobisher* by Cornelius Ketel, 1577
(© The Bodleian Library, University of Oxford).

Many terms used to describe fabrics refer not to the fibre but to the methods of spinning, weaving and finishing the cloth. For example, worsted is a tight, smooth yarn spun from long, smooth fleeces, whereas wool is the fluffy, bulky product of short, crinkly fleeces. The two yarns work quite differently in the fabric. All the textiles in table 2 are created from interwoven threads crossing at right angles. The threads stretched lengthways on the loom are called the warp, while those that are woven from side to side form the weft. A plain weave is produced when each weft thread passes under one warp thread and over the next (fig 2). The ribbed surface of grosgrain is a plain weave. A twill weave is created when (for example) each weft thread passes over three warp threads and under one, creating a tiny area of fabric where the warp is seen prominently on the surface (fig 3). Twills often have diagonal lines of these minute raised areas appearing across the fabric. The smooth gloss of satin is a specialized form of twill. Satin, grosgrain and most other weaves can be woven with wool, worsted or mixed fibres, as well as with silk.

Many woollen and part-woollen cloths were fulled and finished. Fulling involved varying degrees of washing and pummelling. Its aim was to felt the fluffy surface of the wool threads together, hiding the weave and making the cloth stronger and warmer. During the finishing process, a nap might be raised out of this felt which could be left rough or sheared short and smooth. Some materials were produced to suit a specific purpose: for example, the elasticity required for full-length hose called for a woollen fabric with a fairly loose twill weave, only lightly fulled.

There were other materials, such as cotton, leather and fur, which played an important part in clothing the Tudor population. Cotton thread was used as a weft only in such fabrics as fustian. Pure cotton fabrics, woven in the east and known as calicoes, were reaching England by the end of the period, but were still vastly outnumbered by linen and hemp fabrics. Cotton-spinning technology in Europe was primitive: the thread was not strong enough to serve as a warp, which precluded pure cotton fabrics from being manufactured closer to home. Raw cotton fibre had been imported from at least the 13th century and was used for stuffing clothing, padded armour and bedding. In a study of 20 extant doublets, six were found to be padded with cotton wadding.[5]

Leather was used for men's clothing and is the most frequently specified material for doublets in the Essex wills (40 per cent of 284 items), along with canvas (24 per cent) and fustian (21 per cent). Common types include sheep's, calf's, buck's, doe's, buff and spruce. Chamois leather was used for lining fabric hose. The buff leather used for clothing, being naturally tanned, was soft and could be draped like woven cloth. It was not hard and stiff as many modern leathers are. This is represented in a portrait of Martin Frobisher (fig 4), who wears a jerkin with cut tabs at the waist and shoulders, and venetian hose, the fullness of which is softly gathered at the waist. Apart from a 'payre of bodies of sweet leather' made for Queen Elizabeth in 1579, there appear to be no other examples of women's clothing made from leather.[6]

Furs were used extensively by the fashionable for warmth and decoration, mainly as linings. The 1533 Act of Apparel denied it to agricultural workers, who most needed its warmth. Husbandmen were to wear no fur at all, not even the English lamb or rabbit allowed to yeomen. For the middling sort, there was a variety of affordable furs: fox, foyne (beech marten), grey jenet (civet cat), wildcat, budge or bogey (lamb), shanks (from the legs of sheep) and coney (rabbit). From the act, it seems that black jenet, budge and coney were valued above the grey and white versions. Squirrel (the prestige fur of previous centuries) and mink rarely appear in the royal accounts, but leopard was available even to the gentry and other wealthy persons. This is not immediately evident from the portraits of the period, because 'libbards' wombs' – the softer, longer belly fur – were the favoured part of the pelt. In the wills of Elizabethan Essex, men's gowns sport fur but women's clothes have very little. All noblemen were permitted lucerne (lynx) and black jenet, while sable and ermine were reserved for the high nobility and the royal family.[7] The tiny white winter pelts of the weasel were used to make lettice caps for ladies.

Knitting was usual for caps and bonnets, which were often knitted larger than required, fulled to shrink and felted. From at least the middle of the century, knitting was used for working people's stockings and nether hose, women's jackets and men's waistcoats. An Essex woman left her 'best knit sleeves' in her will of 1565.[8] Silk breeches formed part of an unusual collection of knitted garments owned by the Elector Augustus of Saxony in the 1550s, which also included doublets and stockings.[9] Essex men's hose were sometimes knitted; 4 per cent of 106 items are so described.

Visual sources show a wealth of patterned materials worn by the elite. Portraits show both branched and geometric designs. Catherine Parr has a particularly impressive combination of tissued cloth of silver with a very large branched pattern and a rich wrought red velvet with a smaller geometric pattern. Later in the century, the portrait of Elizabeth Buxton shows a glossy, grey damask with a more delicate design of leaves and flowers (fig 5). Paintings rarely show the abundance of striped fabrics worn by all ranks of society, which is evident from documentary sources. Queen Elizabeth owned many gowns, petticoats and kirtles made of striped silk. There are 11 striped gowns in a list of lost items, of which one is a kirtle and bodies 'of great bard velvet', suggesting that both wide and narrow stripes were known. A rare depiction is that of a pink kirtle with narrow red and green stripes, worn by a figure who is probably Jane, fool to Mary Tudor, under her branched damask gown (fig 6). A striped canvas doublet is mentioned in the will of an Essex gentleman in 1584.[10]

There is a handful of references to checked fabrics, which seem to have been used for working clothing only. A statute of 1606 refers to 'all clothes called Check-Kersies, Straights and plain Greys.'[11] A fragment of red and yellow checked wool, found inside one of the leather jerkins on the *Mary Rose*, may have been a lining or a shirt. Chequered velvet is mentioned in Queen Mary's accounts of 1554. The checks were probably formed with areas of cut and uncut velvet rather than woven in different colours.[12]

Dyeing was a huge professional industry; only small items such as stockings might be dyed by tailors or at home. Fleece could be dyed at any of three points in its journey from the sheep to the wardrobe. Dyeing wool before it was spun offered the opportunity to spin multicoloured yarns. This produced the flecked fabrics known as mingle, medley or motley. A shoemaker left a 'greenish mingle-coloured cloak' in his will of 1600.[13] Another approach was to dye the spun yarn, which allowed the weaving not only of 'changeable' fabrics, with a warp of one colour and weft of another, but also of stripes, checks and damasks. Finally, the woven cloth could be dyed in the piece – a much more demanding process, with greater risks of failure. This added considerably to the value of the cloth, particularly if overdyeing with a second colour was needed to reach the desired hue.

The range of colours used in the clothing of the common sort was fairly limited. A great many fabrics were of undyed yarn, known as sheep's colour, white, black, russet or grey. These last two were also fabric names and were perceived as standard wear for country people. However, the descriptions of garments left in the Essex wills reveal a tendency toward a different convention in dress. The main colours were black, white, blue and red, and these were usually confined to specific

5. (left) *Portrait of Elizabeth Buxton, née Kemp* attributed to Robert Peake c. 1588–90 (© Norwich Castle Museum and Art Gallery).

6. A detail from *The Family of Henry VIII* (thought to depict Jane the Fool) by an unknown artist, 1545 (The Royal Collection © 2005 Her Majesty Queen Elizabeth II).

7. A young man's doublet of leather or white kid (inventory no. a.1977.237), possibly German, c. 1610 (© National Museums of Scotland).

8. Heavily pieced doublet or jerkin made from two differently patterned velvet fabrics, c. 1610 (© Manchester Art Gallery). The skirts are interlined with canvas.

garments. For both men and women, the majority of outer garments, such as gowns, coats and cloaks, were black. True black was difficult to dye and highly desirable. Typical fashionable ensembles were made entirely of black fabrics. One example is the gown worn by Mary of Guise in 1551, which was of black damask, lined in black taffeta and edged in black velvet, with a pair of black satin sleeves.[14] A painting of four children illustrates this use of black well, hinting at the variety of textural interest as the light played on the different surfaces (fig 9).

There were many poor attempts at black that had green or brown undertones. These are the blacks that the majority of people could afford. True black might be worn in small ways, such as a hat, partlet or apron.

White canvas and fustian were usual for men's doublets. White was also worn by the fashionable, but for different reasons. The white silks worn by the rich were costly and highly impractical. Later in Queen Elizabeth's reign, she adopted black and white as her colours and it was complimentary to her to wear them at court.

Blue is mentioned predominantly in Elizabethan men's wills, mainly for coats (32 per cent of 157 items) and stockings, although 20 per cent of breeches (25 items) are blue too. Wool dyed with woad was cheap to produce and became associated with servants' livery, which may explain the preponderance of blue coats in accounts of the period, although it was never fashionable. The sumptuary law of 1533 reserved blue (and crimson) velvet for the nobility and garter knights. Henry VIII had a few blue garments among his many crimson, green, black and russet outfits. Queen Mary had a blue gown listed in her 1554 accounts. A page in Henry's household was ordered 'a doublet of blewe tynsell' in 1534. These are, however, the exceptions not the rule.[15]

While blue was a man's colour, red was that of the ordinary woman. Achieved cheaply by dyeing with madder, it was limited almost entirely to one garment, the petticoat, although some Elizabethan kirtles and waistcoats were also red. Of the 1,123 petticoats left in Essex wills, 52 per cent are described as red, while 40 per cent are russet, which could indicate the colour or the fabric. Where petticoat colours are clearly specified (361 items), 87 per cent were red, five per cent were white or black, and two per cent were blue. This habit of wearing red petticoats was not restricted to the poor. The accounts of Mary Tudor, Catherine Parr and Thomasine Petre also contain examples in red, though of much finer fabrics.[16] The use of red was boosted by the belief that it had healthful benefits. Andrew Borde's *A Dyetary of Helth* of 1542 recommends: 'Next your sherte use you to were a

9. *A group of four children making music* by Master of the Countess of Warwick, c. 1565. (© Weiss Gallery).

petycote (waistcoat) of skarlet ... made of stammel or linsye-wolsye.' The beds of those suffering from fevers were often hung with red. It was believed that Queen Elizabeth was saved from small pox by being wrapped in red flannel and it was also used for compresses for the stomach.[17]

Other colours were used more widely by middling and fashionable sorts. *The Fête at Bermondsey* gives a wonderful view of the range of colours in the Tudor palette. The natural dyes of the period were capable of creating vivid colours, but the shades were less saturated than those of today (fig 12). The dyes that produced the most intense colours were the most valued, the prime example of this being kermes (the dried bodies of pregnant shield insects), known as 'grain'. As a red dye, grain could also be used to create dark blue, purple, violet, black and brown. All these colours could be obtained with other dyes, but if kermes had been used, it was always specified, and it showed in the price: in Norfolk in 1593, 'a paier of purple in grayne stockinges dieinge' cost 16d whereas 'dieinge a paier of morrye [wine red] stockings' was half the price at 8d. Likewise, 50 years earlier and higher up the social spectrum, Prince Edward's crimson velvet cost 26s a yard in 1544 because it was 'in grain', while the king's footmen had ordinary crimson velvet at 16s a yard in 1539 (fig 13).[18]

The brightest of red woollens was scarlet, a high-quality broadcloth dyed with kermes. Some scarlets were pre-dyed with green or blue to produce browns and purples, but the most dramatic were white wool dyed with pure kermes. During the 16th century, the term scarlet gradually extended from the fabric to the colour, so that it became possible for Mary Tudor to order 'Skarllyt kyrsseye.' However, scarlet was never used to refer to bright red silks, which were always called 'crimson', a word that derives from kermes.[19] Another cloth that gave its name to a colour was stammell. This was a good quality wool dyed with cochineal, a red dye which at this date was increasingly replacing the more expensive grain: 'Cutchoneale ... wherewith Stammel is died.'[20]

Producing purple, violet or murrey required a blue dye as well as red. Purple in grain silk was as costly as crimson, and its wear was limited by a statute of 1533 to the immediate royal family. Henry VIII always wore a gown of violet in grain silk to take part in the Maundy Thursday ceremony during Lent.[21] Shades of violet could be produced with mixes of madder and woad, which allowed humble people to own garments in this colour. There are 29 examples in the Essex wills.

Tailor-made clothing was not restricted, as it is today, to the wealthy. Having chosen the fabrics and purchased them from a draper or mercer, most

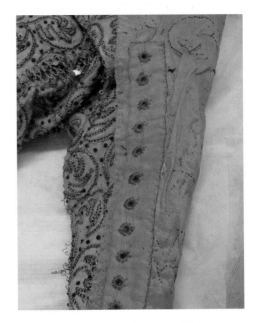

10. Lacing strip inside an embroidered jacket (Middleton Collection no. 11), c. 1600–1620 (© Lord Middleton Collection/Nottingham City Museums and Galleries).

11. A Spanish tailor's workshop, woodcut from *Geometria y traca* by Diego de Freyle, 1588 (by permission of the Folger Shakespeare Library).

12. Woollen yarns dyed using a range of natural dyestuffs available during the 16th century. Renaissance Dyeing, France (www.naturaldyeing.co.uk).

16th-century people commissioned a tailor to make them into garments. Linen garments, such as shirts, smocks, coifs, partlets and sleeves, were the exception, as these were made by women in the home. Lady Margaret Hoby regularly records such tasks in her diary.[22]

Typically, tailors were the sons of craftsmen or the younger sons of minor gentry, who had served a seven-year apprenticeship with a master tailor.[23] Tailoring was a skilled craft, which took years to learn and many more to perfect (fig 11). Some of the methods used by 16th-century tailors are recorded in accounts and pattern books of the period. One skill that the tailor's clients would appreciate was the art of piecing. If a width of fabric was insufficient for a pattern piece to be cut in one, extra were joined to widen it. Cutting a garment from the smallest possible quantity of fabric was a primary concern when the cost of materials was so much higher than the cost of the tailor's time. Silks were usually between 20 and 22 inches wide, which precluded cutting many pattern pieces without piecing. A Spanish tailor, Alcega, wrote in his book that it was advisable for a pattern to be cut with as few pieces as possible and that the nap should run in the same direction for the whole garment.[24]

The remnants left after cutting out a garment were called cabbage. These fragments were never discarded. A velvet doublet in the collection at Platt Hall (fig 8) seems to have been made from the cabbage of two other garments. It has an extraordinary number of pieced components, which are cut from two differently patterned green velvets, the nap of which runs in all directions. The desire to avoid waste is illustrated by another common practice. Garments were often made from a combination of fabrics – with more expensive choices where they showed and cheaper alternatives where they were hidden. Even the royal wardrobe accounts have regular references to garments which are 'lined with', 'turned up with', 'let down with', 'faced with', and 'edged with' a variety of fabrics.

Sir William Cavendish, husband to Bess of Hardwick, had holland shirts made for him in the early 1550s with a finer holland for the borders and cuffs. Similarly, the Crayforde girls, the daughters of a gentleman, had smocks made in the 1570s of canvas, which was a fairly heavy linen (though not as heavy or stiff as modern canvas), but with finer, more expensive linen for their sleeves.[25]

Tailors made prototype garments in cheap fabrics to ensure that the fit and style were appropriate before the top fabric was cut out. These were called patterns by Queen Elizabeth's tailor, Walter Fyshe, who used buckram, canvas or fustian for them. Once fitted, the patterns would be unpicked and transferred to brown paper or laid directly on the top fabrics to be cut out.[26]

Close examination of extant 16th-century garments has revealed further techniques which seem to have been common practice. Before use, linen or silk thread was passed through a lump of beeswax. This strengthened it and helped prevent knots and fraying. The most usual method of sewing long constructional seams together was back stitch. Another common practice was to complete the different elements and then join them by whipping the edges together. This method was useful when sewing thick fabrics or for attaching pleated skirts, as it avoided having bulky turnings next to a seam. Raw edges on unlined outer garments, which would not be subjected to the rigours of washing, could be overcast to prevent fraying. Wax was also used for this purpose. Searing candle was a regular order in Queen Elizabeth's Great Wardrobe and is also listed in the accounts of Norfolk tailors Peckover and Gallyard in the 1590s.[27]

Raw edges were sometimes left untreated. This was most usual in cloaks of well-fulled wool. Leaving the hem raw ensured that the fabric would hang well. Where a modern dressmaker would normally hem or face a garment, a Tudor tailor would be as likely to bind or 'edge' it. Strips of the garment fabric or a special binding ribbon, known as 'lyor', could be used. Alcega wrote that extra fabric must be allowed if a garment is to be edged rather than hemmed, assuming that the edging will be made of the same fabric. Binding protected the garment fabric on necklines and hems, where constant friction and grime wore them away. It also produced a smooth finish where multiple layers of fabric converged (for example, top fabric, interlining and lining).

Garments were frequently interlined. Standing collars, for example, were stiffened with paste buckram, and firm buckrams and canvases were used to add substance (fig 8). Bulky woollens, such as freize, kersey and cotton, interlined pleated skirts and full sleeves. Raw fleece and cotton were both used for stuffing and padding (fig 7). Where boning was used, it took the form of bents (dried grasses) or whalebone. Fashionable outer clothing was nearly always lined (fig 10). As with top fabrics, economy was of the essence, and linings were pieced. A tailor's bill of 1590 charges for 'making your frese yerkyn, fustion to lyne it, taffeta to face it and edge the skyrtes.'[28]

Surface decoration features on clothing throughout the 16th century, but it is during the Elizabethan period that it becomes notably elaborate. These treatments were not the exclusive preserve of the elite. Guards and welts were strips cut from broad widths of fabric. They were applied in single or multiple rows around the edges of garments for both ordinary and gentlefolk. Guards around skirt hems were particularly common. Colour combinations were often subtle, with the guards being the same colour as the garment but of a different fabric, adding textural interest. Black velvet on black wool or black silk was a favourite. Welts were similar to guards, but were usually narrower and tended to be rounded (as with piping for cushions today). They were often cut from the same fabric as the garment they embellished and could be set into seams. A servant bequeathed his 'best welted canvas doublet' in 1582.[29]

Slashing was very popular during the first half of the century, especially for men's wear. The slashes were generally fairly large, allowing a profusion of silk lining, or 'pullings out', to emerge. As the century progressed, the slashing became more refined, with smaller and more numerous cuts worked into complex designs, or 'cutt allover with a verye busye cutt', as one of Queen Elizabeth's garments was described.[30] The raw edges of the slashes were not finished or hemmed, although sometimes the back of the fabric might be brushed with size (a light glue). If the slashes were carried out diagonally across the grain, there would be little fraying. Sometimes the frayed edges were part of the intended effect, as was the case with a black satin forepart with matching sleeves for Queen Elizabeth which was 'cutt and ravelyd' in 1562.[31]

As the taste for smaller designs grew, pinking competed with slashing in popularity. Sharp blades of various shapes and sizes were used to cut the fabric. These were probably laid over a lead block to prevent the tools from losing their edge. Printing, not with ink, but with hot irons, which embossed a pattern on the surface of silk fabrics, was also popular (fig 15). A few examples of printed garments survive from the early 17th century. The Victoria & Albert Museum in London has a magnificent suit of printed cream-coloured satin and the Museum of London has a pair of sleeves of printed velvet, lined with printed satin. The accounts of Henry VIII and Queen Elizabeth all contain printed garments.[32] A strapwork effect was also popular (fig 14). Narrow strips of fabric or braid were interlaced to create it, although smocking techniques may have been employed to achieve the same look.

During the first half of the 16th century, embroidery was restricted to linen garments, such as smocks, shirts and partlets. Blackwork and white work were the

13. *Jane Seymour* by Hans Holbein, 1537 (© Royal Cabinet of Paintings Mauritshuis). Jane wears crimson velvet and has a row of pins down the side of her bodice. Her veil is pinned up on one side.

a new gown of Ryssell worsted, turned up with black velvet
1537, The Lisle Letters, 896

14. Strapwork fabric worn by *William, Lord Fitzwilliam of Milton and Gainspark (c. 1570–1643/4) and later 1st Baron Fitzwilliam of Lifford* by William Segar (circle of), c. 1595 (© Weiss Gallery).

15. A combination of slashing, stamping and spangles embellish the lustrous silk forepart and sleeves worn by *An unknown lady* by William Segar, c. 1585–1590 (© Weiss Gallery).

most common forms, the designs being simple geometric patterns, followed by arabesque and naturalistic styles. Later, blackwork was embellished with silver or gold thread. Work with red or blue silks on linen was especially popular in the 1560s. The vogue for natural motifs incorporated flowers, birds, fruit, insects and small creatures, which were typical of the late Elizabethan era (fig 16). Some of the most beautiful and skilfully worked examples of polychrome embroidery come from the last quarter of the century. Embroidery included spangles or 'oes', similar to modern sequins, although smaller, and made from real silver or silver gilt (fig 15). Spangles were relatively inexpensive; the Norfolk tailors, Peckover and Gallyard, used great quantities on wedding clothes they were making in the 1590s. Their accounts include payments for gold oes, silver oes, fine oes and superfine oes.[33]

Small pearls were also used to enhance embroidered work. Pearls were symbols of purity and became a great Elizabethan favourite. Real pearls were graded by size and usually described as great, mean, ragged and seed.[34] Queen Elizabeth was observed in 1598 'dressed in white Silk, bordered with pearls the size of beans.'[35] Not many people could afford pearls of this size, but fakes made of glass (venetian pearls) were produced in large numbers.[36]

Most Tudor ladies aspired to be accomplished needlewomen and often worked small items in the home (such as sweet bags to hold scented powders, cushion covers and coifs). Nevertheless, the embroidery for most garments was usually undertaken by professionals.

Lace was an important component of Elizabethan dress. In the 16th century, the term was used to refer to three different items of dress.[37] The laces used to tie garments together (discussed as a fastening on page 18) were often referred to as 'points'. Decorative braids made of metal thread were also known as 'laces'. These were often laid on top of seams. The third use of the term 'lace' referred to the intricately worked white linen thread fabric known as bonelace, as the bobbins used to make it were bone. This is what is known as lace today. The earliest mention of bobbin lace in England is in 1547, when a small purse trimmed with 'bone worke lace' was recorded in the inventories taken after the death of Henry VIII.[38] By 1577, bonelace was appearing in a will in Essex: 'a pair of white sleeves edged with white bonelace.'[39] Narrow laces (made in the same way as bonelace) in gold and silver threads, called billiment laces, were used to trim small items, such as coifs and gloves, as well as larger garments, such as the 'black cloth gown with the great billiment lace' in the will of a widow in 1591.[40] The very elaborate and large designs seen trimming ruffs and collars of the 1580s onwards are usually needle lace, rather than the bone lace made with bobbins (fig 17).

Tailors were not the only source of clothing in the 16th century. A few simple clothes were made in the home. Materials for them were bought from chapmen, who sold door-to-door. They distributed more linen than woollen cloth, which suggests that while shirts and smocks were sewn at home, wool was usually bought and made up elsewhere.[41] A travelling tailor could be hired to make garments for a whole household during his stay, as did 'the fellow that helped to make the marriage clothes' for the Bacons in 1597.[42]

A great many clothes were recycled. *The Lisle Letters* document the frugal re-use of every worn-out garment and the grateful acceptance (by a noble family) of made-over cast-offs from other people.[43] Botchers were often old or infirm tailors who refurbished old clothes.[44] A payment of 2d is recorded for 'the lame taylor' who mended a maid's petticoat for the second time in Wales. Clothes might be made over for a new owner after a bequest. Manuel Chamberlyn of Essex left his best clothes to his fellow servants and 'all my other old raiment to the poor people of Magdalen Laver'.[45]

Garments represented stored wealth for rich and poor. They were a source of ready cash in times of crisis. Frippers or pawnbrokers were happy to extend loans against pledged clothes. A contemporary claimed there were two or three of them on every street in London. William, Lord Vaux (fig 1, page 14), was unable to attend the House of Lords in 1593 because he could not afford to release his robes from the pawnbroker. Clothes which were not redeemed by repayment of a loan went into circulation as second-hand goods.[46]

The high value of clothes made their care a priority for all 16th-century people. Protective measures helped eke out their longevity. These measures included sewing fringes and guards, which could take the dirt and wear and then be easily replaced, to the bottom of skirts. A widow's will of 1584 describes her 'train gown with a dun guard'.[47]

When they were not being worn, clothes were stored in chests and coffers, often in their own boxes and bags. The royal wardrobe accounts include many entries for storage bags such as 'two Cases of buckerame for two riche Gownes' for Queen Mary in 1558.[48] Clothes put away for storage were brushed rather than washed. Henry VIII's wardrobe accounts for 1534 list 'one dussen brushes, and one dussen and a halfe of rubbers delivered to like use into our said warderobe of our roobis.' There were wardrobe staff whose specific duties were to brush Queen Elizabeth's clothes and lay sweet bags amongst the garments in store.[49]

Given that most 16th-century garments were made from fabrics that are professionally cleaned today, it is not surprising that brushing them was preferable to washing. This does not mean that clothes were dirty or, indeed, that the people who wore them lacked basic hygiene. There is ample evidence of laundering and cleaning in the 16th century. Contrary to popular belief, Queen Elizabeth was fastidious and kept high standards of personal cleanliness. Paul Hentzner noted that at 'Windsor Castle … there are worthy of notice here two bathing rooms, cieled and wainscoted with looking glass.'[50]

Linen was worn next to the skin because it was washable. Every baby, child, man and woman, regardless of rank, would have worn a shirt or a smock beneath their other clothes, forming an absorbent barrier between the body and the more expensive outer garments. Apart from linen stockings, these were the only garments that could be washed regularly in hot water. The more shirts and smocks an individual owned, the less frequently washday came around (fig 20). The wealthy owned such garments by the dozen and even the poorest of the testators in the Essex wills who left shirts or smocks owned at least two or three. When travelling from Italy to the French court in 1536, the Italian nobleman Ippolito d'Este took the best part of his household with him. The journey was arduous, taking them across open countryside and snowy mountains, yet Ippolito still wore a clean shirt every day and even his stable boys, the lowest ranking of all the servants, were given changes of shirts during the journey.[51]

Published manuals offered precise advice on removing stains from fabrics. Treatments included soap, alkalis (lye and lime-based), buffering agents (from wine lees), acids (orange and lemon juice), wetting agents (for example, ox gall), absorbents (such as fuller's earth) and dispersants (such as alcohol and egg white). These were used in careful combinations, requiring considerable skill and experience.[52]

If the stains could not be removed, more drastic action might be taken. The accounts of Bess of Hardwick describe the 'tornynge of a velvet gone and a gone of clothe and a clothe gone.'[53] The garment would have been unpicked, the lining removed and the fabric turned before the gown was sewn back together. Turning, altering and translating were all terms for the various techniques for rejuvenating

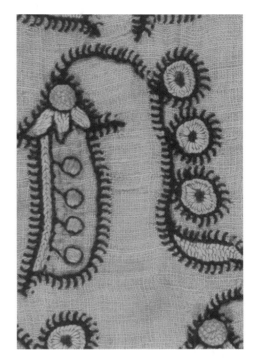

16. Linen embroidered with black and white silk in a repeated peapod design (Middleton Collection no. 15), c. 1570–1596 (© Lord Middleton Collection/Nottingham City Museums and Galleries).

17. Italian linen reticella lace (T.171.486-1903), late 16th century (© V&A Images/Victoria & Albert Museum, London).

clothes. The Norfolk tailors Peckover and Gallyard were paid for dyeing stockings and gowns and 'skowering owt of the spotes' of a gown.[54]

The number of garments owned by individuals varied enormously according to rank. At the top of society, an exaggerated account estimated that 6,000 gowns were left by Queen Elizabeth when she died, yet there were 1,900 items listed in an inventory of 1600.[55] At the other end of society, ten labourers' inventories in Oxfordshire between 1550 and 1596 suggested that the average man owned clothes worth a couple of shillings to a pound. His wardrobe comprised a pair of leather breeches, a coat, a waistcoat, a couple of shirts, stockings, shoes and a hat.[56]

Perhaps typical of the middling sort was Grace Cockete of Newport, Essex. In her will, dated 6 June 1562, she left at least four outfits, with several choices of petticoat, including a trained gown, a kirtle upperbodied with damask and a pair of damask sleeves, two frocks, four pairs of best shoes, 13 items of linen neck and headwear, five best smocks and sundry other items of velvet. While this may seem a surprisingly good stock of clothes, what is most noteworthy is the ease with which Grace is able to list her three red petticoats in rank order: to 'Margaret Coper my best red petticoat,' to 'Grace Rochell my next red petticoat' and to 'Robert Jackson's wife my worst red petticoat.' It is a vivid insight into the mind of a 16th-century person that she knew her family, friends and neighbours would recognize the hierarchy in her wardrobe and expected Mistress Jackson to feel flattered that, although someone else was worthy of the 'best', Grace's 'worst' petticoat was of sufficient value to be bequeathed to her.[57]

18. *Mary, Lady Guildford* by Hans Holbein, 1527 (© The St Louis Art Museum, Missouri. Museum Purchase).

19. A placard worn by *An unknown noblewoman* by George Gower (circle of), 1578 (© Weiss Gallery).

20. *Splendor Solis*, School of Nuernberg (inventory no. 78D3, folio 31 recto), c. 1531/2, 75 (© Bildarchiv
Preussischer Kulturbesitz/Kupferstichkabinett, Staatliche Museen zu Berlin/Joerg P Anders).

CONSTRUCTING THE GARMENTS: THE PATTERNS

'TEND YOVR NEDILL'

Inscription on a silver thimble found at Acton Court

The tools used by the 16th-century tailor have changed little in 400 years. Take away the mechanized sewing machine and the electricity to power a modern iron, and the sewing kit of today would be reassuringly familiar to the Tudor tailor. All he required was a good pair of shears or scissors, needles, pins, thimbles, wax or chalk for marking out, pressing irons and measuring sticks. Making garments today requires only this familiar equipment.

A Tudor tailor might also use a pair of dividers to mark out patterns, a shaping board (to assist in pattern cutting or for laying out the work underway), strips of parchment for measures, a stiletto for making eyelet holes, and a range of special tools for cutting, pinking and stamping designs on silks. Replicating surface decoration techniques today may require specially commissioned tools. However, a sharpened screwdriver, for pinking, and lead flashing (to serve as a cutting surface) are available at builders' merchants. Stamps designed for embossing leather may be heated and used for printing. Scalpels or rotary blades (use a cutting board under the fabric) are the best tools available today for slashing fabric.

The 21st-century sewing kit (left) and the 16th-century sewing kit (right).

Reproduction pinking tools by Dan Brown (www.greenmanforge.com) and Dave Hodgson (www.bodgeramour.co.uk). A lead-covered block is placed under the fabric to preserve the blade's edge.

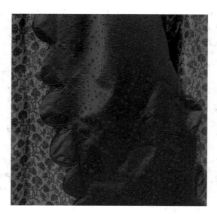

Detail of a hanging sleeve lined in pinked satin. This pinking was worked with a sharpened screwdriver.

Detail of a satin waistcoat with stamped design, embellished with spangles. Made by Lizzie Adcock (www.arumliliedesigns.co.uk)

Although the 16th-century tailor sewed his garments entirely by hand, the modern maker has the additional choice of using machine stitching. There are, however, elements of Tudor clothing construction for which it is difficult, if not impossible, to use a sewing machine. It is better, for example, to set in a cartridge-pleated sleeve or assemble the stiffened elements of hats and hoods by hand.

Sourcing materials

Choosing the materials for reconstructing 16th-century garments is one of the most important, and exciting, parts of the process. Using fabrics appropriate to a 16th-century garment will make the construction easier. A fabric that is appropriate to the period and the persona to be represented will also produce a costume with integrity. Unfortunately, many of the materials available to the Tudor tailor are no longer produced, or their modern equivalents are prohibitively expensive, and compromises must be made. Observation of colour, finish and pattern used in extant garments and depicted in paintings will provide a feel for the materials used in Tudor clothes, and this will make it easier to spot good substitutes. Lateral thinking is often the key to finding the right fabrics and trims. Fabrics may look better and be more accurate to the period if the 'wrong' side is used. Braids and lace can be improved by cutting them down or laying one over another. Jewellery findings may be customized by being opened up, flattened out or cut down.

The weight of modern sheeting is a good guide to the closely woven linen required for most shirts and smocks. Cotton is a cheaper and more easily available alternative, but it does not behave in the same way, nor is it so durable, as linen. For very fashionable underclothes, finer linen is necessary. Modern lawn makes an acceptable substitute, but finely woven ramie fibre feels much closer to the original. Unbleached, or partially bleached, linens are appropriate for smocks and shirts that are intended to represent those worn by the lower sort. It is advisable to wash all linen and cotton before it is made into garments, to allow for shrinkage.

Wool is one of the more difficult fabrics to purchase today, as its use tends to be limited to suits and winter coats. Wools with an evident weave (plain or twill) and a light, loose nap are best for common clothing. Wools with dense, even, short naps, such as modern meltons and doeskins, can be used to represent broadcloth for fashionable clothing. Worsted and venetian make good aprons, partlets, middle- and upper-class kirtles, doublets, hose and summer gowns.

Another material used extensively in 16th-century garments was fustian, a mixture of linen and cotton or worsted and cotton. The closest modern equivalent of the inexpensive type, which was used for linings, is brushed cotton. The more costly Naples fustian, used for fashionable doublets and gowns, had a raised, velvety nap. This material is best represented by good-quality cotton moleskin.

One of the most easily available silks today is dupion, an Indian silk with a slubbed surface. Although this has a long history in India, it was not used in England until recent times and is best avoided. Taffeta and satin are safer choices. Cheap, lightweight versions can be made to look far more substantial and expensive if mounted on calico.

The interlinings of clothing also require appropriate materials. Foundation fabrics include buckram, canvas and wadding, and it is useful to select the different types of boning and wiring required before you begin to put a garment together.

Reproduction stamping tools made by Dave Hodgson (www.bodgeramour.co.uk).

Basic foundation materials, starting from left: Top row: fleecy domet, white domet, black domet, polyester wadding. Middle row: light cotton wadding, heavy cotton wadding, buckram, silk organza. Bottom row: cotton canvas, linen canvas, linen buckram, calico.

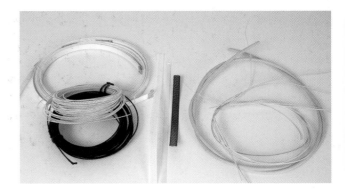

Stiffening materials, starting from left: Steel boning, millinery wire, plastic boning, cane.

Left: Binding raw edges. Right: To work a flat fell seam, both seam allowances are pressed to one side, then one of the allowances is cut down to half its width and the other folded over it and sewn down to cover all raw edges.

Attaching a pleated skirt to a bodice or doublet with whip stitch. Both skirt and body parts must be lined and completed before the two are joined.

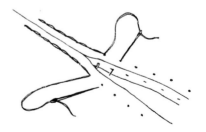

Butt stitch is used for joining thick pieces of leather. Two needles are used simultaneously, working with waxed thread through pre-prepared holes which enter the leather on the top edge and emerge through the middle of the cut edge.

Useful techniques

Basting

Basting is often mentioned in the instructions. This usually refers to the temporary stitching carried out by hand to keep layers together during the construction process. These stitches are removed once the garment is finished.

Binding and facing

For finishing edges, both binding and facing are used. With binding, a strip of fabric encloses the raw edges and is visible from the outside of the garment. A facing is applied to the inside of the garment and is not visible on the right side.

Whipping

Some of the pleated skirts of gowns and jackets may be too bulky to be machine stitched. If so, the 16th-century method of whipping the two together is useful. The skirt and body parts are finished and lined separately. The skirt is pleated and the tops of the pleats whipped together. The body is then pinned to the skirt, right sides facing, and the tops of the pleats are whipped to the edge of the body waist.

Working with leather and fur

Thin leather may be sewn in the same way as fabric. However, instead of the seams being pressed open, they are opened out and tapped down with a hammer. The seam allowances may be glued down for a flat finish. Thicker leathers require a different treatment. The edges that are to be joined are cut without seam allowances and are sewn together, using butt stitch. A leather-working tool with a flat spike called an awl is used to make the holes for the stitches. Two needles are threaded with waxed linen thread and the stitches are worked in tandem. The tension is pulled up evenly as the stitches progress.

Fur linings and facings are made up and finished around the edges before being sewn into the garment. When pieces of fur are joined there is no need for seam allowances at the edges that are to be sewn together. These edges are whipped together (fur sides facing) by hand, or with a small zigzag stitch on the machine. The outside edges of the facing or lining should have 6mm (¼ in) seam allowances. Working from the fur side, lay cotton tape (or bias binding for curved edges) on the edge and whip it in place by hand or use a small zigzag machine stitch. Turn the tape to the back of the fur and catch it down by hand.

Grading and notching

Seam allowances sometimes call for grading and notching. Grading is used where a number of layers of fabric have been sewn together. Bulk is minimized by trimming each of the layers down by slightly different amounts. Notching is used on curved seam allowances: concave curves are snipped and small wedges removed from convex curves.

Buttons

Matching buttons to complete a garment can be made by hand with cloth or thread. To make a cloth button, mark a circle on a piece of the fabric by drawing around a cotton reel. Cut this out as a square. Gather the circle up loosely with running stitch (a) and poke the corners of the square into the middle, using the point of a small pair of scissors (b). Pull the gathering up tightly and secure with a few stitches (c). Use the remaining length of thread to sew the button loosely to the garment. Work around the 'stalk' with buttonhole stitch to finish.

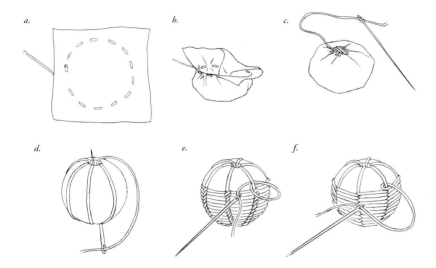

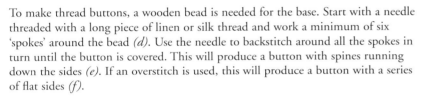

Notching curved seam allowances. Above left: snips are made in concave curves allowing the fabric to open up. Above right: notches are taken from convex curves to reduce bulk.

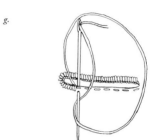

To make thread buttons, a wooden bead is needed for the base. Start with a needle threaded with a long piece of linen or silk thread and work a minimum of six 'spokes' around the bead *(d)*. Use the needle to backstitch around all the spokes in turn until the button is covered. This will produce a button with spines running down the sides *(e)*. If an overstitch is used, this will produce a button with a series of flat sides *(f)*.

Buttonholes and eyelets

Buttonholes (see pic *(g)*, right) should be marked out and prepared by sewing a box of small running stitches around the area to be cut. Cut the buttonhole and work around the slit with buttonhole stitch. Eyelets are made by forcing a stiletto or knitting needle through the fabric. The hole is then reinforced by whipping around it with plain or buttonhole stitches (see pic *(h)*, right).

Hooks and eyes

Hooks and eyes are sewn on by stitching through the looped parts and catching down the outside edges of the hooks or eyes to prevent them from pulling when fastened. It is advisable to sew hooks and eyes alternately on each side to help prevent them from coming undone when the garment is worn.

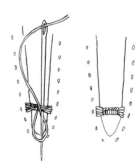

Levelling skirts

Level skirts are best achieved by tying a piece of elastic around the waist of the wearer or a stand adjusted to the same height. If a farthingale is to be worn, put this on the wearer or stand first. Loosely arrange the skirt under the elastic so that the hem is about 5cm (2in) higher than required. Arrange the fullness evenly around the waist and gently tug the skirt down until the hem is level and the correct distance from the floor. Mark the skirt at the waist just below the elastic with chalk or pins. If the bodice waist dips, mark the shape on the skirt by pinning the bodice or waistband pattern over the top of the skirt at the centre front and arranging pins to follow the shape immediately below it. Carefully remove the skirt and spread it out on a flat surface. The line will be a little irregular and should be smoothed. If the skirt is a calico toile, the excess material should be is cut away and the line transferred to a paper pattern. If the top fabric is used, baste a line 5cm (2in) below the chalk/pin line. Cut the excess fabric away leaving a 5cm (2in) seam allowance above the chalk/pin line.

Buttonhole bar.

Alternate hooks and eyes sewn to the inside edge of a garment.

Enlarging a body piece at waist by slashing and spreading.

Lengthening a body piece by slashing and spreading.

Using the patterns

Sizes for the patterns in this book are

Women:
Bust 92cm/36in
Waist 71cm/28in
Hips 97cm/38in
Height 160–170cm/5ft 2½in–5ft 6½in
This is a modern size 12–14.

Men:
Chest 96cm/38in
Waist 87cm/34in
Height 170–178cm/5ft 7in–5ft 10in

- The scale used for the patterns is ⅛ inch to 1 inch for garments and ¼ inch to 1 inch for hats, headdresses, cuffs and collars.
- None of the patterns include seam allowances. These must be added as directed in the making instructions.
- CF = centre front
- CB = centre back
- SH.P = shoulder point (the top of the shoulder)
- Before beginning to cut out and make up any of the patterns, it is recommended that you read the instructions through carefully, to familiarize yourself with the process and ensure that all the necessary equipment and materials are to hand.
- The fabric yardages supplied with each pattern give the maximum amounts needed without taking into account any placing of the pattern pieces in opposite directions (top and tailing) or piecing, unless specified. Some yardages may be reduced if these measures are taken. More material may be required for matching large fabric patterns, such as branched designs.
- Many patterns carry the instruction 'cut 2', for body, sleeve and leg pieces. This means that you should cut two mirror images so as to end up with left and right parts.

Enlarging a sleeve by slashing and spreading.

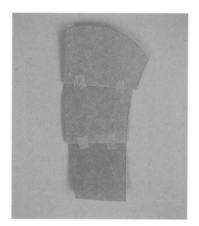

Shortening a sleeve by folding away the excess length.

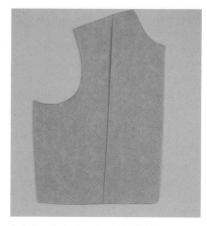

Reducing a body piece at waist by slashing and overlapping.

Resizing and fitting the patterns

If the difference between the wearer's size and the pattern size is more than 5cm (2in), the first task, after scaling up, is to resize the pattern pieces. To add width or height, cut and spread the pattern pieces. To narrow or shorten them, fold the excess away. Once these adjustments have been made, place the pieces on a new sheet of paper and draw around them, smoothing the curves. Calico mock-ups (toiles) are cut from the paper patterns with generous seam allowances at the edges to allow for adjustment. The instructions for making the garments assume that any pattern resizing has already happened and only secondary fittings are necessary.

A dressmaker's dummy is useful when a real body is not available to fit; these have a modern, immovable body shape but can be adapted. Cheap stands made from polystyrene are available from shop fitting and display suppliers. Choose a dummy which is one to two sizes too small and remove its fabric cover. Cut away the bust with a bread knife or small saw. Pad the stand with wadding to create the personal measurements required and replace the fabric cover. This dummy will behave much like a real body under the boned and stiffened layers of the garments under construction. Once the calico toile has been shaped to fit the wearer perfectly, it is used to cut the garment pieces from the top fabrics.

It is helpful to make cardboard mock-ups of hats. Bonnets and coifs, in particular, look surprisingly small when they are under construction, and look much bigger once they are on the head, so it is very easy to make them too large. Many of the hats and headdresses are constructed on buckram bases, which require wired edges. These may be achieved using a wide zigzag stitch on the sewing machine or by hand, using a spread-out version of buttonhole stitch. In both cases, the wire is attached to the edge of the buckram, rather than on top of it.

Stitch techniques

Running stitch is the simplest of hand stitches and is used for seams in light fabric that will not be under too much strain. Backstitch is used for constructional seams that require strength. Whip stitch, another strong stitch, can be used for the same purpose. Slip stitch and hemming stitch are both used for sewing in linings and for hemming. Slip stitch is quicker, hemming stitch is stronger and less likely to catch. Herringbone stitch is useful for catching down bulky hems and seam allowances that will be covered by linings, especially on curved edges. Pad stitch is used to secure wadding and padding: stitches travel on the inside and show on the right side as tiny 'prick stitches'. A French seam is a two-stage seam, useful for constructing unlined garments such as shirts, as the raw edges are enclosed in the second stage. The fullness of lightweight fabrics may be gathered up by working two rows of small running stitches or large machine stitches, tying off the threads at one end and pulling up the others to the right length. For longer lengths or thicker fabrics, box or knife pleats are used. Cartridge pleats are always carried out by hand. Two parallel rows of stitches are worked along the lined or folded edge to be pleated: the larger the stitches the fatter the pleats will be. Recommendations are given with each set of instructions as to which of the techniques are most suitable.

Accuracy

The patterns that follow have been devised after careful examination of extant garments, visual material and documentary evidence from the 16th century, as well as secondary sources. However, there is a great deal of relevant research awaiting publication, original clothing lying unreported in museum collections, and further experimentation with reconstructions to be undertaken. The patterns are merely best estimates based on the information available today.

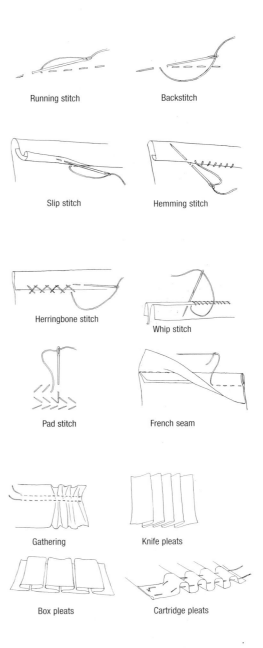

Running stitch

Backstitch

Slip stitch

Hemming stitch

Herringbone stitch

Whip stitch

Pad stitch

French seam

Gathering

Knife pleats

Box pleats

Cartridge pleats

Shirts and smocks

a. Basic shirt with collar,
cuffs and tied fastenings
b. Smock with collar,
cuffs and buttoned fastenings
c. Collar and cuff with frill
d. Collar with tied fastening
e. Collar with button and loop fastening
f. Collar with toggle and eyelet fastening
g. Smock with simple hemmed neck and sleeve

Basic shirt

Materials
- Smock: 3.5m (3¾ yd) of 112cm (45in) wide linen
- Shirt: 3.5m (3¾ yd) of 112cm (45in) wide linen

1. Cut out all pattern pieces, adding 12mm (½ in) seam allowances all the way around. Cut the slit for the front opening, turn in a narrow hem and stitch down. Work a buttonhole stitch bar 6mm (¼ in) up from bottom of slit (see diagram on page 51).
2. Sew underarm gussets into sleeves (see diagram right), leaving opening at wrist if required, and press.
3. For plain sleeves, finish with a narrow hem at the bottom. For sleeves with cuffs, hand hem opening at wrists and gather the bottom of sleeves to fit cuffs. Pin one long side of the cuff onto gathered edge of sleeve, right sides together, and sew onto sleeve. Repeat for the other sleeve. Trim down seam allowances, fold cuff over, turning in all raw edges, and hand sew down. Press.
4. Sew neck gussets into body, and finish shoulder seams. Sew side gussets into body, finishing side seams but leaving opening for sleeve where marked on pattern. Press.
5. Gather neck to fit collar, and sew on collar as for cuffs. Press.
6. Turn body inside out and pin sleeves into body. Sew sleeves to body. Open out and press.
7. Hem bottom of body.
8. Work fastenings at collar/cuffs.

Smock

Make as above, but omitting neck and side gussets. There is no need to gather the neckline before attaching the collar, as the neckline is cut to fit. For a low-cut neckline, do not cut the slit for the front opening. Leave the neckline unfinished, with a hole just big enough for the head to pass through. Mark the correct neckline under the bodice and finish with a narrow hem.

Collars with frills
1. The collar band needs to be cut as two separate layers with a 12mm (½ in) seam allowance all around rather than on the fold, as indicated on the pattern.
2. Cut the frill. The cut width of the frill will depend on the style chosen. If a sufficiently fine fabric is selected, the frill may be cut twice as wide, plus seam allowances, and then folded down the middle, pressed and made up as double thickness, which will avoid the need to hem. The length should be two to three times the length of the finished collar, plus seam allowances.
3. If the frill consists of a single layer, finish one long side and both ends with a narrow hem. Gather or pleat frill to collar measurement, distributing the fullness evenly.
4. Pin gathered edge to one of the collar bands, right sides together, and sew into place. Place on top of the other collar band, so that the frill is sandwiched between both collar bands, and sew on, using the first stitch line as a guide. Trim seam allowances, turn bands down over raw edges and press.
5. With right sides together, pin the collar onto shirt/smock neckline, catching one of the band layers only. Sew into place. Snip into seam allowance of smock neck if necessary. Turn in ends of collar bands and pin the second layer down over the stitch line, covering the raw edges. Work fastenings.

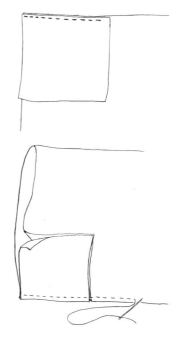

Putting a gusset into a sleeve. Lay the gusset onto the top right-hand corner of the cut-out sleeve and sew down the outside edge, stopping short of the bottom of the gusset by the width of the seam allowance. Backstitch to secure. Fold the sleeve in half along the width, right sides together. Fold the corner of the sleeve which has the gusset sewn to it over on itself and pin the other edge of the gusset to the left-hand corner of the sleeve. Sew the gusset to the sleeve along the outside edge and continue the row of stitching to complete the sleeve seam. If making up with French seams, trim the seam allowances down to half and repeat the process, enclosing all the raw edges.

Pattern 1: Basic Shirt

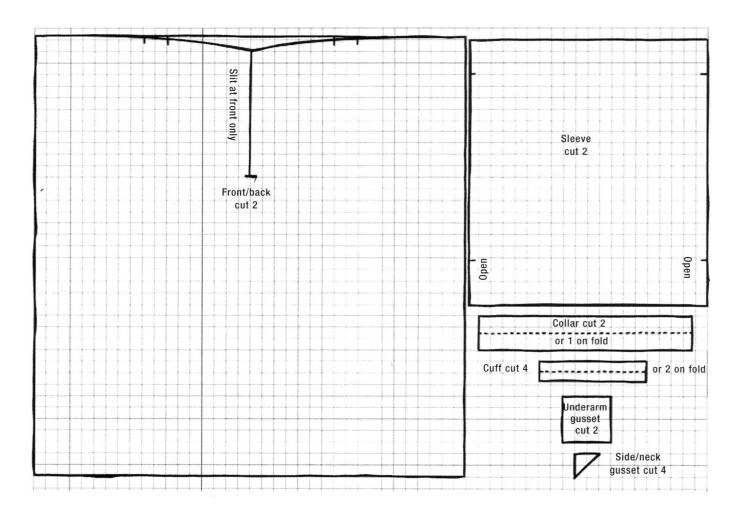

Pattern 2: Smock

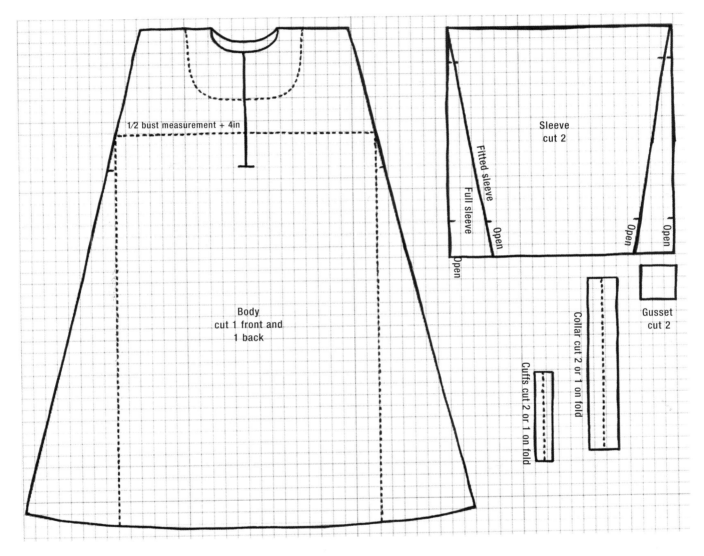

1/2 bust measurement + 4in

Body
cut 1 front and
1 back

Sleeve
cut 2

Fitted sleeve

Full sleeve

Open

Open

Open

Open

Gusset
cut 2

Collar cut 2 or 1 on fold

Cuffs cut 2 or 1 on fold

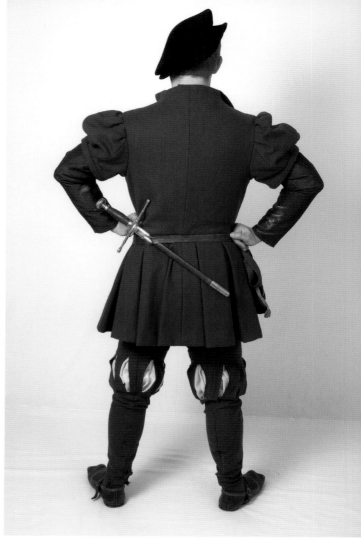

Full-length bias-cut hose with slashed detail above knee. Worn with a short-sleeved wool jerkin with full box-pleated shirt and grown-on collar, over a chamlet doublet with grown-on collar.

Basic men's clothing

Full-length footed bias-cut hose

Materials
- 2.3m (2½ yd) of wool at least 125cm (50in) wide will be required to cut out these hose without piecing.
- 2.3m (2½ yd) of cotton or linen, at least 125cm (50in) wide, for lining

Making up the hose – machine method
1. Pin and sew the back seams together. Select a stitch with a slight zigzag or wavy line. Press seam allowance open at either end; don't worry about the middle.
2. Pin the foot into place. This should be done with the hose turned wrong side out. Start at the heel and continue up one side of the ankle gusset – remember that the slit has minimal seam allowance and should be pinned on the very edge. Pin the other side of the gusset and the rest of the foot. The foot section of the hose will need to be eased onto the sole.
3. Sew into place, finishing the top of the gusset by hand. Trim seam allowance down to 6mm (¼ in) and press open around gusset using a sleeve board or rolled up piece of fabric.
4. Turn one leg through so that it is right side out and place it inside the other leg, right sides together. Pin together around crotch and sew, leaving CF open above codpiece mark. Snip into seam allowance at curve and press open at CB.
5. Cut out waistband pieces with 12mm (½ in) seam allowance at centre back

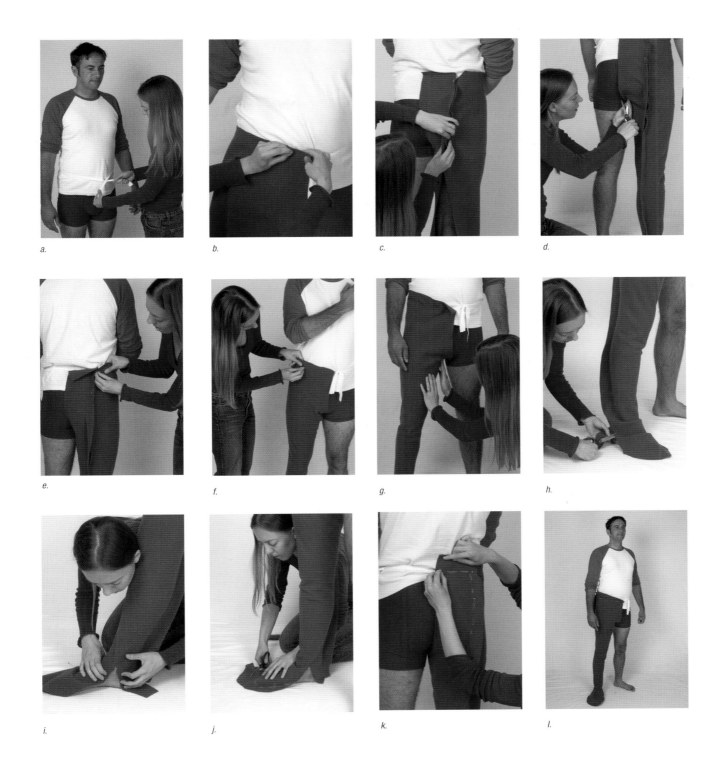

a.

b.

c.

d.

e.

f.

g.

h.

i.

j.

k.

l.

Fitting the hose

It is only necessary to fit one leg unless the wearer is obviously asymmetrical. Tie a tape around the waist of wearer (a). Pin the hose to the tape around waist (b). Draw the fabric around leg and pin together down the back of the leg to just above the ankle. Check that the foot piece will lie correctly over the foot and is not veering off to one side, re-pinning if necessary (c). Smooth the fabric up to the top of the inside leg and snip into the seam allowance around crotch (carefully!) (d). Re-pin the hose around back of waist, pulling the wool up to get rid of any excess slack (e). Do the same at front (f). Check that the crotch seam will sit right up between the legs. This is very important: if the seam sits too low it will be difficult for the wearer to move easily and the seam may rip. Re-pin the back seam,

gradually smoothing the material, adjusting and re-pinning to eliminate wrinkles (g). Position the hose foot over the foot of the wearer and snip part way up the gusset opening (h). Check that the opening is in line with the ankle bone and that the fabric is not twisting before continuing to cut to the top of the gusset opening (i).Mark around the foot with chalk and cut off any excess seam allowance (j). Mark all sewing lines with chalk (k). When all lines are marked, un-pin and check that all marks are clear. Cut off any excess seam allowance, leaving 12mm (½ in) all around, except at top edge where 2.5cm (1in) should be left. Lay the fitted and trimmed leg on the unfitted one, right sides together, and cut the excess material off the unfitted leg (l).

Pattern 3: Full-length footed bias-cut hose

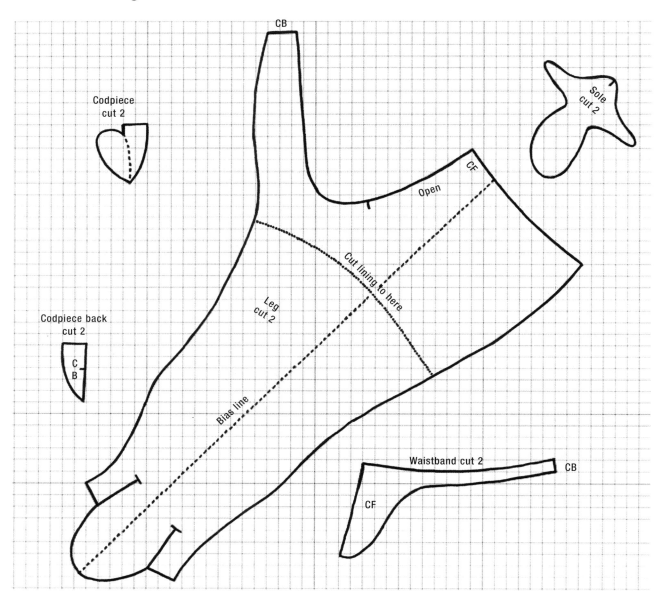

Pattern 4: Basic doublet/jerkin

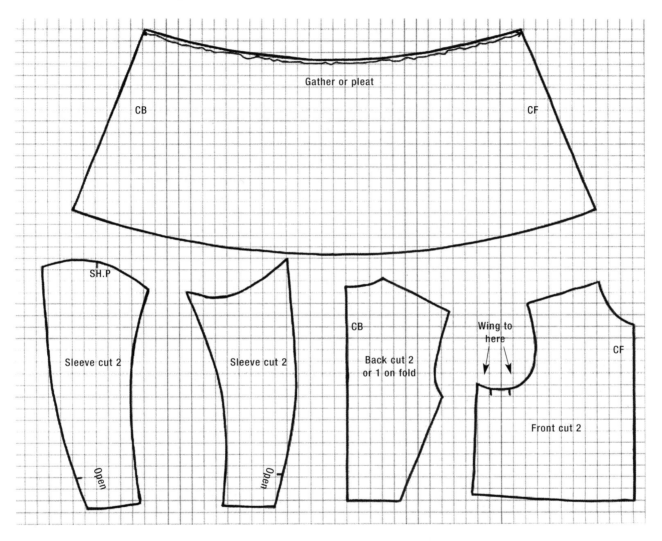

Canvas waistband basted into the inside waist of the hose.

Pins hold the codpiece stuffing into place, where it will be secured with stitches.

only. Press seam allowance open.

6. Pin waistband inside hose and baste into place. Turn waistband and seam allowance at front opening to inside of hose, pin and hand baste into place (see picture, top left).

7. Make up hose lining and hem with a loose back stitch or machine zigzag. Pin into hose, turning seam allowance under, and handsew into place.

8. Work eyelets.

Making up the hose: hand method

Sew the main seams, using a back stitch. Before sewing foot into bottom of leg, turn seam allowances under all the way around, baste and press. Turn seam allowance under all around bottom of hose, including sides of slits, baste and press. Pin the foot into the bottom of the hose leg and whip stitch together.

Making up the codpiece

1. Sew back sections of codpiece together, right sides facing, and press seam allowance open. With right sides facing, sew codpiece sides together down centre front edge. Clip into seam allowance and press seam open at top and bottom.

2. Pin codpiece to back, right sides together. Sew together, leaving the top open. Trim seam allowance down and turn through.

3. Stuff firmly with wool or cotton fibre. Pin the codpiece to the back along the dashed lines, trapping the stuffing inside (see picture, bottom left). Handstitch into place.

4. Turn top edges of codpiece in, hand sew down and press flat. Work a pair of eyelets in each corner.

5. Attach to hose, just above centre front opening with strong stitches at bottom of codpiece.

To make hose with slashed detail, cut the pattern 5cm (2in) longer in the upper leg to allow for puffing. The lining should be cut to reach the knee and a band of gathered material sewn on for the puffs. Make up the lining first and fit the hose on top of it to mark the slashed area. The hose should be stitched to the bottom edge of the lining to keep the slashes sitting over the puffs correctly.

Doublets and jerkins

Alternative sleeves can be taken from the other doublet and jerkin patterns.

Materials

For a simple doublet without skirts:

- 1.1m (1¼ yd) of calico, top fabric and lining, each 112cm (45in) wide (plus canvas for the collar and short skirts, if included)

For a jerkin with long skirts:

- 2.2m (2½ yd) of calico, top fabric and lining, each 112cm (45in) wide (plus canvas for collar, if included)

1. Cut pattern pieces out in calico, top fabric and lining, adding 12mm (½ in) seam allowance all around except at centre fronts of body pieces where 4cm (1½ in) should be added and hems of skirts (if included) where 2.5cm (1in) should be added. If collar or short skirts are included, cut these pieces in canvas without seam allowances and baste them to calico pieces. Lay the calico pieces on the wrong side of the top fabric pieces and baste around the sewing line.

2. Sew body pieces together – side seams, back seam (if present), then shoulder seams. Sew sleeves together, leaving opening at wrist, as marked on pattern. Trim down the seam allowance of the calico. Press all seams open.

3. If wings are included, fold these in half along the length, wrong sides together, and baste down. Press. Baste wings into place on sleeve head.

4. Sew sleeves and collar into body. Trim calico seam allowance down around armholes and snip into curves.

5. Make up lining as above (excluding wings).

6. Sew skirt pieces together leaving front edges open. Press seams open. Turn up hem of skirt and seam allowance at front edges. Pin, baste or herringbone stitch down and press. Sew skirt pieces of lining together, leaving front edges open, and press seams open. Lay lining onto skirt, with wrong sides together, and pin in place, turning the seam allowance under at hems and front edges. Handsew lining to skirt. Press.

7. Pin skirt to bottom of doublet, wrong sides together, sew. Grade seam allowances and snip into curves.

8. Pin lining into doublet and hand sew into place. Work fastenings.

9. For a simple doublet without skirts, work pairs of eyelets around waist for points to fasten hose. If doublet has skirts, cut lacing strip in linen canvas using the pattern on page 99. Turn in ends, fold in half along the length and press. Work pairs of eyelets in strong linen thread. Hand sew strip into doublet waist overstitching securely at ends, ensuring the stitches do not go through the top fabric.

c.

a.

b.

e.

d.

a. Long skirted sleeved jerkin and full-length hose
b. Full-length bias-cut hose
c. Long-skirted sleeveless jerkin with wings
d. Doublet (use skirt pattern from pattern 16, Elizabethan man's doublet, page 99)
e. Short bias-cut hose

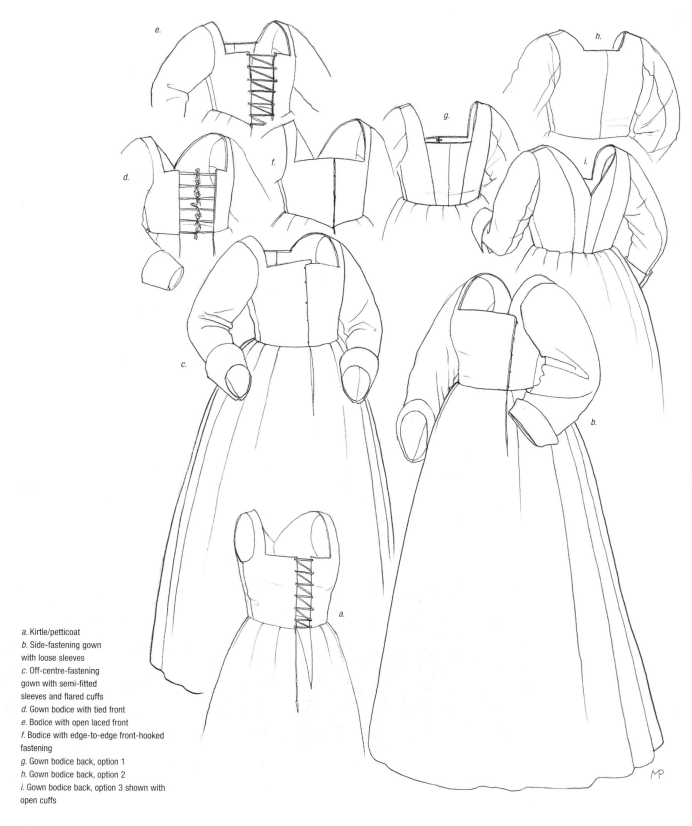

a. Kirtle/petticoat
b. Side-fastening gown
with loose sleeves
c. Off-centre-fastening
gown with semi-fitted
sleeves and flared cuffs
d. Gown bodice with tied front
e. Bodice with open laced front
f. Bodice with edge-to-edge front-hooked
fastening
g. Gown bodice back, option 1
h. Gown bodice back, option 2
i. Gown bodice back, option 3 shown with
open cuffs

Basic women's clothing

Kirtles and petticoats

The garment worn by all women over the smock consisted of a fitted bodice with attached skirt. In the early Tudor period this was called a kirtle. By the 1550s, the word 'petticoat' was being used to describe this item of clothing and 'kirtle' referred to a garment that was worn over, or instead of, a petticoat by wealthier, more fashionable women. Bodices were usually stiffened and lined, but do not need to be boned, especially for the earlier periods or if the wearer is slight. Petticoat and kirtle bodices usually close at the front, though back or side lacing is necessary for kirtles that are to be worn under front-opening gowns.

There are two sorts of skirts: those made up of shaped panels and those made up of straight panels. Shaped front or back panels should be used for styles from 1500 to around 1550. From 1550 to 1580 only the front panel needs to be shaped, and from then on all the panels can be cut as simple rectangles. Hems of petticoats and kirtles should have a circumference of at least 275cm (110in) round (two of the panels given in the pattern), and subsequent layers should increase in layers by 15cm (6in). For fuller skirts, cut two back panels. Lining the skirt is optional.

Petticoat and kirtle skirts may also be made up separately from the bodices, in which case they will need to be attached to a waistband with hooks or ties for fastening.

Petticoats

Materials

- Either 2.6m (3yd) of top fabric, 150cm (60in) wide or 3.25m (3½yd) of top fabric, 112cm (45in) wide (skirt panels will be pieced)
- 3.25m (3½yd) of lining, 112cm (45in) wide (if lining both bodice and skirt)
- 50cm (½yd) of canvas, 112cm (45in) wide for interlining bodice

1. Cut skirt panels in top fabric (and lining if required), adding 12mm (½in) seam allowance down the sides and around the hem and 2.5cm (1in) along the top edge. Cut bodice pattern pieces in calico, top fabric and lining, with a 2.5cm (1in) seam allowance all around, except lacing edges of bodice, which need 4cm (1½in). Cut bodice fronts in canvas without seam allowance or straps. Baste to calico fronts. If plastic boning is to be used it can be sewn directly to the canvas. Alternatively, sew channels onto canvas/calico layer for

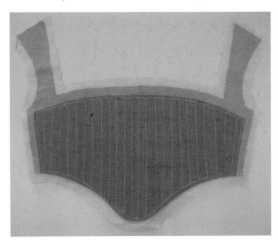

The calico interlining of this bodice has been stiffened with linen canvas and an additional layer of linen buckram, which stops short of the neckline by ¾in. The buckram is held in place with multiple rows of stitching.

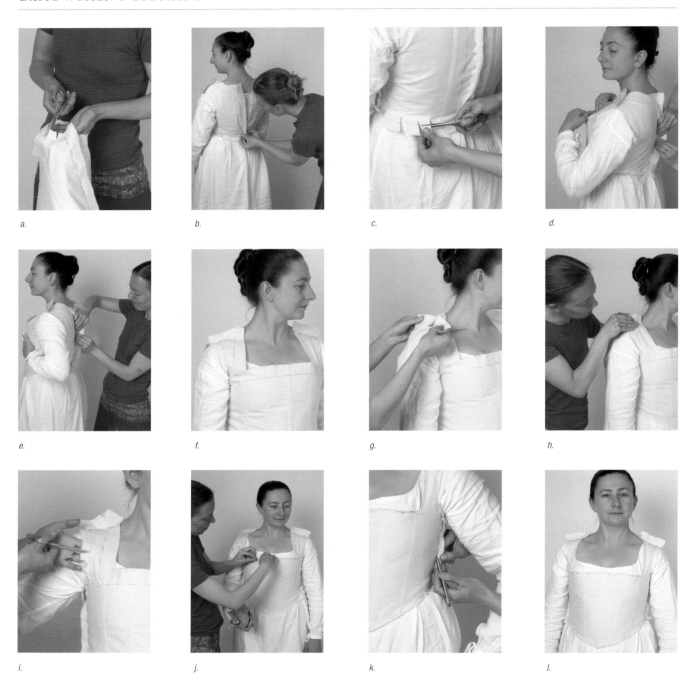

a.

b.

c.

d.

e.

f.

g.

h.

i.

j.

k.

l.

Fitting a bodice toile

Make up the bodice in two layers of calico with generous seam allowances. Sew channels for boning if required and insert bones. Snip into seam allowance under arms before bodice is fitted (a). Pin the bodice together along the fastening edges. These could be at the front and sides rather than the back (b). Snip into the seam allowance around the waist at the back, so the bottom of the bodice sits on the natural waist without wrinkles (c). Re-pin the fastening edges a little closer together. Ask the wearer to lift her bust into the correct position as this is done (d). The wearer should continue to hold her bust until the re-pinning is complete (e). If the neckline of the bodice gapes around the shoulder strap or there are wrinkles around the armhole, the shoulder seam will need to be adjusted (f). Unpick the shoulder seam (g). Adjust the strap so that it sits smoothly and snugly against the body, and re-pin (h). Snip into the seam allowance around the armhole until it is just big enough to be comfortable. do not make the armhole too large. Re-pin the strap if necessary (i). Fold the seam allowance under around the neckline and waistline to the correct levels (j). Mark all seams and edges with a pencil (k). The completed toile should be closely fitted and wrinkle-free (l).

inserting bones. Bones should be cut 12mm (½ in) shorter than length of bodice to avoid digging in at waist or poking up at the top.

2. Start with making up the bodice. Baste calico pieces to wrong side of top fabric pieces.

3. Sew bodice together along back seam (if present), side seams and shoulder seams, right sides facing. Insert prepared bones if used, making sure that they sit 6–8mm (¼–⅜ in) above waistline, to prevent digging in and getting in the way of attaching the skirt. Check the bodice for fit before pressing seams open. Sew up the lining in the same way as bodice.

4. Turn the seam allowance under around neckline and baste or herringbone stitch in place. Pin bodice lining into bodice, wrong sides together. Baste around armholes, neckline and front edges, leaving the bottom 7.5cm (3in) near the waist unbasted. Bind off armholes with a strip of binding made from self fabric.

5. Make up the skirt: pin seams together, leaving a 25cm (10in) opening at centre front, and then sew and press seams open. Make up lining in same way.

6. To put the lining in by machine, pin lining into skirt, pinning around hem, with right sides together and matching seams. Sew around hem. Trim the seam allowance of the lining down by half, snip notches into any curved seam allowance, and turn the skirt the right way round. Put the skirt over an ironing board, top fabric side down, and roll the hem of the skirt between the fingers to get the lining sitting above the hem edge by 3mm (⅛ in). Press. Pin and baste layers together around top edge. Handsew the layers together around the opening and strengthen at the bottom with a thread bar worked with buttonhole stitch (see diagram on page 51).

7. To put the lining in by hand, press the seam allowance up around the hem of top fabric skirt. Pin lining into skirt, with wrong sides together. Turn lining seam allowance under around hem, setting it back from the edge by 3mm (⅛ in), and then pin and handsew into place. Pin and baste layers together around top edge. Handsew the layers together around the opening and strengthen at bottom with a thread bar worked with buttonhole stitch (see diagram on page 51).

8. If the skirt is not too bulky it can be pleated up and machine sewn to the bottom of the bodice. The seam allowances around the waist should be graded and the bodice lining handsewn down, covering raw edges and machine stitching. If the skirt is bulky or a hand method is preferred, the skirt can be whipped onto the bottom of the bodice as described on page 50.

9. Work eyelets and remove any visible basting.

A back-lacing kirtle with separate sleeves which tie to the top of the shoulder straps. The light brown woollen sleeves have been slashed and lined with contrasting black linen for decorative effect.

A woollen damask gown with short puffed sleeves and hooked front fastening. A square partlet without ties is pinned on top of the gown. The puffed sleeve pattern may be found on page 81.

The full skirt of this gown has been knife-pleated before being sewn to the bodice.

Tudor woman's gown with loose sleeves

Materials
- 4.1m (4½ yd) of top fabric, 150cm (60in) wide or 4.6m (5yd) of top fabric, 112cm (45in) wide
- Either 4.5m (5yd) of lining fabric, 112cm (45in) wide (if lining both bodice and skirt) or 150cm (1½ yd) of calico, 112cm (45in) wide, for interlining bodice

1. Cut skirt panels in top fabric (and lining if required), adding 12mm (½ in) seam allowances down the sides and around the hem and 2.5cm (1in) along the top edge. Cut bodice pattern pieces in calico, top fabric and lining with 2.5cm (1in) seam allowances all around, except the front edges of bodice which need 4cm (1½ in). Sew tapes onto calico for boning channels along front edges. Pin calico pieces onto wrong sides of top fabric pieces and baste around sewing lines.
2. With right sides facing, sew bodice together along side, side back, centre back and shoulder seams. Press seams open. With right sides facing, sew sleeves together along back seam, and then press seam open. Pin sleeves into bodice, matching SH.P of sleeve to shoulder seam of bodice. Sew sleeves in, clipping into seam allowance under arm. Put the lining together in the same way.
3. Make up skirt and sew to bodice, following guidelines above and making sure the opening in the skirt corresponds to the opening in the bodice.
4. Insert prepared bones into channels if included, making sure they are 12mm (½ in) shorter than the channel. Turn the seam allowance in around the neckline, fronts of bodice and bottom of sleeves, and pin and baste or herringbone stitch down. Press. Pin lining into bodice, setting it back from the edge by 3mm (⅛ in), and handsew into place.
5. Work eyelets, sew in rings, hooks and eyes or ties depending on preferred method of fastening. Remove any visible basting.

Tudor gown with semi-fitted sleeves and flared cuffs

1. Cut cuffs in top fabric and calico, adding 12mm (½ in) seam allowances all around. Cut cuffs in canvas without seam allowances. Baste canvas to calico cuffs. Baste prepared calico cuffs onto wrong sides of top fabric. Cut cuffs in lining, adding 12mm (½ in) seam allowance all around. Fold cuffs in half, right sides together, and sew back seam. Press seams open. Turn seam allowance in around top and bottom of top fabric cuffs, and then pin, baste and press. Pin lining into cuffs, setting it back by 6mm (¼ in) at bottom edge and 3mm (⅛ in) at top edge. Handsew lining into place.
2. Follow making up instructions for the early Tudor gown above.
3. Pin cuffs to bottom of sleeves and whip together by hand.

If a more fashionable fitted sleeve is required, the bottom of the sleeve and the cuff will need to be left open and the sleeve closed with eyelet holes and either lacing or hooks and eyes.

Pattern 5: Basic petticoat/kirtle/gown

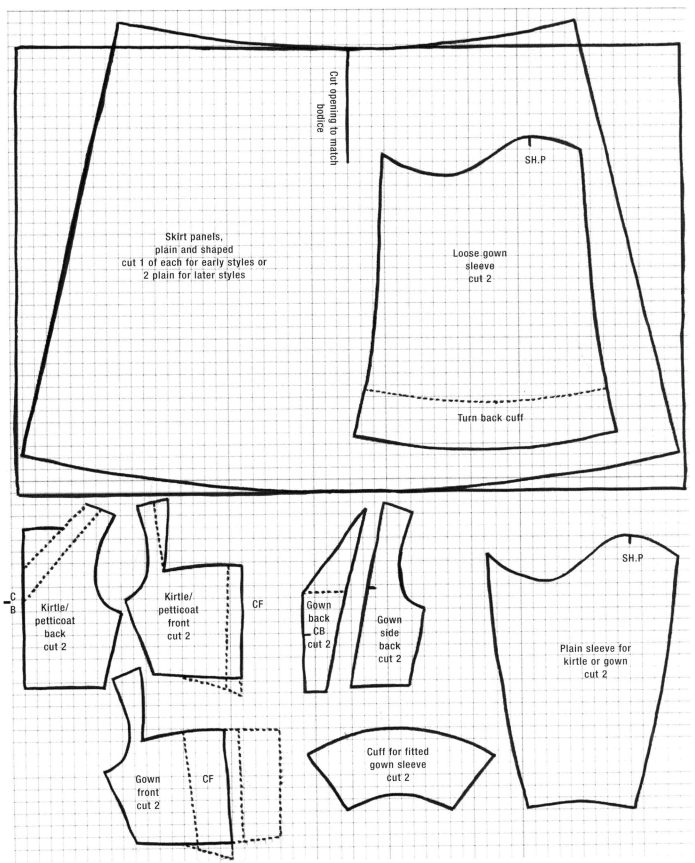

Cut opening to match bodice

Skirt panels,
plain and shaped
cut 1 of each for early styles or
2 plain for later styles

SH.P

Loose gown
sleeve
cut 2

Turn back cuff

C
B

Kirtle/
petticoat
back
cut 2

Kirtle/
petticoat
front
cut 2

CF

Gown
back
CB
cut 2

Gown
side
back
cut 2

SH.P

Plain sleeve for
kirtle or gown
cut 2

Gown
front
cut 2

CF

Cuff for fitted
gown sleeve
cut 2

Pattern 6: Partlets

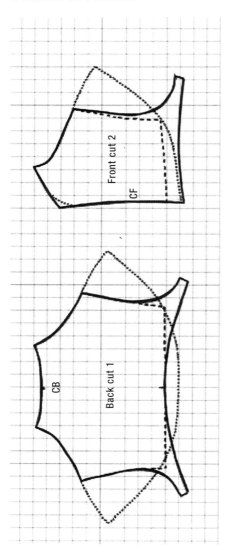

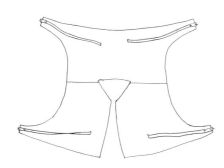

Partlets

Patterns are given for three styles, as shown in the diagrams below.

A square partlet without ties pinned in place on the gown.

Materials
- 50cm (½ yd) of top fabric, 112cm (45in) wide
- 50cm (½ yd) of lining, 112cm (45in) wide

1. Cut one back and two fronts in top fabric and lining fabric, adding 12mm (½ in) seam allowances all around.
2. Join the shoulder seams of each layer, snipping into curves of seam allowances, and press open (if using velvet, press over a towel or velvet board to avoid crushing the pile).
3. If making up the underarm tied version, cut four lengths of tape, about 25cm (10in) long (linen or cotton is best, as it will not slip) and pin to the narrow points under the arm scye with the ties lying in toward the body (see diagram bottom left).
4. Pin the partlet and the partlet lining together, with right sides facing. If you are using velvet and sewing by machine, it is worth basting the two together first, to prevent the fabric from 'walking'.
5. Sew all the way around, leaving an opening of between 10 and 12.5cm (4 and 5 inches) at the centre back for turning through.
6. Take out any basting. Snip into curves, trim off corners and turn through. Roll the edges of the partlet between the fingers to get the lining sitting just behind the top fabric. Press.
7. Hand sew the opening in the centre back closed.
8. Sew hook and eye (or buttonhole stitched bar) to the front corners of the partlets.

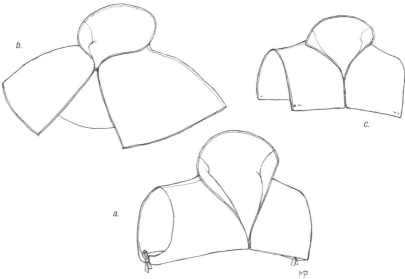

a. Square with underarm ties, fastened with hook and eye at front
b. Round, fastened with hook and eye at front
c. Small square without ties (suitable for lower-middle class), pinned onto gown bodice

Loose gown or frock and loose kirtle

Patterns are given for gown and two sleeve options. These gowns were frequently fur lined or trimmed. Decorative guards can be applied to front edges and along the slashed seams of version A. The front edges can be closed simply with a girdle, with hooks and eyes or pairs of ribbon ties.

Version A
Materials
- 6m (6½ yd) of top fabric, 112cm (45in) wide
- 6m (6½ yd) of lining, 112cm (45in) wide
- 1m (1yd) of calico, 112cm (45in) wide, for interlining sleeves
- 70cm (¾ yd) of silk or linen, 112cm (45in) wide, for sleeve puffs
- The loose gown requires 6m (6½ yd) fabric, 112cm (45in) wide or 5m (5½ yd) if there is no nap and the pattern can be top and tailed. If 150cm (60in) wide fabric is used the gown will require 3.3m (3½ yd)

1. Cut four body pieces in both top fabric and lining fabric, adding 12mm (½ in) seam allowances all around. Cut sleeves in calico and top fabric, adding 12mm (½ in) seam allowances all around. Baste calico to sleeves, with wrong sides together and making sure to include all of the marks shown on pattern.
2. Make up top fabric and lining layers separately: sew side seams, centre back seam and shoulder seams of body pieces, and press seam allowances open. The sleeve seams are left mainly open and will be caught together by hand at a later stage; for now, sew only the first 8.5cm (3½ in) at top and 5cm (2in) at the bottom. Fold the rest of the seam allowance to the inside, pin and baste down. Press. Snip into seam allowance in sleeve head either side of where it will be cartridge pleated (indicated on pattern), fold the allowance in this area under pin, baste down and press. Turn up the seam allowance at sleeve wrist, snipping into the curve. Pin, baste down and press.
3. Fold seam allowance in around neck edges and down the centre front edges of gown, and pin, baste down and press. If gown is to be fastened with pairs of ties, baste these into place now. Pin lining into gown (wrong sides together) folding seam allowances in around neck edge and centre front edges, pin into place and handsew down, taking care to do a few good strong back stitches through the ties, if present, and stopping 7.5 or 10cm (3 or 4in) above the hem. Baste layers together around armholes.
4. Put sleeve lining inside sleeve (wrong sides together). Pin lining into place just back from the folded edge and hand sew down. Baste layers together under the arm.
5. Cut the lengths of silk or linen for puffs, adding 12mm (½ in) seam allowances all around. Sew together along long edge and turn through. Turn allowances in at short edges and press down. Gather at either end and at marked intervals, using small running stitches. Pull up tightly and tie threads off. Position the puffed strips inside the sleeves, placing the gathered sections behind the points where the edges are to be caught together. Using strong thread, sew the puffs in at these points, catching the sleeves together at the same time. Catch the puffed strips down with a few stitches on the inside of the sleeves in between the gathered sections to avoid gaping.
6. Pleat sleeve head to 50cm (20in), using cartridge pleats. Pin sleeves into gown, matching shoulder points. Sew underarm section first and then the sew the pleated section in by hand.
7. Put gown onto a stand or large (preferably padded) hanger. Leave for as long as possible to allow the hem to drop.
8. Pin lining and gown together around hem and level off, either on a stand or on a model. Trim hem back where necessary. Turn hem of gown up, pin and baste into place, press. Bring gown lining down over hem, turn seam allowance under to sit about 6mm (¼ in) above the edge, pin and handsew down. Add protective binding or fringe to hem if desired.
9. Sew hooks and eyes to centre front edges if required.

A loose English gown with version B sleeves, fur collar and silk ties, worn over a loose kirtle.

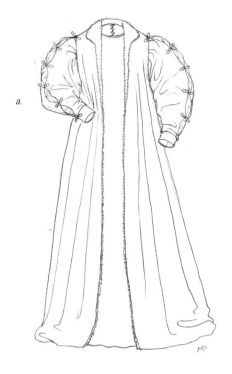

a.

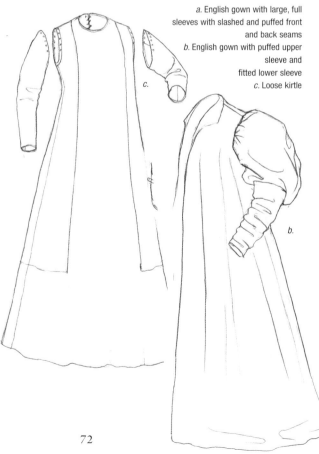

c.

b.

a. English gown with large, full sleeves with slashed and puffed front and back seams
b. English gown with puffed upper sleeve and fitted lower sleeve
c. Loose kirtle

Version B
Materials
• 6m (6½ yd) of top fabric, 112cm (45in) wide
• 6m (6½ yd) of lining, 112cm (45in) wide
Note: You will only require 5m (5½ yd) if there is no nap and the pattern can be top and tailed.

1. Cut four body pieces in top fabric and lining fabric, adding 12mm (½ in) seam allowances all around (pattern is the same for front and back). Cut the sleeve in top fabric and in lining fabric, adding 12mm (½ in) seam allowances all around. Mark puff line with basting.
2. Mark up top fabric and lining layers separately: sew side seams, centre-back seam and shoulder seams of body pieces. Fold each of the sleeve pieces in half and sew up back seams. Press seam allowance only.
3. Turn allowance up at sleeve cuff, snipping into curve, then pin, sew and press. Put sleeve lining inside sleeve (wrong sides together) matching centre back seams. Handsew lining in at cuff. Match up the basted bottom of puff lines and pin together. Sew layers together with a backstitch which travels about 12mm (½ in) on the inside and leaves small stitches on the right side.
4. Pleat sleeve head to 51cm (20in), either with 5 or 6 box pleats (basting into position when happy) or using cartridge pleats. Sew sleeves into gown, matching shoulder points. Snip into sleeve allowance under arm. Bring sleeve lining up inside sleeve to cover raw edges around armhole, pin and sew down. Follow steps 7–9 for Version A.

Loose kirtle
The pattern for the loose kirtle is based on an extant example dated 1570–80 in the Germanisches Nationalmuseum, Nurnberg. The details of this kirtle can be found in Janet Arnold's *Patterns of Fashion*, pages 109–110. Like the fashionable fitted kirtles of the Henrician period, the kirtle has a forepart and border around the hem of decorative fabric and a hind part of plainer, less costly material. The original kirtle has a pair of fitted sleeves which are laced to eyelet holes worked around the armholes. If sleeves are required, use the sleeve pattern given with the waistcoat pattern on page 85, and make them up in the same decorative fabric as the kirtle. Bind the edges at sleeve head, and work eyelets around sleeve heads.

Materials
• 3.1m (3½ yd) of foundation fabric and lining (top and tailed or pieced), each 112cm (45in) wide
• 3.1m (3½ yd) of decorative fabric and calico, each 112cm (45in) wide
• 70cm (¾ yd) of lining, 112cm (45in) wide, for sleeves

1. Cut fronts and backs in foundation fabric and lining fabric, adding 12mm (½ in) seam allowances all around. Cut decorative panels in calico and top fabric; the front panel should be cut on the fold to avoid a seam running down the centre. Baste the calico to the decorative fabric.
2. Sew kirtle together along side and front seams, right sides facing (leave the back seam and shoulder seams open), and sew. With right sides facing, sew the decorative fabric panels together at sides only. Press all seams open. Press seam allowance on decorative panel under along the sides of the long front section and around the top of the hem section, clipping where necessary. With wrong sides facing, pin decorative fabric to kirtle, and turn the raw edges under. Pin

Pattern 7: Loose gown or frock

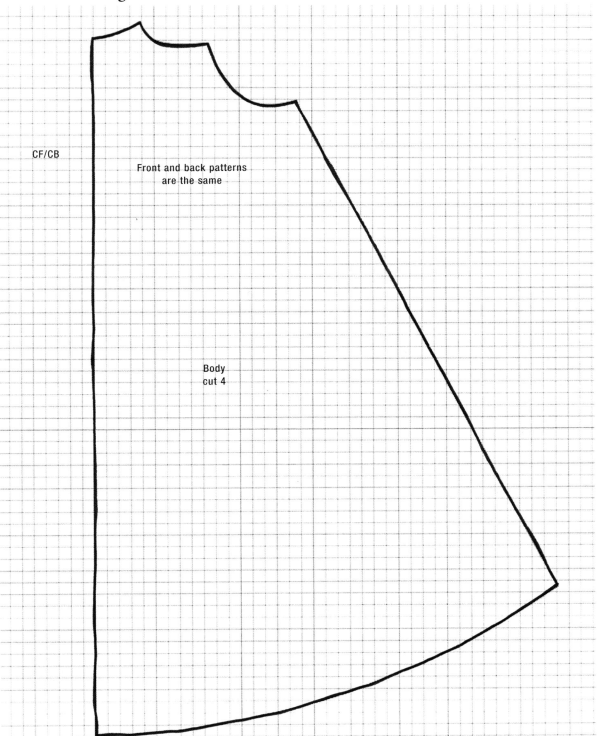

CF/CB

Front and back patterns
are the same

Body
cut 4

and hand sew down. Sew the shoulder seams and the back seam, leaving the
top half open where indicated on pattern, and press allowances open.

3. With wrong sides facing, make up the kirtle lining, press seams open, and pin
    into kirtle. Baste around all edges. Baste layers together around hem, neck,
    armholes and centre back edges. Press. Bind off armholes, neck and centre
    back edges with a strip of the decorative fabric, or a plain silk that goes with it.

4. Bind hem with a strip of the decorative fabric, a strip of velvet or velvet
    ribbon. Work eyelets down centre backs, spacing them 2.5cm (1in) apart.

Pattern 7: Loose gown or frock

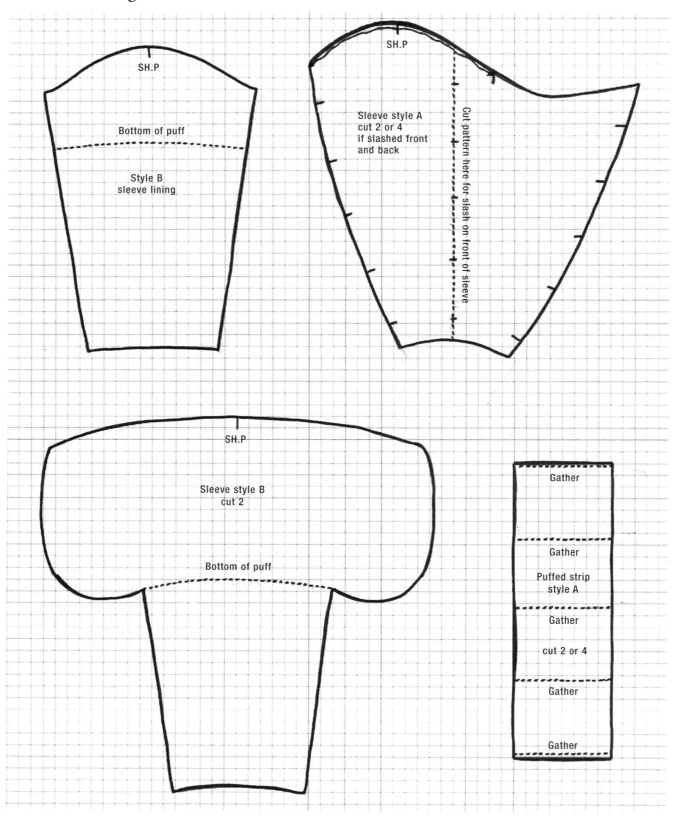

SH.P

Bottom of puff

Style B
sleeve lining

SH.P

Sleeve style A
cut 2 or 4
if slashed front
and back

Cut pattern here for slash on front of sleeve

SH.P

Sleeve style B
cut 2

Bottom of puff

Gather

Gather

Puffed strip
style A

Gather

cut 2 or 4

Gather

Gather

Pattern 8: Loose kirtle

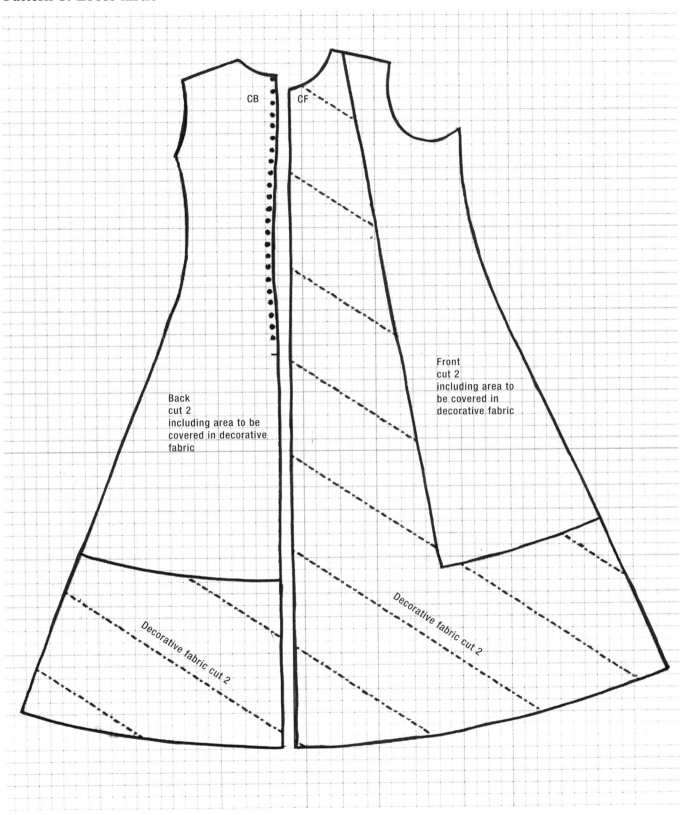

CB

CF

Back
cut 2
including area to be
covered in decorative
fabric

Front
cut 2
including area to
be covered in
decorative fabric

Decorative fabric cut 2

Decorative fabric cut 2

a.

c.

Loose gown with collar/revers

The body pieces of this pattern are very basic and can be used for the whole period. When this gown is worn open, or closed at the waist only, it has revers which run into the collar and can display a contrasting lining. When fastened up to the neck, the collar is a smaller 'Peter Pan' style. A long plain sleeve is given with the pattern, though any of those provided for the fitted English gown and doublet bodice may be used. Wings can be included for Elizabethan styles. For simple coats, cut length to dotted line and make up without collar, or use a standing collar.

Materials
- 4.7m (5¼ yd) of top fabric and lining, each 112cm (45in) wide
- 1.5m (1⅔ yd) of calico/facing fabric, each 112cm (45in) wide

Note: Follow instructions for making up sleeves given with sleeve patterns; if wings are included they should be made up and basted to the sleeve heads before sewing sleeves into gown.

1. Cut body pieces, wings (if included) and collar in top fabric, leaving 12mm (½ in) seam allowances all around except body hems, where 2.5cm (1in) should be allowed. Cut body panels in lining, adding 12mm (½ in) all around. Cut collar and facing in calico and facing fabric, adding 12mm (½ in) seam allowances all around. (To avoid a seam between the collar and revers, cut the front body pattern along dashed rever line and tape the pattern pieces together), as shown in the diagram.) Mark all sewing lines with chalk or basting.
2. Make up body of gown by sewing the centre back seam, side seams and shoulder seams. Press all seams open. With right sides together, pin collar onto gown and sew, clipping into seam allowance around neck. Press seam open. If any guards are to be applied, they should be sewn on now. Turn raw edges under around fronts and collar, pin and baste down. Press.
3. Make up lining as above. If the collar and rever facing have been cut as one, sew the body pieces together first and then, with right sides together, pin the facing to the gown and sew. Press all seams open.
4. Put the gown, inside out, on a stand or large padded hanger. Place the lining over the top, right side out. Leave for as long as possible to allow hem to drop.
5. Pin lining to gown. Match the shoulder seams, centre back neck and underarm seams first, and then put a couple of pins in down the side seams and centre back seam and pin around the hem. Don't worry about turning the lining under at this stage. When lining is pinned into place, take gown off stand or hanger and spread out on a flat surface. Turn raw edges of lining in around collar, down centre fronts and pin, setting it 6mm (¼ in) back from gown edge. Handsew into place. Baste lining to gown around armholes. Put in sleeves, following instructions given with sleeve patterns.

b.

d.

a. Loose gown with puffed, paned sleeves
b. Loose gown with plain sleeves and wings
c. Back view of loose gown with puffed, paned sleeves
d. Loose gown fastened high under chin, fur lining or facing

Pattern 9: Loose gown with collar/revers

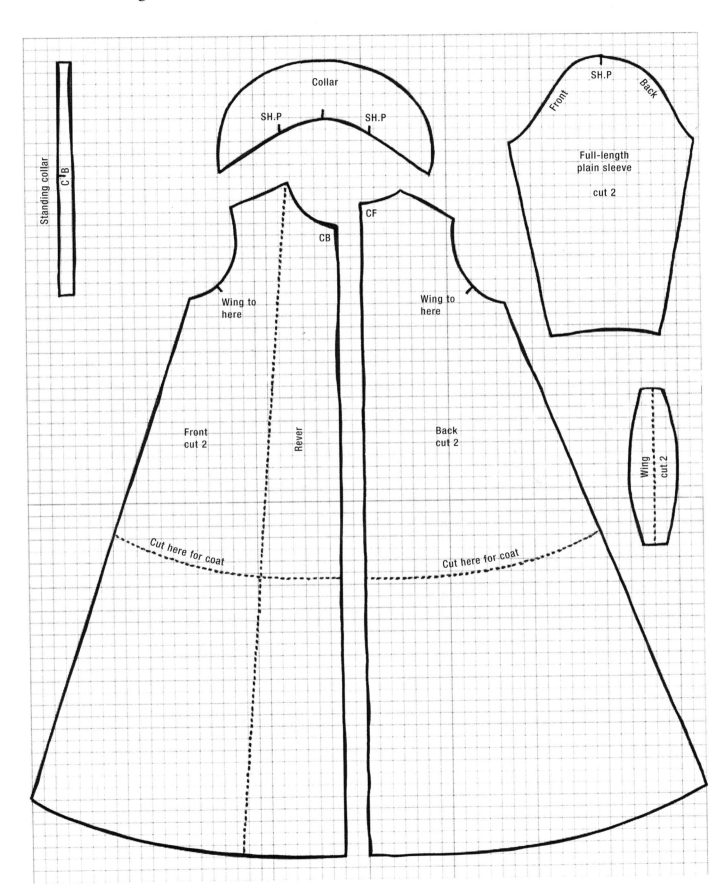

Standing collar

C B

Collar

SH.P   SH.P

CB

CF

Wing to here   Wing to here

Front cut 2   Rever   Back cut 2

Cut here for coat   Cut here for coat

SH.P

Front   Back

Full-length plain sleeve

cut 2

Wing cut 2

a. Fitted English gown with puffed, paned
upper sleeves and tied front fastening
b. Fitted English gown with plain half-
length sleeves and hooked fastening
c. Fitted English gown with plain full-length
sleeves, tied fastening and pleated back
section to skirt

Fitted English gowns

The pattern for the full length sleeve is given on page 77. Sleeves from the other loose gown patterns or doublet bodice may also be used here. The front skirt can be cut away, as indicated by dashed line on pattern, to reveal the forepart. The back section of the skirt can be full and pleated; for this, extend centre back of back panel so that it measures 3 times the width of the back bodice panel at waist. Pleat up, using box pleats or large cartridge pleats. An opening for a pocket is included in the pattern. This can either be a simple slit through which to reach a purse or a pocket may be sewn in: use the pattern on page 102 and sew in before the lining is put in.

Fitted English gown with plain sleeves

Materials
- 3.7m (4 yd) of top fabric and lining, each 112cm (45in) wide

1. Cut all pattern pieces in top fabric and lining fabric, adding 12mm (½ in) seam allowances all around except at front edges of skirt, where 7.5cm (3in) should be allowed. Sew on any applied decoration to sleeve.
2. Make up top fabric and lining layers separately. Sew the front body to the front skirt at waist and sew the back body to the back skirt at waist. Clip seam allowance and press open. Sew side seams (leaving open for pocket where marked) and shoulder seams of gown, then sew back seams of sleeves and sleeve linings. Clip seam allowances at shoulder. Press all seams open.
3. Fold seam allowance in around neck edges and down the centre front edges of gown. Pin, baste down and press. If gown is to be fastened with pairs of ties, baste these into place now. Pin lining into gown (wrong sides together), folding seam allowances in around neck edge and centre front edges. Pin into place and handsew down, taking care to do a few good strong back stitches through the ties, if present, and stopping 7.5 or 10cm (3 or 4 in) above the hem. Baste layers together around armholes and bind raw edges with a bias strip of lining fabric.
4. Snip into seam allowance at underarm on both sleeve and sleeve lining. Pin and baste the seam allowance down all the way around the sleeve head. Press. Put sleeve lining inside sleeve (wrong sides together), matching underarm seams. Pin the lining into the sleeve around sleeve head, turning raw edges under, and handsew in place. Pin and baste layers together at hem. Bind sleeve hem with self fabric.
5. Gather sleeve head to fit armhole circumference of gown, using small cartridge pleats. Pin completed sleeves into armholes and stitch into place by hand.
6. Put gown onto a stand or large (preferably padded) hanger. Leave for as long as possible to allow the hem to drop.
7. Pin lining and gown together around hem and level off, either on a stand or on a model. Trim hem back where necessary. Turn hem of gown up. Pin and baste into place, and then press. Bring gown lining down over hem, turning seam allowance under to sit about 6mm (¼ in) above the edge. Pin and handsew down. Add protective binding or fringe to hem if desired.
8. Sew hooks and eyes to centre front edges if ties were not used.

A fitted English gown made in black worsted trimmed with a black velvet guard, with puffed, paned sleeves. This gown fastens at the waist only and is worn over a black-lacing wool kirtle.

Sleeve foundation with tapes sewn on to take bones.

Completed panes ready for cartridge pleating and attaching to gown (hand method only)

Fitted English gown with puffed and paned sleeves

Materials

As for previous gown, but with an additional
- 30cm (12in) of calico, 112cm (45in) wide, for interlining sleeve foundation
- 25cm (10in) of fabric, 112cm (45in) wide, for sleeve puff (top and tailed or pieced)

Make up gown as before, except for armholes, where the lining and top fabric should be basted together but not bound off.

1. Cut sleeve foundation in lining fabric, adding 12mm (½ in) seam allowances all around. Cut panes and bands in top fabric and lining fabric, adding 12mm (½ in) seam allowances all around. Cut sleeve puff in lightweight fabric, adding 12mm (½ in) seam allowances all around.
2. Sew tapes onto sleeve foundation where indicated on pattern, setting them back from the edges by 12mm (½in) Sew short tapes on first, then sew long tape over the top, but not at the points where it crosses the short tapes, otherwise the bones will not be able to pass through. Sew underarm seam and press open. Gather up sleeve head to fit the circumference of the gown armhole. Insert bones into tapes (plastic or thin strips of cane are best). The long bone which goes around the whole sleeve should be overlapped and taped together with zinc oxide tape. The vertical bones should have the ends finished off with zinc oxide tape.
3. Make up sleeve puff by sewing the underarm seam, pressing open and then gathering both edges. The top edge should measure the same as the gown armhole and the bottom edge should measure the same as the sleeve band. Pin gathered puff onto foundation.
4. Make up panes*. Press the seam allowances down along the long sides. Pin lining pieces to panes, turning raw edges under, and handsew down. Press. Work two rows of gathering stitches at either end of all of the panes, pull up to 6mm (¼ in) at top and bottom of all panes. Pin the panes onto the sleeve and arrange the gathering of the puff so that the fullness sits between the panes. Baste all the layers together around top and bottom edges.
5. Make up sleeve bands. Sew short sides together and press seam allowances open. Turn the seam allowance under around the bottom edge of the band, baste and press. With wrong sides together, pin band lining inside band. Sew lining into band along bottom edge, turning raw edge under and setting back by 3mm (⅛ in). Press.
6. Pin band to bottom of sleeve, right sides together (without catching the lining in at this stage) Sew. Trim seam allowances and bring band lining up inside band to cover raw edges. Pin and sew into place.
7. Pin sleeves into gown and sew in. Bind raw edges together at armhole with bias strip of lining fabric.

*Hand method of gathering and attaching panes: panes can be completed individually, cartridge pleated at top and bottom and sewn onto rest of sleeve after it has been sewn into the gown. The evidence from effigies suggests that this was the period method.

Pattern 10: Fitted English gown

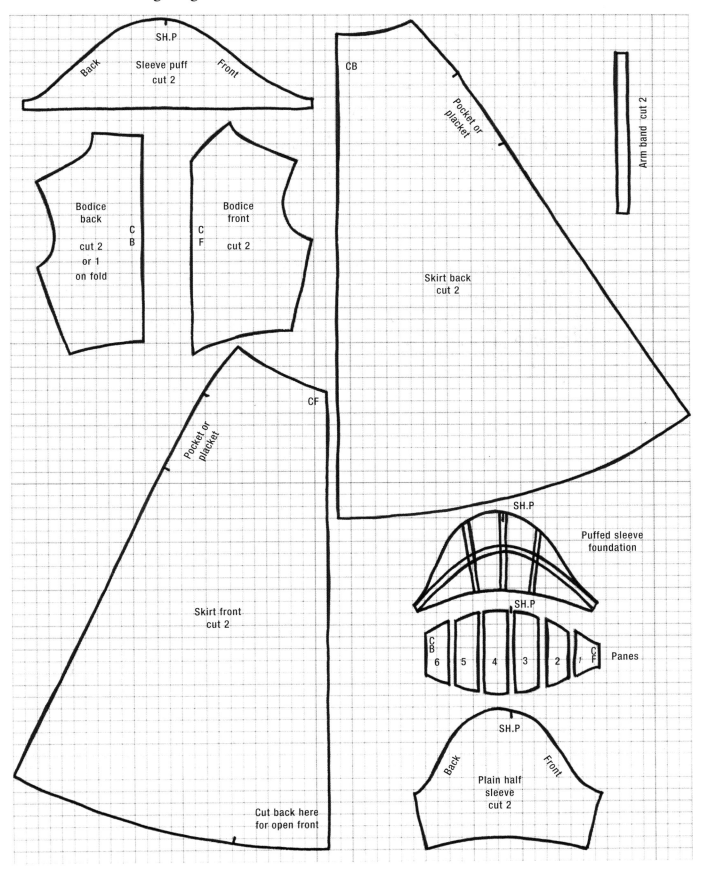

Back Sleeve puff cut 2 SH.P Front

CB Pocket or placket

Arm band cut 2

Bodice back cut 2 or 1 on fold C B C F Bodice front cut 2

Skirt back cut 2

Pocket or placket CF

SH.P Puffed sleeve foundation

SH.P

Skirt front cut 2

C B 6 5 4 3 2 1 C F Panes

SH.P Back Plain half sleeve cut 2 Front

Cut back here for open front

Doublet bodice made in wool with collar, skirts, slashed
shoulder rolls and hooked fastening.

Wool gown with doublet bodice and flounced skirt worn
over a medium roll.

Doublet bodice

Materials
- 1.4m (1½ yd) of calico, top fabric and lining, each 112cm (45in) wide
- 70cm (¾ yd) of wadding, 112cm (45in) wide, for sleeves (if necessary)
- 11cm or ⅛ yd of canvas, 112cm (45in) wide, for interlining collar

Doublet may be closed with either hooks and eyes or buttons and buttonholes. If skirts are required, use the skirt patterns from the late Elizabethan bodice. The collar may be omitted and neck cut lower.

Making up the bodice with collar, wings and skirts
1. Cut all pattern pieces in calico, adding 12mm (½ in) seam allowances all around except fronts of body, which should have 2.5cm (1in), plus button stand on one side (if closing doublet with buttons). Cut bodice fronts and collar in canvas without seam allowances. Baste the canvas to the calico pieces around outside edges. Sew bone channels through these layers where indicated on pattern. Cut wadding for sleeves without seam allowance, and baste to calico sleeves. Cut all pattern pieces except wing in lining, adding 12mm (½ in) seam allowances all around.
2. Cut all pattern pieces except lacing strip in top fabric. Lay the prepared calico pieces onto the top fabric. Pin and baste together. Sew the bodice together at centre back seam, side seams and shoulder seam, checking for fit before pressing all seams open. Any applied decoration that covers the seams should be sewn on now. Sew on collar, clipping seam allowances.
3. Turn seam allowances in around skirt pieces, leaving top edge open. Pin, baste and press. Handsew linings onto skirts. Pin and sew skirts to bodice waist. Insert prepared bones into channels Turn seam allowance in up centre fronts and around collar. Pin and baste. Press.
4. Sew sleeves together, pressing seams open. Fold seam allowances in at cuffs, clipping into curves. Pin, baste and press. Pleat sleeve head to fit armhole measurement, using small box pleats. With wrong sides together, fold wing in half and baste along curved edge. Baste wing to top of sleeve matching SH.Ps. Pin sleeves into bodice and sew in.
5. Make bodice lining up as above. Pin lining into bodice, turning raw edges under and clipping curves where necessary. Handsew into place. Press.
6. Make up lacing strips. Pin calico lacing strips to lining lacing strips and baste together. Fold seam allowances in and press. Fold strip in half widthways and press. Handsew around edges. Work eyelets, spacing them 3cm (1¼ in) apart. Hand sew lacing strips into bodice along dashed lines, taking care to catch interlining but without allowing the stitches to come right through to the right side of the fabric.
7. Sew on hooks and eyes or work button holes and sew on buttons.

If the doublet is to have shoulder rolls rather than wings, these can be made up and attached at the end. The rolls use the same pattern as the wings. They should be folded in half, right sides together and stitched along the curved edge from either end, leaving a 5cm (2in) gap in the middle. Trim the seam allowance down and turn the rolls through. Stuff the rolls firmly with wool/cotton or polyester wadding and sew up opening. Pin the rolls onto the bodice and hand stitch in place, catching them at the corners and in the middle. The sleeve may be cartridge pleated instead of box pleated when the wings are omitted.

Pattern 11: Doublet bodice

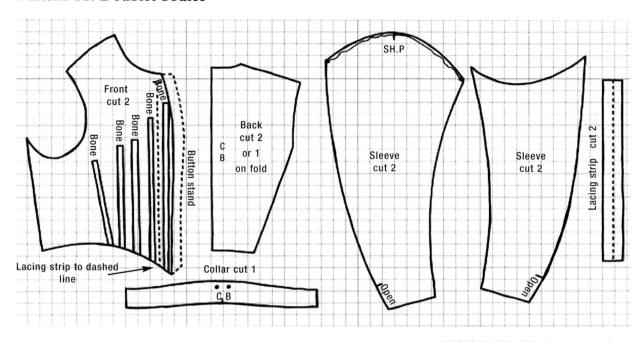

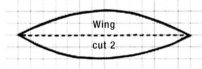

a. Doublet bodice with wings, collar and hooked fastening
b. Doublet bodice with shoulder rolls, low neck and buttoned fastening

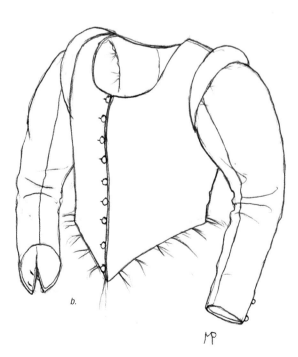

Wool waistcoat with narrow wings and round collar worn over wool kirtle.

Waistcoat

Materials

- 1.4m (1½ yd) of top fabric and lining, each 112cm (45in) wide

1. Cut all pieces in top fabric and lining with 12mm (½ in) seam allowances all around, except fronts, which should have 2.5cm (1in). Mark the slashes for the godets with chalk.
2. Make up waistcoat and waistcoat lining pieces separately. Sew the back and fronts together. Sew the sleeves together. Press seam allowances open.
3. Make up wings. Press the seam allowance down along the straight edge. Pin lining in and hand sew along straight edge only. Baste the layers together along curved edge. Baste wings to sleeves, matching up shoulder points. Sew sleeves into armholes. Clip seam allowance under arm.
4. Slash into waistcoat and waistcoat lining where marked for godets and press the raw edges back by 6mm (¼ in) at the bottom, grading to nothing at top of point. Pin godets in place behind slashes. Sew godets in, top-stitching close to the folded edge of the slash.
5. Make up collar and cuffs, if required. Turn seam allowances under around outside edges and cover with lining, leaving the bottom edges open. Hand sew down. Sew collar and cuffs to waistcoat. Clip curve in neck. Grade seam allowances around wrist and turn up, basting into place.
6. Pin lining in to waistcoat, covering all raw edges, and sew into place.
7. Sew pairs of hooks and eyes down centre front, setting them back 3mm (⅛ in) and spacing them 2.5–4cm (1–1½ in) apart.

Waistcoat with straight cuffs and curved collar.

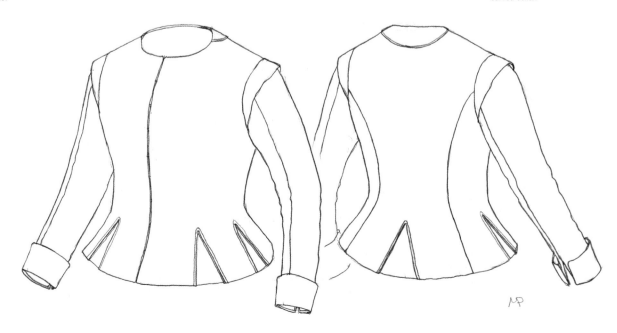

Pattern 12: Waistcoat

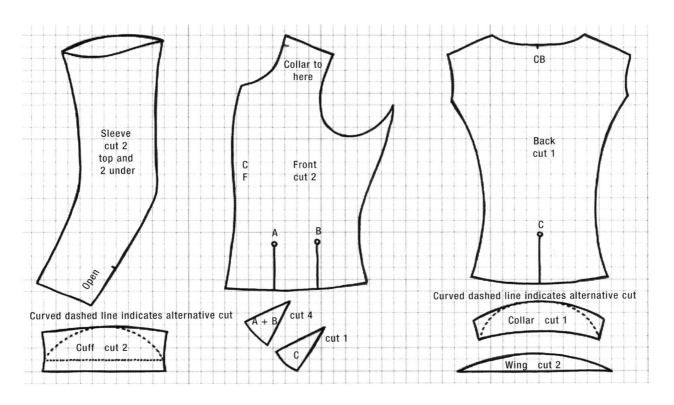

Sleeve
cut 2
top and
2 under

Open

Curved dashed line indicates alternative cut

Cuff   cut 2

Collar to
here

C
F

Front
cut 2

A   B

A + B   cut 4

cut 1

C

CB

Back
cut 1

C

Curved dashed line indicates alternative cut

Collar   cut 1

Wing   cut 2

Detail of waistcoat showing
hooked front fastening and
gussets over hips.

Velvet gown with satin collar, paned upper sleeves and slashed lower sleeves, worn over jerkin with box-pleated skirt and half-length paned hose.

Henrician men's clothing

Henrician man's doublet

Patterns for two styles of doublet are given, the first of which is a low-necked version with a side-fastening placard. Since this style leaves a smooth area of material across the chest, it lends itself to the display of fine materials and surface decoration, such as slashing and puffing. The same fancy materials and decoration can be applied to the bottom half of the sleeves as well, since they could be seen through the shorter gown sleeves. This style is typical of the first thirty years of the century. It is fastened at the shoulder, side seam and next to the armhole with hooks and worked thread bars or with ties threaded through pairs of eyelet holes. Pairs of eyelets are worked around the waist for trussing the doublet to the hose.

The second style is a high necked version with a 'grown-on' collar and optional large puffed upper sleeves. This style is seen in many of Holbein's drawings of courtiers made during the 1530s. These doublets may be fastened at the front with small buttons, edge to edge with hooks and eyes, or tied with pairs of points. This style is seen both with and without skirts.

Both styles can either have openings at the wrist fastened with buttons or hooks and eyes, or can be cut loose enough to fit over the hand without the need for any opening.

a. Gown worn over 'U' front jerkin, side-fastening doublet and full-length hose

b. Side-fastening doublet and full-length slashed hose tied together at waist

c. Gown back with rounded collar

d. Sleeveless jerkin with 'U' front

e. Jerkin with puffed upper sleeves and high front, hooked fastening

f. Doublet with puffed upper sleeves, high front, buttoned fastening

Doublet with grown-on collar, slashed detail on sleeves and no skirts, pointed to hose.

Materials

- 1.4m (1½ yd) of top fabric and lining, each 112cm (45in) wide
- 25cm (¼ yd) of canvas, 112cm (45in) wide, for interlining skirts (if included). If including puffed upper sleeves, add 50cm (24in) of top fabric, 112cm (45in) wide

Making up the side-fastening, low-necked doublet

1. Cut body pieces and sleeves out in calico and top fabric, adding 12mm (½ in) seam allowances all around. Cut body pieces in canvas without seam allowances. Pin canvas to calico pieces and baste together.
2. If slashing is to be done on top fabric, it should be carried out at this stage and the completed top fabric should then be basted to any additional interlining, which will show through cuts.
3. Pin calico pieces to the wrong side of top fabric pieces and baste together. Any applied decoration, such as braid or cord, should be sewn on at this point.
4. Sew body pieces, right sides together, at centre back seam if present, then side seams and shoulder seams. Press seam allowance open. Sew sleeves together, snipping into curves in the seam allowance. Press.
5. Pin sleeves into body, right sides together and matching SH.P on sleeve head with shoulder seam on body. Sew in place. Snip into seam allowance under arm.
6. Turn raw edges in at neck, centre front, around waist, at bottom of sleeves and around armhole and shoulder of placard, snipping into curves where necessary. Pin and herringbone stitch or baste down. Press.
7. Cut out lining, adding 12mm (½ in) seam allowance to lining fabric. Sew lining pieces together as for mounted top fabric. Press seam allowances open. Pin lining into doublet, snipping allowance where necessary. Hand sew into place. Sew a tie inside the doublet at the bottom of the side seam and another to the bottom of the narrow side panel. This will help to keep the doublet in place around the waist.
8. If fastening with ties, work eyelets in left front and attach ties to right front; if fastening with hooks, sew these to inside of the left front and work thread bars on right front. Work pairs of eyelets around waist.
9. If including puffed upper sleeve, sew the back seam up and press allowances open. Pleat the top and bottom edges to fit sleeves, and sew onto sleeves.

Making up the front-fastening, high-necked doublet

1. Cut out body pieces, sleeves and skirts (if required) in calico and top fabric, adding 12mm (½ in) seam allowance all round. Cut body pieces and skirts in canvas without seam allowance. Baste canvas pieces onto calico pieces. Follow steps 2–5 above.
6. Sew skirt pieces right sides together, if included, at centre back and side seams. Press seam allowance open. Pin skirt to bottom of doublet, right sides together, sew and press seam allowances open, snipping into curves where necessary.
7. Turn raw edges in at neck, centre front, around waist and at bottom of sleeves, snipping into curves where necessary. Pin and herringbone stitch or baste down. Press.
8. Cut out lining, adding 12mm (½in) seam allowances all around. Sew lining pieces together as for mounted top fabric. Press seam allowances open. Pin lining into doublet, snipping allowance where necessary. Hand sew into place. Work fastenings at CF and pairs of eyelets around waist, or into separate lacing strip (use pattern on page 99) if skirts are included.

Pattern 13: Henrician man's doublet

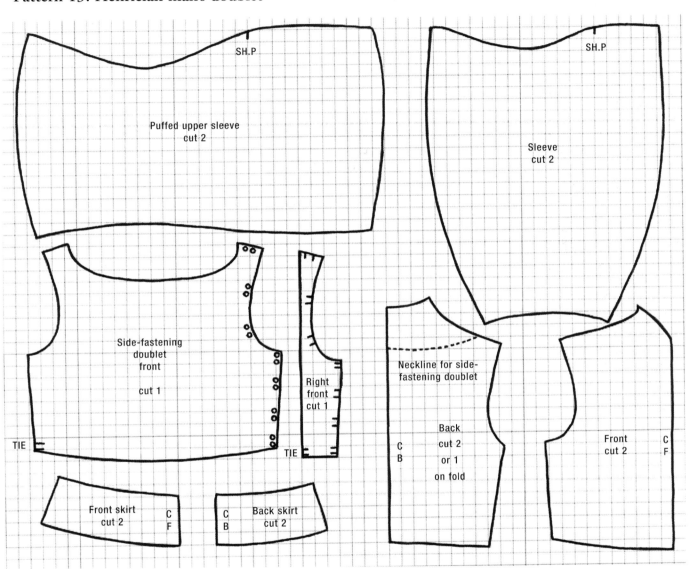

Puffed upper sleeve
cut 2

SH.P

Sleeve
cut 2

SH.P

Side-fastening
doublet
front

cut 1

Right
front
cut 1

Neckline for side-
fastening doublet

Back

cut 2

or 1

on fold

C
B

Front
cut 2

C
F

TIE

TIE

Front skirt
cut 2

C
F

C
B

Back skirt
cut 2

Pattern 14: Henrician man's jerkin

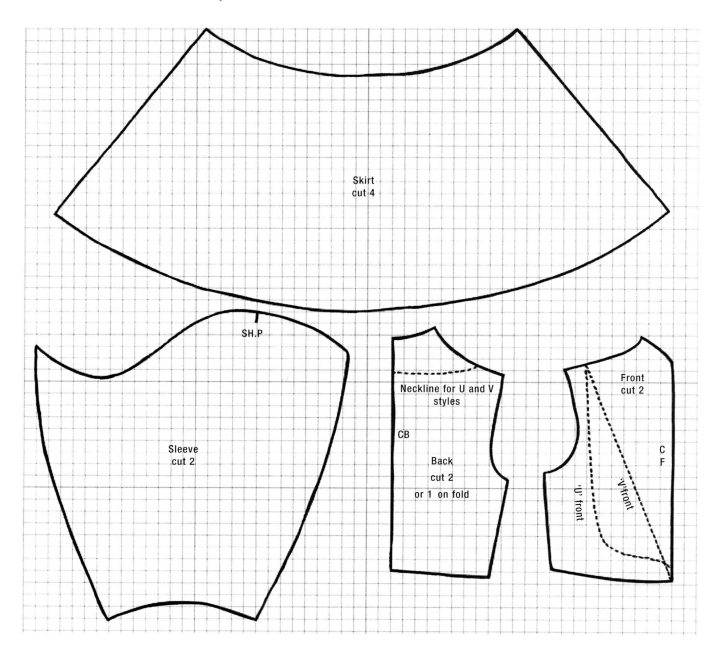

Skirt
cut 4

SH.P

Sleeve
cut 2

Neckline for U and V
styles

CB

Back
cut 2
or 1 on fold

Front
cut 2

CF

'U' front

'V' front

Henrician man's jerkin

Materials, without sleeves

- 3.1m (3½ yd) of top fabric and lining, each 112cm (45in) wide
- 2.5m (2¾ yd) of canvas or wool, 112cm (45in) wide, for interlining skirts
- If including large sleeves add 1.4m (1½ yd) of top fabric, lining and light wadding, each 112cm (45in) wide

1. Cut out body pieces, sleeves (if required) and skirts in calico and top fabric, adding 12mm (½ in) seam allowances all around. Cut interlining for skirts and sleeve (if required) without any seam allowances and baste to calico by hand. This basting will remain in place and should be fairly thorough. If the interlining is too large and encroaches into the seam allowance it should be trimmed back.
2. Pin calico pieces to the wrong side of top fabric pieces and baste together.
3. Sew body pieces together, centre back seam if present, then side seams and shoulder seams. Press seam allowances open. Sew skirt pieces together, leaving the centre fronts open. Press all seam allowances open. Any applied guards of trims should be sewn on now.
4. If including puffed upper sleeves given with doublet pattern, follow instructions above. Sew sleeves together, snipping into curves in the seam allowance. Press seam open. Pleat sleeve head, using box pleats, to fit armhole. Baste pleats into position when happy with the arrangement. Pin sleeves into body, right sides together, matching SH.P on sleeve head with shoulder seam on body, and sew in. Snip into seam allowance under arm.
5. Pin seam allowance under at centre front edges of skirt and all around hem. Baste into place and press.
6. Cut out lining, adding 12mm (½ in) seam allowances all round. Sew lining pieces together as for mounted top fabric. Press seam allowances open.
7. Spread out skirt on a clear flat surface, right side down, and place lining on top. Pin lining to skirt along the top edge and turn the raw edges under along the centre front and hem, pinning just back from the edge by 3–6mm (⅛–¼ in). Secure the layers at the top with basting and handsew the lining into place down around other edges. Pleat skirt up to waist measurement using box pleats. Baste the pleats into place.
8. If the skirt is not too bulky it can be machine sewn onto the bottom of the body. The seam allowances around the waist should be graded before covering over with the lining. If the skirt is bulky or a hand method is preferred, it can be whipped onto the bottom of the body as described on page 50.
9. Turn seam allowances under around body and sleeve cuffs, snipping into curves where necessary. Pin and herringbone stitch or baste into place. Press. Pin lining into doublet, snipping allowance where necessary. Hand sew into place.
10. Sew in hooks and eyes or eyelet holes.

Velvet jerkin with long slashes over chest, small slashes around borders and long plain sleeves.

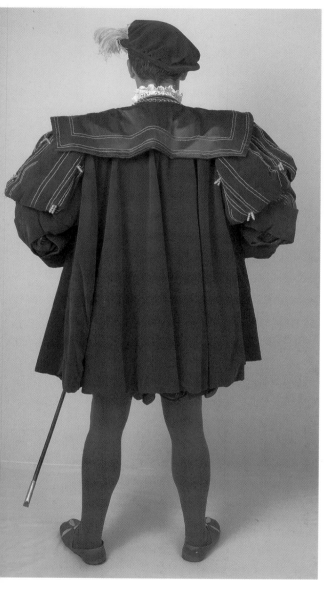

Back view of costume on page 86.

Henrician man's gown

These gowns are typically lined or faced with fur. However, the facings and collar can also be of a contrasting plain fabric, such as velvet, satin or tinsel (for the very wealthy). The facings can also be of self fabric. Single or multiple rows of velvet guards, usually black, make for typical and striking decoration.

Materials
- 5.1m (5⅔ yd) of top fabric, 112cm (45in) wide
- 4.1m (4½ yd) of lining, 112cm (45in) wide
- 1.5m (1⅔ yd) of facing fabric, 112cm (45in) wide
- 90cm (1yd) of wadding, 112cm (45in) wide, for interlining upper sleeve
- 40cm (½ yd) of canvas, 112cm (45in) wide, for interlining upper sleeve
- 2m (2¼ yd) of cane or boning for upper sleeve

Making up gown with fabric collar and facings
1. Cut body pieces, sleeves and upper sleeves in calico and top fabric, leaving 12mm (½ in) seam allowance all around except body hems, where 2.5cm (1in) should be allowed. Cut collar pieces in calico and facing fabric, adding 12mm (½ in) seam allowances all around. (It is preferable not to have a shoulder seam on the collar/rever. If there is enough fabric to cut the collar in one piece, tape the pattern pieces together matching the marks on shoulder seam.) Cut sleeve facing pattern along dotted line to create two patterns; cut both pieces twice in facing fabric, adding 12mm (½ in) seam allowances all around. Mark all sewing lines. Cut upper sleeves in thick wadding without seam allowance. Cut a piece of canvas without seam allowance for each upper sleeve. This is to stiffen the top row of pleats and should fill the section in between the bone channel and the top of the pattern. Cut all pattern pieces except upper sleeve and sleeve facing in lining adding 12mm (½ in) all around.
2. Stitch the canvas pieces onto the calico upper sleeves. The canvas shape should not encroach into the seam allowance, so trim back if necessary. Sew on a 2.5cm (1in)-wide tape to form the bone channel. The tape should stop short of the underarm seam by 2.5cm (1in). Pin the wadding onto the upper sleeves and trim off 4cm (1⅝in) at either end to expose bone channel. Baste wadding onto sleeve, taking care not to sew through the bone channel.
3. Baste calico pieces to top fabric/facing fabric. Baste in all slash and pleat lines, and baste in line on sleeve where upper sleeve comes to.
4. Make up body of gown by sewing the centre back seam, side seams and shoulder seams. Sew underarm seams of upper sleeves. Press all seams open. If any guards are to be applied they should be sewn on now. Turn up hem of gown and bottom of sleeves, pin and baste down. Press. Make up collar/rever by sewing shoulder seams (if present). Turn in seam allowances of collar around outside edge and hem (leave inside edge). Baste down and press. Make up the lining.
5. Put the gown, inside out, onto a stand or large padded hanger. Pin lining onto gown. Match the shoulder seams and underarm seams first, put a couple of pins in down the side seams and centre back seam and then pin around the hem. Don't worry about turning the lining under at this stage. When lining is pinned into place take gown off the stand or hanger and spread out on a flat surface. Turn lining up around hem and pin, setting it 6mm (¼ in) back from gown edge. Handsew into place. Baste lining to gown around armholes, neck and down centre fronts.

Pattern 15: Henrician man's gown

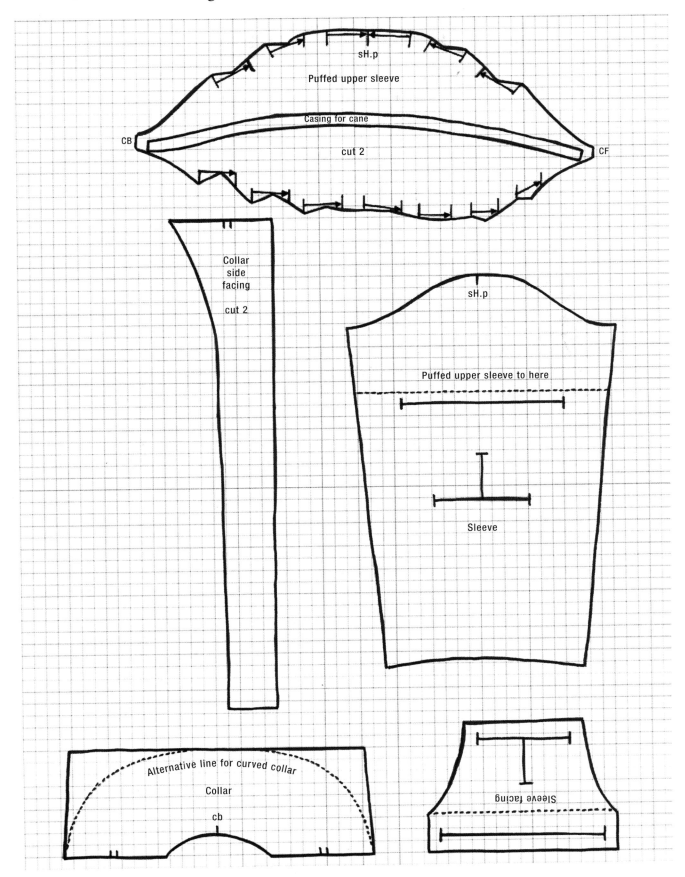

sH.p

Puffed upper sleeve

Casing for cane

CB

cut 2

CF

Collar
side
facing

cut 2

sH.p

Puffed upper sleeve to here

Sleeve

Alternative line for curved collar

Collar

cb

Sleeve facing

Pattern 15: Henrician man's gown

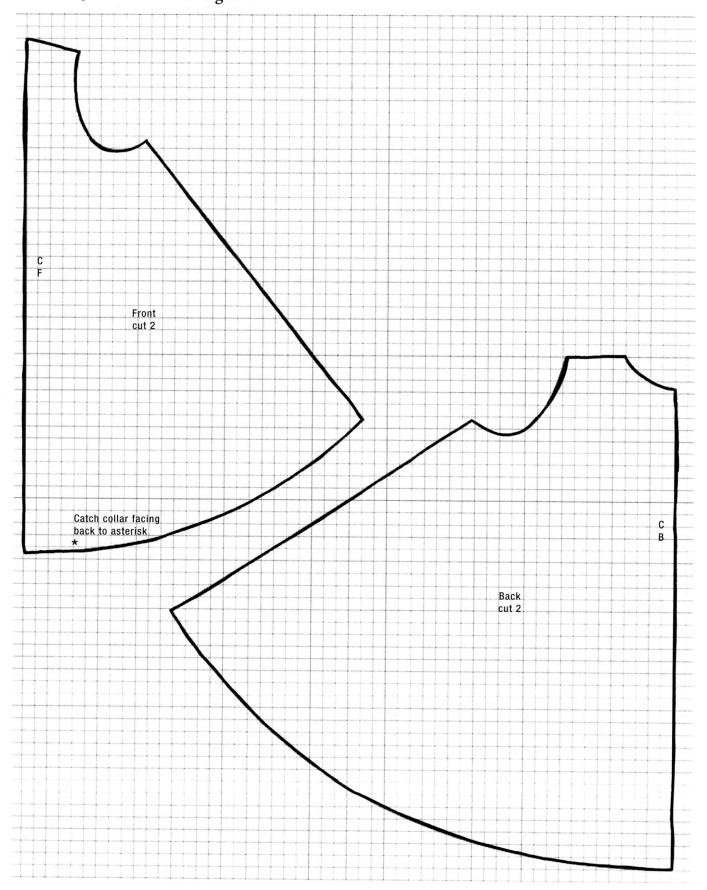

C
F

Front
cut 2

Catch collar facing
back to asterisk
*

Back
cut 2

C
B

6. Pin collar lining onto collar, wrong sides together. Fold raw edges under along outside edge and hem and pin, setting it back 3mm (⅛ in) from edge. Handsew down and press. Pin collar to gown, right side of collar to wrong side of gown. Sew collar to gown. Grade seam allowances and snip into curve around neck. Sew the collar lining down over raw edges. Turn collar back over gown and with a few stitches catch bottom of collar facings to gown fronts where marked on pattern.

7. With right sides together, pin sleeve facings onto sleeve over the areas to be slashed. Turn sleeve over and baste the slash lines through to the facings. Sew a box of stitching around slash lines, making it about 6mm (¼ in) wide. Cut the slash lines with a sharp blade, stopping short of each end by 6mm (¼ in). Snip into these corners with sharp scissors. Turn facings through to wrong side and press. Where the two facings meet in the middle, between the slashed areas, turn one of the raw edges under and pin it over the other. Handsew into place, making sure that the stitches catch the calico layer only and do not pass through to the right side. Baste around the edges of the facings. Sew underarm seams of sleeves. Press seams open.

8. Leave sleeves inside out and slide the sleeve linings over them, pinning around sleeve head (wrong sides together) and baste into place. Pin the sleeve lining to the sleeve along the centre back seam in a couple of places to keep it from moving around. Insert a sleeveboard or hardback book into the sleeve, positioning it under the slashed area. Carefully cut the lining away over the slashed area and bring the facing fabric through to the inside, fold the raw edges of the facings over the cut edges of the lining and pin into place. Handsew into place, making sure that the stitches catch the calico layer only and do not pass through to the right side. Pin and hand sew lining to bottom of sleeve, setting it back by 6mm (¼ in) from edge.

9. Pleat upper sleeves, ensuring that the sleeve head measures the same as the gown armhole and that the lower edge measures the same as the basted line on the sleeve. Adjust if necessary. Baste pleats into place. Cut two pieces of boning, each 1m (40in) long. Thread through the tapes on the inside of the upper sleeve, overlapping by 10cm (4in), and tape around overlap with zinc oxide tape. Turn in the seam allowance at the bottom of the sleeve and baste down.

10. Turn upper sleeves right side out and pin onto sleeves, matching up shoulder points and underarm seams. Baste the layers together around sleeve heads. Handsew bottom edges of upper sleeves to basted line on sleeves. Pin sleeves into armholes of gown, matching shoulder points and underarm seams. Sew sleeves into gown. Bind all raw edges at armhole together with a bias strip of lining fabric.

Making up gown with fur collar and facings
The construction of the gown does not differ from the method described above. The fur facings must be prepared first and all edges finished using the method described on page 50. The facings can then be handsewn to collar and sleeves.

Detail of gown back showing square satin collar trimmed with gold cord and paned upper sleeves, caught together with gold aiglets.

Elizabethan men's clothing

Doublet

The size of the peascod is dictated by the curve on the front of the body and the amount of wadding used in the lining. Only two layers of wadding are shown on the pattern. This will produce a moderate peascod, for a more pronounced shape increase the amount of layers, reducing each one a little in size so that the top fabric can sit smoothly over the padding.

Materials

- 2.6m (2¾ yd) of calico, top fabric and lining, each 112cm (45in) wide
- 60cm (⅔ yd) of canvas, 112cm (45in) wide
- 60cm (⅔ yd) of wadding, 112cm (45in) wide, for padding
- 60cm (⅔ yd) of light-weight wading, 112cm (45in) wide, for interlining sleeve
- 70cm (¾ yd) of boning if required

1. Cut out pattern pieces in calico and top fabric, adding 12mm (½ in) seam allowances all around except at fronts, which should have 4cm (1½ in). Cut canvas for body fronts, collar and skirts and lightweight wadding for sleeves without seam allowances. Pin to calico pieces and baste together. Sew on tapes for bones (if used). Cut out body, sleeves, skirts and collar in lining fabric, adding 12mm (½ in) seam allowances all around. Cut wadding for body as shown by dashed lines on pattern.
2. If slashing or pinking is to be done on top fabric, it should be carried out at this stage. The completed top fabric should then be basted to any additional interlining, which will show through cuts. Now make up the top layer. Baste prepared calico pieces to top fabric pieces. Any applied decoration, such as braid or cord, should be sewn on at this point.
3. Fold wings in half along the length, with wrong sides together, and baste down. Turn hems and sides of skirt/tabs over and pin. Baste or herringbone stitch. Press. Sew skirt linings to skirts, leaving top edges open. Press.
4. Sew body pieces together: side seams, back seam, then shoulder seams. Check for fit. When happy with the fit, trim the seam allowance at the fronts down to 12mm (½ in), allowing for overlap required for buttons. Press. Sew sleeves together, leaving opening at wrist as shown on pattern and snipping into curves in the seam allowance. Press.
5. Gather sleeve head to fit armhole. Baste wings into place on sleeve head. Sew sleeves and collar into body. Snip into seam allowance under arm.
6. With right sides together, pin completed skirts onto doublet waist and sew. Grade the seam allowances around waist. Herringbone stitch seam allowance of skirt/tabs up onto the body interlining, being careful not to allow the stitches to come through to the top fabric.
7. Pin facings to front edges, right sides together, and sew. Trim down seam allowance, notch curve of peascod, turn through and press. Turn in seam allowance at bottom of facing and stitch neatly in place to conceal raw edges of skirts.
8. Work buttonholes at fronts and cuffs. A single eyelet should be worked at the bottom of the front edge, replacing the bottom button and button hole. This is to enable the hose to be fastened to the doublet at this point. If bones are to be used, insert them into the tapes.
9. Now make up the padded lining. The pieces of wadding which are to sit against the buttonhole edge will need to be trimmed back a little to allow for this. Pin the first (largest) layer of wadding to the wrong side of a front lining

Inside of doublet lining with a layer of cotton wadding, pad-stitched into place, and additional cotton-wadding belly pieces basted into place.

Right side of doublet lining after wadding has been pad-stitched into place.

Inside of doublet showing lacing strip and lacing tab in place.

a. Doublet and trunkhose with canions front
b. Doublet and trunkhose with canions back
c. Jerkin (shown with squared-off wings)
d. Venetian hose

piece and pad stitch together. Repeat for the other front and the back. Position the extra pieces of wadding on the fronts, one on top of the other and loosely baste together around the edges. Sew lining pieces together and press seams open.

10. Pin lining into doublet and sew into place.

11. Cut lacing strip in canvas. Turn in seam allowances, fold in half along the length and press. Work pairs of eyelets in strong linen thread. Hand sew strip into doublet waist, overstitching securely at ends and ensuring the stitches do not go through the top fabric. Cut two pieces of canvas for lacing tabs, each 10 x 7.5cm (4 x 3in). Fold 12mm (½ in) in all the way around and press. Fold each piece of canvas in half to produce 2.5cm (1in) x 4cm (1½ in) tab. Handsew around edges and work an eyelet near the edge. Hand sew inside doublet waist 12.5cm (5in) back from CF.

12. Sew on buttons. Sew a pair of eyelets into centre back of collar for attaching ruff. Use the doublet pattern without sleeves for the jerkin, and make up with an unpadded lining.

Pattern 16: Elizabethan man's doublet/jerkin

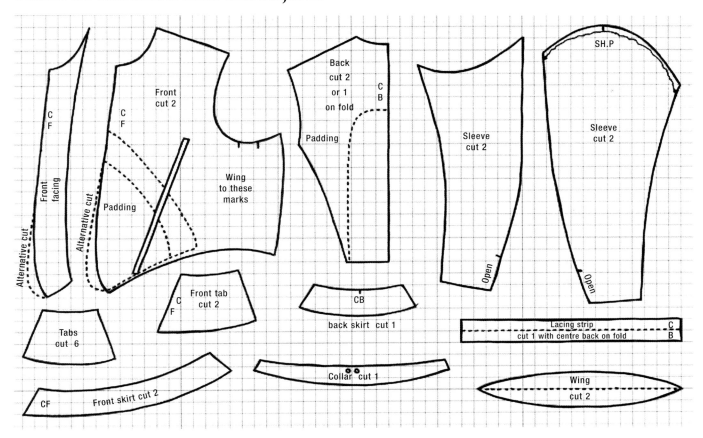

Far left: Back view of doublet with skirts and trunkhose made in silk with knitted netherhose.

Left: Velvet jerkin with embroidered guards worn over silk damask doublet and satin trunkhose with slashed panes.

Right: Pocket detail of Venetian hose.

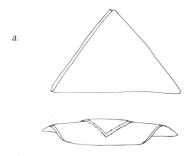

a.

b.

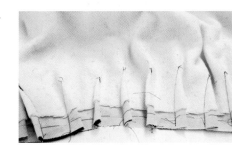

c.

d.

e.

Trunkhose

For styles without canions, cut the foundation pattern 2.5cm (1in) below dashed line.

Materials

- 4.2m (4½ yd) of calico, 112cm (45in) wide
- 1m (1¼ yd) of top fabric and lining, 112cm (45in) wide, for panes
- 70cm (¾ yd) of top fabric, 112cm (45in) wide, for trunkhose lining
- 80cm (¾ yd) of top fabric, 112cm (45in) wide, for canions
- 1.3m (1½ yd) of fabric, 112cm (45in) wide, for foundation lining
- 1.2m (1⅓ yd) of wadding, 112cm (45in) wide, for padding trunkhose lining and making sausage shapes

1. Cut all pattern pieces in calico and top fabrics, adding 12mm (½ in) seam allowance all around (cut foundation pieces on bias). Cut the panes with generous seam allowances along the bottom edges to allow for any necessary adjustments. Number the calico panes, using a pencil, in the seam allowance on the bottom edge before cutting out. Cut linings for panes. Cut cotton wadding without seam allowance for trunkhose lining. Cut two 52.5 (21in) squares of wadding for padded sausage shapes. Roll up and secure with a few stitches, as shown in diagram *a*.
2. Make up panes first. Any slashing or pinking on the panes should be carried out on the top fabric. Baste top fabric to calico. Any applied decoration or decorative edging should be sewn on at this stage. Turn seam allowances under along top edge of panes and on both sides. Pin and baste or herringbone stitch down. Press. Pin linings to panes and handsew in.
3. Baste canion top pieces to foundation pieces (diagram *b*). Sew foundation together at outside seams only. Press seam allowances open.
4. Baste cotton wadding to calico trunkhose lining pieces around outside edges. Baste to top fabric. Sew up side seams of trunkhose lining, leaving opening for pocket where marked. Press seam allowances open. Mark position of darts on wadding side of trunkhose lining.
5. Pad stitch the area of trunkhose lining to be darted, using matching thread. Sew darts into bottom of trunkhose lining, missing every third dart. The bottom edge of the trunkhose lining should measure the same as the line along the top of the canions on the foundation. Check before completing all the darts how much is left to go, and distribute this amount evenly amongst the remaining darts (see diagram *c*).
6. Make up the pocket. Cut two strips of the trunkhose lining fabric measuring 15 x 17.5cm (6 x 7in), press 12mm (½ in) under all the way around. Sew these strips into the centre of the calico pocket (see diagram *d*). Fold pocket in half and sew seam, leaving open at mark. Press seam allowance open. Position seam in the centre of the pocket and sew along bottom edge. Pin pocket into opening in trunkhose lining and handsew in place (see diagram *e*). Baste pocket to trunkhose lining at top.
7. Gather waist of trunkhose lining, using two rows of gathering stitches, to fit waistband, distributing the fullness evenly. Position panes on trunkhose lining and pin top and bottom. The panes should lie flat against the lining without tension or slackness. Trim off any extra seam allowance on panes (see diagram *f*).

8. Take pins out from panes on bottom edge only. Gather the panes at the bottom edge using two continuous rows of gathering stitches to fit to the darted area at the bottom of the trunkhose lining. Ensure that the gathering is evenly distributed along bottom edge of panes before pinning back on lining. The edges of the panes should sit next to each other and not overlap. Baste into place.

9. With right sides together, pin trunkhose lining and panes onto foundation layer, along top edge of canions. Sew into place and layer the seam allowances to reduce bulk (see diagram *g*).

10. Pin wadding sausage into position on top of darts and secure with a few stitches at either end and in the middle (see diagram *h*). Remove pins at tops of panes from trunkhose lining. Bring lining up over sausages and pin to foundation around waist and along front and back edges. Baste together.

11. Baste waistband top fabric pieces to calico pieces. Sew waistbands together, right sides facing, along centre back seam, press seam open. Sew to trunkhose.

12. Cartridge pleat the tops of the panes by running two parallel rows of stitching along top edge of panes, about 12mm (½ in) long in strong thread. Pull up to the same measurement as waistband. Pin the pleated panes to the bottom edge of the waistband and sew each cartridge pleat in place with a couple of stitches in strong linen thread. Position the sides of the cartridge pleats flat against the foundation rather than butting the ends of the pleat up against the waistband in the usual way (see diagram *i*).

13. With right sides facing, pin the outside seams of trunkhose together, and sew. Press seam allowances open.

14. Turn one of the legs through to the right side and feed it into the other leg. Pin the two legs of the trunkhose, right sides together, along crotch seam and sew, leaving fly open from mark. Press seam allowances open at back and snip into seam allowance under crotch.

15. Make up linings for foundation. When marking out the pattern on the lining fabric (on bias), do not include the dip at front waist but mark straight across and add 2.5cm (1in) extra height to waist. This is because the waistband lining is cut as one with the main lining to cut down on bulk. Cut with 12mm (½ in) seam allowances all around. Make up foundation lining and press seam allowances open. Pin foundation lining into place inside trunkhose and baste together at waist, fronts and bottom of legs. Bind raw edges using silk ribbon or binding.

16. Work a pair of eyelets at either side of front opening, about half way down, and in pairs along waistband to correspond with doublet lacing strip.

17. Make up fly flap in trunkhose lining fabric, mounted on linen. Bind around all edges with silk ribbon or binding. Pin fly flap into position and hand sew into place.

f.

g.

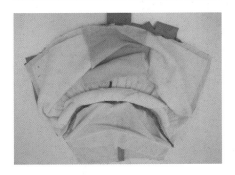

h.

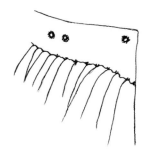

i.

Pattern 17: Elizabethan men's trunkhose

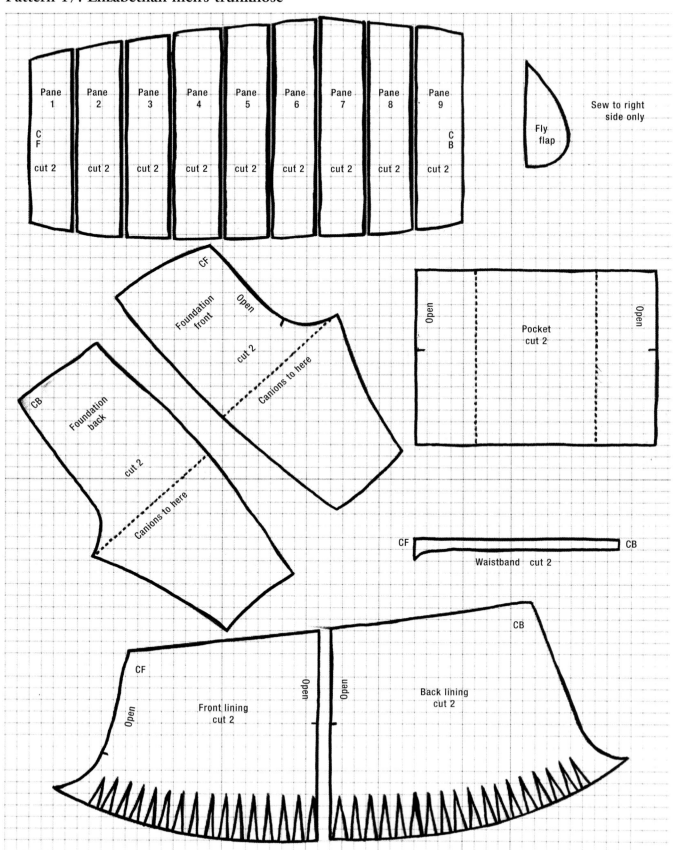

Pattern 18: Elizabethan man's Venetian hose

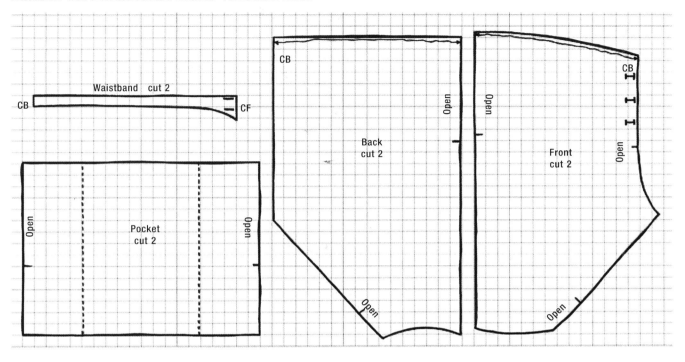

Waistband cut 2

CB   CF

Pocket cut 2

Open   Open

CB

Back cut 2

Open   Open

Open

CB

Front cut 2

Open

Open

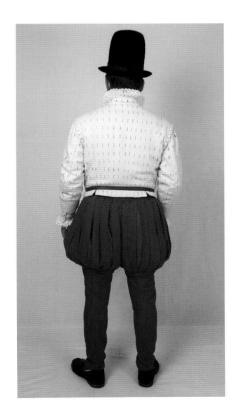

Left: Back view of doublet with narrow skirts and trunkhose made in wool with bias-cut netherhose.

Right: Wool doublet with pinked decoration and thread buttons. Trunkhose with wool panes and worsted lining.

Silk doublet with tabs worn with woollen Venetian hose.

Venetian hose

The calico interlining should be omitted if if these are to be made in heavy wool. These hose do not have an added button stand, the edges overlap only slightly when the hose are buttoned.

Materials
- 1.5m (1⅔ yd) of calico and top fabric, each 112cm (45in) wide
- 2m (2¼ yd) of lining, 112cm (45in) wide, including pocket

1. Cut leg and waistband pieces in calico, top fabric and lining, adding on 12mm (½ in) seam allowances all around. Baste calico pieces to top fabrics around sewing lines. Cut pocket in calico, adding 12mm (½ in) seam allowances all around.
2. With right sides facing, pin front leg pieces to back leg pieces down side seams only. Sew together, leaving the opening for pocket where marked. Press seams open. Sew on any applied braids. Make up pocket and sew into hose as described in step 6 of trunk-hose instructions.
3. Pin and sew inside leg seams, leaving opening where marked, and press open. Turn one leg right side out and feed it into the other leg. Pin around crotch seam and sew legs together, leaving the fly opening where marked. Turn up the raw edges at the bottom of the legs, clipping into curves. Baste and press. Press the top 5cm (2in) of seam open at centre back.
4. Make up the lining in the same way. Pin lining into hose, with wrong sides facing. Turn lining seam allowance under along the fly opening and the opening around the bottom of the legs. Handsew in place. Baste layers together around waist. Gather waist to fit waistband.
5. With right sides facing, sew waistbands together along centre back seam. Press seam open. Sew lining into waistband along top edge only. Pin waistband to gathered waist of hose, right sides facing. Sew waistband to hose. Trim seam allowances down. Turn seam allowance of waistband in at centre front and pin waistband lining down along this edge and along bottom of waistband, covering all raw edges. Handsew down.
6. Work pairs of eyelets around waistband for trussing to doublet. Work buttonholes and sew on buttons at fly and waistband front edge. Sew on hooks and eyes or worked thread bars at inside leg opening.

Fashionable Henrician lady: petticoat and kirtle

Petticoat

If no farthingale is to be worn the petticoat should be lined in a substantial material, such as wool or canvas.

Materials

- 3.1m (3½ yd) of calico, top fabric and lining, each 112cm (45in) wide
- 2.1m (2⅓ yd) of wadding to pad skirt, if required, 112cm (45in) wide

1. Cut all pieces in top fabric and lining, adding 12mm (½ in) seam allowances all around. Cut skirt wadding without seam allowances.
2. Make up bodies: pin centre back seam, side seams and shoulder seams right sides together and sew. Make up skirt: pin front panels to back panels, and centre front to centre front, right sides together, and sew, making sure the top 25cm (10in) of the front seam is left open. Make up lining in same way. Press all seams open.
3. Pin lining inside main fabric bodies and baste the two layers together around all edges except the waist. Bind around these edges with a strip of bias, cut from the top fabric, leaving the last 5cm (2in) of binding unstitched at bottom of fronts. Pin bodice lining back from waist edge.
4. Turn up hem of skirt, herringbone stitch down and press. Turn skirt inside out and pin lining in. This is made easier if the skirt is put over an ironing board and the lining is first pinned into position on the skirt at the seams and then in between. Pin lining in at top and bottom edges. Remove skirt from ironing board and turn the hem of the lining under, pinning it back from the edge of the skirt by 6mm (¼ in). Handsew in place. Baste layers together along top edge and handsew lining in place down each side of centre front opening. Press.
5. Pin pleats into skirt, following guide on pattern. Check that it measures the same around the waist as the bottom of the bodice. Baste pleats into place.
6. With right sides together, pin bodice to skirt along waist. Sew bodice to skirt without catching the bodice lining. Grade seam allowances and bring bodice lining down over raw edges on the inside waist, pinning and and then handsewing down. Finish sewing the ends of the binding down. Work a pair of eyelets at centre front on both sides.
7. Remove any visible tacking.

Kirtle

The overall measurements of the bodice should be 5cm (2in) smaller than the actual body measurements to allow for lacing in, and for the give in the fabric. It is important not to cut the bodies too long in the sides; the waistline of the bodies should sit just below the bottom of the ribcage. This may feel quite short, but it is necessary to prevent the bottom edge of the bodies from digging into the flesh around the waist. These kirtles can be made as either back or side lacing, the important thing being that the front neckline has an unbroken line. The benefit of side lacing is that both front and back necklines can be unbroken.

The bodice neckline is covered with a strip of decorative fabric which will show above the neckline of the gown. The front panel and back hem of the skirt should be made of the same fabric if the gown skirt is split, or the hem likely to be seen.

a. Kirtle with train
b. Petticoat
c. Kirtle bodice with side lacing
d. Kirtle bodice with back lacing

Pattern 19: Henrician lady's petticoat

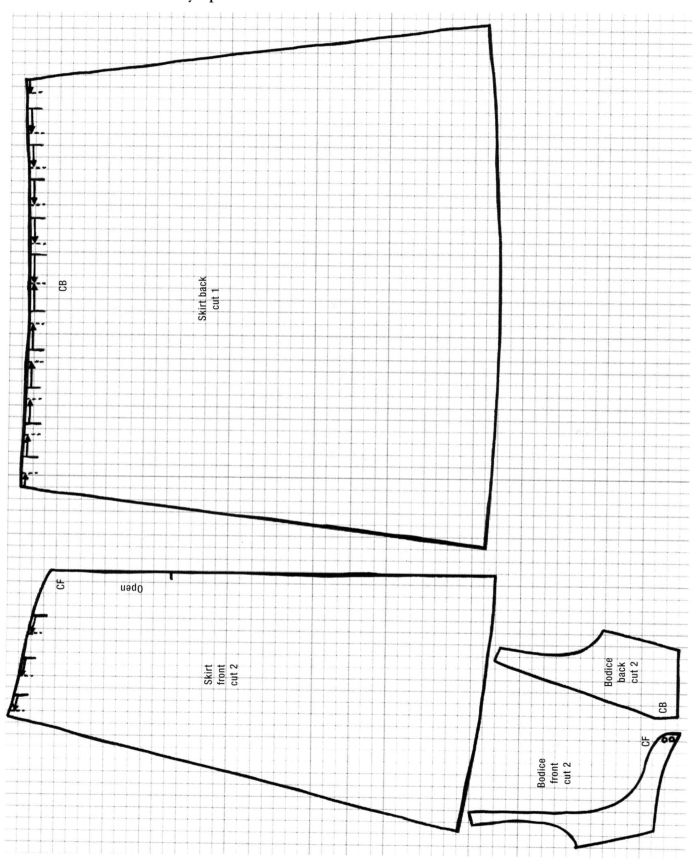

CB

Skirt back
cut 1

CF

Open

Skirt
front
cut 2

Bodice
back
cut 2

CB

Bodice
front
cut 2

CF

Materials, for untrained kirtle

- 3.75m (4⅛ yd) of calico, lining and top fabric (small amount of piecing on skirt), each 112cm (45in) wide
- 1.5m (1¾ yd) of canvas, 112cm (45in) wide, to interline body and forepart
- 7.5m (8½ yd) of boning; cane or plastic is best for all areas except the centre front, where a steel bone is recommended to re-enforce the point at waist and to help create the dip between the breasts evident in portraits of the time.
- 1m (1yd) of fine piping cord
- Add 1.1m (1¼ yd) of calico, top fabric and lining, 112cm (45in) wide, if including train

1. Cut bodice and skirt pieces in calico and top fabric with 12mm (½ in) seam allowances all around, except lacing edges of bodice which need 4cm (1½ in). Cut front skirt panel and bodice pieces in canvas without seam allowances. Baste canvas layers to calico pieces. Mark bone channels on bodice pieces. Baste prepared calico pieces to top fabric pieces.
2. Sew bone channels in bodice pieces, either by machine or by hand using backstitch – do not sew curved bust outline. Press.
3. For back-opening bodice, sew side-back seams and shoulder seams of bodice together; for side-opening bodice, sew back seam and shoulder seams together. Press seam allowances open. Make up lining in the same way.
4. Insert bones, making sure that they sit 6–8mm (¼ –⅜ in) above waistline, to prevent digging in and getting in the way of attaching the skirt. Sew in curved bust line. Before setting steel bone into centre front channel, bend top over so that it curves in toward the body from about 4cm (1½ in) below the top edge.
5. Cut a bias strip of lining fabric measuring 1m (1yd) by 5cm (2in) wide. Place the piping cord down the middle of the strip, fold in half and trap cord in place with a row of stitching, making sure the cord is sitting tightly against the folded edge. Sew the piping to right side of neckline. The bias strip should be trimmed so that it sits back from the centre back by 6mm (¼ in); leave the cord untrimmed at this stage. Grade seam allowances and turn the bias strip to the inside of the neckline, clipping in to the corners. Baste or herringbone stitch down.
6. Pin the the strips of decorative fabric to neckline. Fold the raw edges under where the shoulder strap meets the front of the bodice and around the outside edges. Handsew down. Baste layers together around neckline. Turn seam allowances under around neckline, clipping into corners. Herringbone stitch down and press.
7. Sew skirt panels together leaving 25cm (10in) openings at back or sides, depending on where the bodice is lacing. Sew skirt lining panels together in same way. Press seam allowances open.
8. Pin lining into skirt, baste around top and bottom and handsew openings. Pin pleats into top of skirt, as indicated on pattern. Check skirt over petticoat or farthingale to see that it is hanging correctly, adjusting pleating and levelling hem if necessary. Finish hem with a binding of self fabric or velvet.
9. Sew pleats into place. With right sides together, pin pleated skirt to bottom of bodice (it will be necessary to clip into the seam allowance of the skirt at the dip in C.F) and sew together. When sewing around point of bodice, square off the point with one or two stitches rather than trying to sew a sharp point. This gives the seam allowance more room to lie flat and the point will look sharper.
10. Turn seam allowances under at lacing edges and baste down. Pin lining into bodice and handsew in place, making sure not to catch any of the hidden piping cord. Work eyelets. Put kirtle on wearer and gently pull on both ends of the piping cord until the neckline of bodice sits closely against the skin. Secure ends of cord with a few small stitches set 12mm (½ in) back from the centre back, going right through all layers. Trim ends of cord off.
11. Sew any applied decoration such as jewels or braid around neckline.

Fashionable Henrician petticoat in taffeta. The minimal bodice ensures that no unnecessary bulk is added to the body. The skirt is interlined with cotton wadding.

Pattern 20: Henrician lady's kirtle

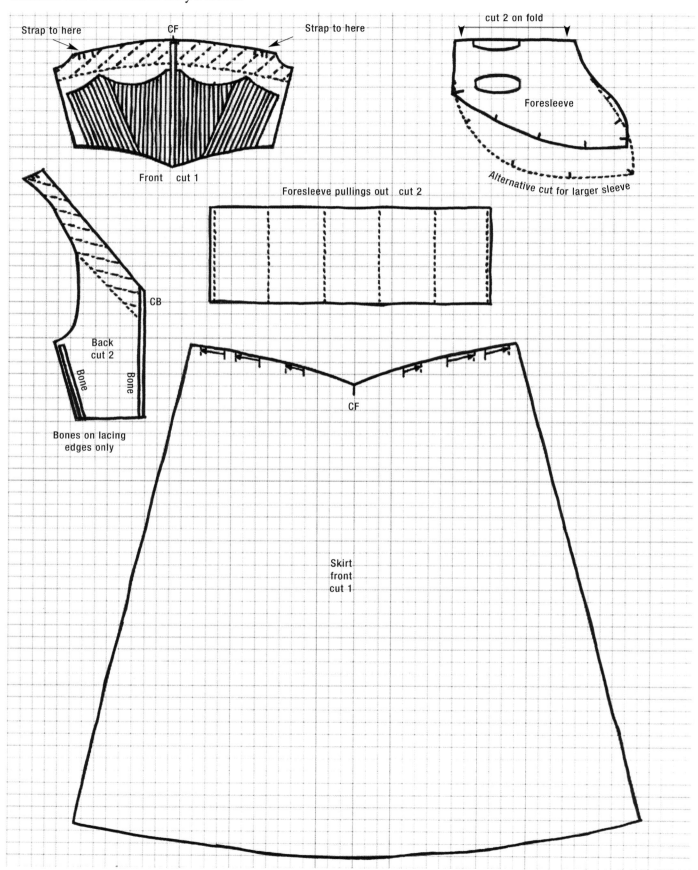

Strap to here

CF

Strap to here

cut 2 on fold

Foresleeve

Alternative cut for larger sleeve

Front   cut 1

CB

Foresleeve pullings out   cut 2

Back
cut 2

Bone

Bone

Bones on lacing
edges only

CF

Skirt
front
cut 1

Pattern 20: Henrician lady's kirtle

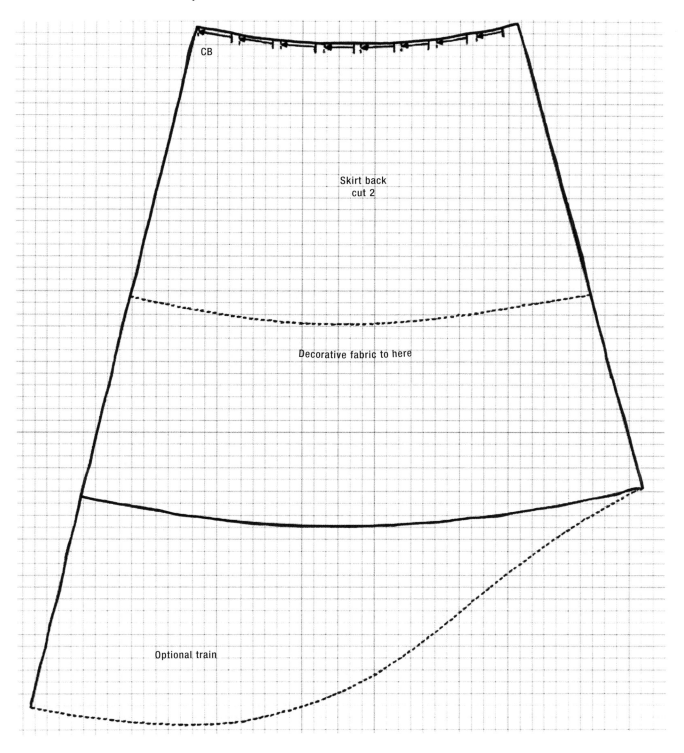

CB

Skirt back
cut 2

Decorative fabric to here

Optional train

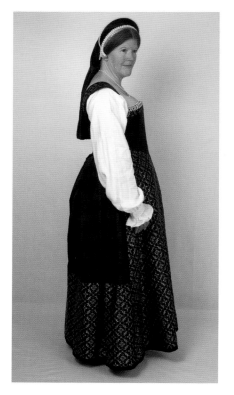

Top left: Kirtle without train in black taffeta with damask forepart and border around hem and neckline. Top middle: French gown in damask with medium-sized velvet turnbacks. Foresleeves match forepart of kirtle. Top right: Back of French gown showing train. Bottom left: Back of French gown. Bottom middle: Detail showing damask forepart of kirtle and matching foresleeves. Bottom right: Neckline of kirtle bordered with damask and jewels.

Fashionable Henrician lady: French gown

Trained gown

Materials
- 9.6m (10yd) of calico and top fabric, each 112cm (45in) wide
- 8.5m (8¾ yd) of lining, 112cm (45in) wide
- 30cm (12in) of canvas, 112cm (45in) wide
- 1.8m (2yd) of wool or cotton wadding, for padding the pleats
- 1.15m (1¼ yd) of contrast fabric, 112cm (45in) wide, for lining sleeve turnbacks

1. Cut all pieces in calico, top fabric and lining, adding 12mm (½ in) seam allowances all the way around, except for side and back skirt panels which need 2.5cm (1in) seam allowance at top. Sew tapes for bones onto bodice fronts where marked. Cut wadding for the top 45cm (18in) of skirt back panels, without seam allowances. Baste to calico skirt panels. Cut placard in canvas without seam allowances and baste to calico stomacher. Sew tapes to placard for bones. Baste calico pieces to top fabric pieces.
2. Sew bodice pieces together. When sewing the side and side-back seams, backstitch just below the neckline edge rather than running the stitching into the seam allowance. This will allow the seam allowance to be folded down smoothly. Do the same for the shoulder strap at the corner where the strap meets the front neckline. Press seam allowances open. Make up bodice lining in the same way.
3. Sew seams of top fabric sleeves, right sides together. Press seams open. Pin sleeves into bodice, matching the sleeve back seam with mark on bodice. Sew into place, snipping into seam allowance under arm.
4. For sleeve linings, first cut four lengths of narrow linen or cotton tape, 7.5cm (3in) long, for loops to tie foresleeves to. Fold in half and pin to turn-back lining where marked on pattern. Pin sleeve lining to turn-back lining, right sides facing, and sew together, catching the ends of the tape loops into the stitching. Press seam allowance open.
5. With right sides facing, pin sleeve lining to sleeves around bottom edge, and sew around. Grade seam allowances and turn through. Roll the bottom edge of the sleeve between your fingers so that the top fabric sits just behind the turn-back lining. Press.
6. Sew skirt panels together. When sewing the front panel to the side panel, backstitch just below the top line rather than sewing into the seam allowance. Sew skirt lining panels together in same way. Press seam allowances open.
7. With right sides facing, pin skirt and skirt lining together down centre front edge and around hem. Sew together. Grade seam allowances, snipping and notching curves and trimming corners. Turn through. Roll the hem between your fingers so that the lining sits just behind the top fabric. Press.
8. Lay the skirt out on a flat surface and then smooth out and pin along top edge, about 10cm (4in) down from top. Baste the layers together along top of front panel only. Run a few lines of large basting stitches from waist to hem to keep the layers together.
9. Turn the seam allowances in along tops of side and back panels. Pin together and handsew in place. Press. Pleat front section of skirt as indicated in pattern, basting pleats down along top edge.

Top: The neckline of the kirtle sits snugly against the body, while that of the gown sits smoothly beneath it.

Above: Foresleeves bound in contrasting silk with slashed detail and jewels.

Left and below: Back views of French gown showing the eight large cartridge pleats ready to be positioned and sewn into place.

10. Work two rows of parallel stitches in strong thread to create eight very large cartridge pleats. Pull threads so that pleats are partly formed, but do not tighten to finished width at this stage.

11. Pin the bodice on a model or stand over the layers it will be worn with. Pin the skirt to bottom of bodice and check that everything is sitting correctly, making any necessary adjustments to pleats in the front panel. Take pins out and remove gown from model/stand.

12. With right sides facing, pin the pleated front panel of the skirt to the bottom of the forebodies. Sew together. Grade seam allowance. Insert the bones into the tapes in the forebodies.

13. Turn seam allowances under around neckline and bodice fronts. Baste or herringbone stitch down. Press. Pin lining into bodice and bring sleeve lining up to cover raw edges around armhole, snipping where necessary. Handsew into place. (Alternatively, the neckline can be bound.)

14. Put gown back on model/stand and arrange the cartridge pleats evenly along the bottom of the bodice. Only the top of each pleat will be sewn to the bodice, the rest will sit underneath and create bulk. Catch into place with a few pins. Carefully remove gown from model/stand and handsew the tops of the cartridge pleats to the bottom of the bodice, using strong thread.

15. Work eyelets in forebodies. Work buttonhole bars where indicated on pattern.

16. Turn seam allowances of placard piece under, baste into place and press. Pin lining in and handsew into place. Sew hooks to one side of placard. Attach the other side to gown by hand, using strong thread and securing at top and bottom with back stitches.

22. Bind hem of gown skirt with 2.5–4cm (1–1½ in) wide velvet strip or ribbon.

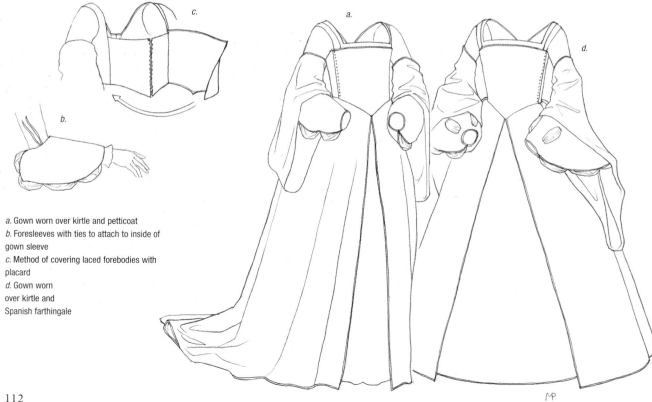

a. Gown worn over kirtle and petticoat
b. Foresleeves with ties to attach to inside of gown sleeve
c. Method of covering laced forebodies with placard
d. Gown worn over kirtle and Spanish farthingale

Pattern 21: Henrician lady's gown

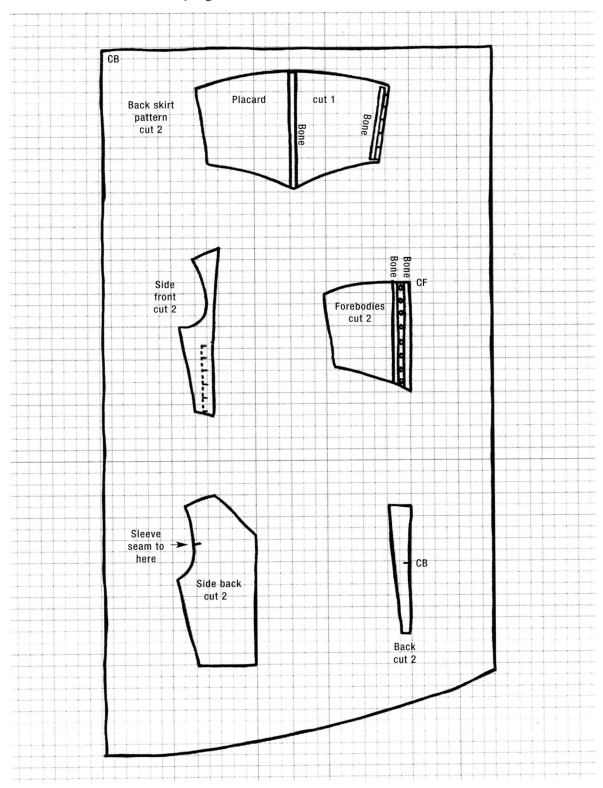

CB

Back skirt
pattern
cut 2

Placard   cut 1

Bone

Bone

Side
front
cut 2

Bone
Bone

CF

Forebodies
cut 2

Sleeve
seam to
here →

Side back
cut 2

CB

Back
cut 2

Pattern 21: Henrician lady's gown

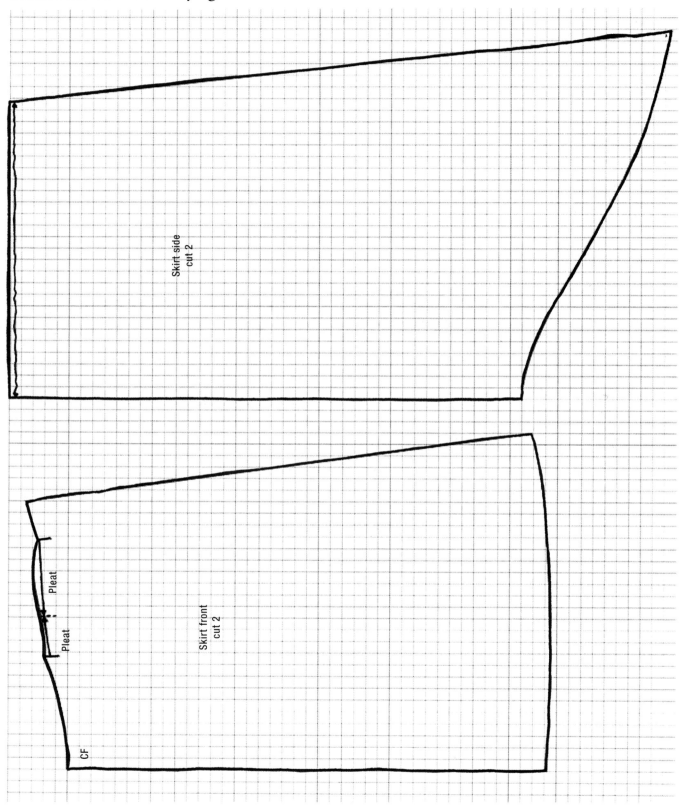

Skirt side
cut 2

Skirt front
cut 2

Pleat

Pleat

CF

114

Pattern 21: Henrician lady's gown

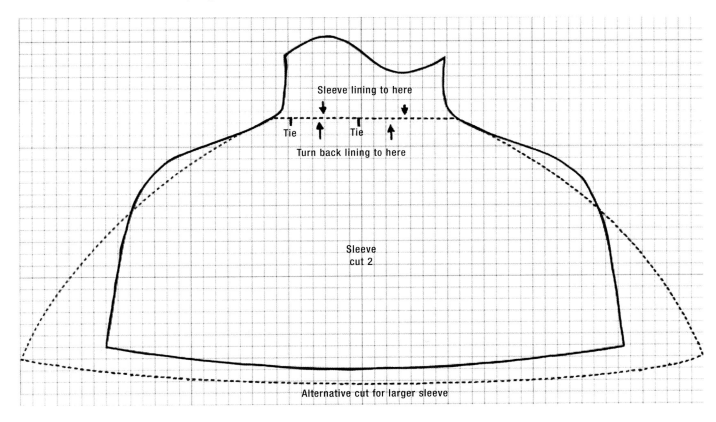

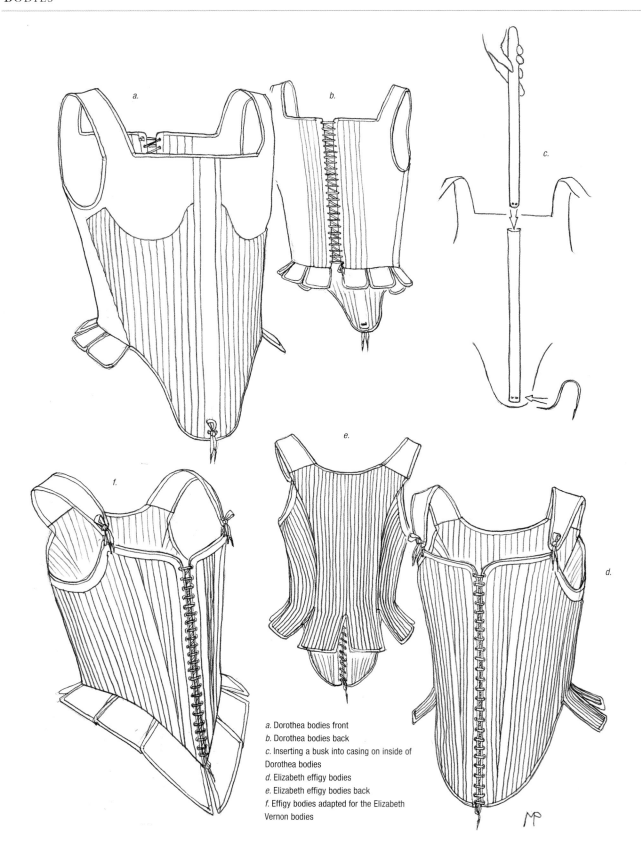

a. Dorothea bodies front
b. Dorothea bodies back
c. Inserting a busk into casing on inside of
Dorothea bodies
d. Elizabeth effigy bodies
e. Elizabeth effigy bodies back
f. Effigy bodies adapted for the Elizabeth
Vernon bodies

Bodies

Notes on scaling up the bodies patterns

The overall measurements should be 5cm (2in) smaller than the actual body measurements to allow for lacing in and for the give in the fabric. It is important not to cut the bodies too long in the sides: the waistline of the bodies should sit at the bottom of the ribcage. This may feel quite short but is necessary to prevent the bottom edge of the bodies from digging into the flesh around the waist. The cut actually helps to create the elongated look of the late Elizabethan period as it further exaggerates the long point at the front.

Materials

For each pair of bodies you will need:

- 75cm (¾ yd) of foundation fabric and top fabric, each 112cm (45in) wide
- 5m (5½ yd) of binding

- For the Dorothea bodies, 9m (10yd) of boning
- For the Effigy bodies, 18.5m (20yd) of boning
- A couple of steel bones are recommended at the front for all styles to reinforce the pointed waist and prevent it from curling up.

Dorothea bodies

The original bodies have a busk casing sewn to the inside of the front. A separate busk would be inserted and tied in at the bottom. If this method is to be used, the two bone channels at centre front should not be stitched, nor bones inserted. The busk casing is made up separately and sewn on at the end.

1. Cut pattern pieces in canvas and top fabric, leaving 12mm (½ in) seam allowances all around except at centre back, where 4cm (1½ in) should be left. Mark all sewing lines and bone channels on right side of canvas pieces.
2. Baste top fabric pieces to canvas pieces around sewing lines, wrong sides facing.
3. Sew bone channels, either by machine or by hand, using double running stitch to make a solid line of stitching, and working from the canvas side. Do not sew curved bust outline. Press.
4. Sew side-back seams and shoulder seams together and press seam allowances to one side. Trim one of the seam allowances down to half, fold the other allowance under and handsew down (flat fell seam).
5. Insert prepared boning and sew in curved bust outline.
6. Bind tabs and sew on to waist.
7. Bind armholes and top edge of the bodies. Bind around point at front waist, handsewing binding over tabs on inside.
8. Press the seam allowance at back edges to inside. Trim the canvas seam allowance down to 2.5cm (1in). Fold the top fabric over it, covering all raw edges, and handsew down. Work eyelets down centre backs and around waist, if desired for tying to the farthingale.
9. If including a separate busk, work a pair of eyelets through the bodies at bottom of centre front, as marked on pattern. Cut the busk casing in canvas, adding 12mm (½ in) seam allowances all around. Press the seam allowance under on all edges. Work a pair of eyelets at bottom and hem the top edge. Sew busk casing to inside of bodies down centre front by hand, making sure the eyelets match up.

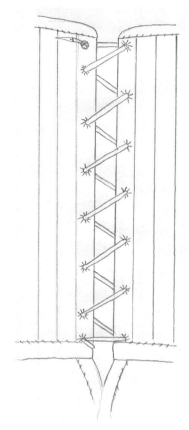

Method of lacing with a single lace (viewed from the inside). The top and bottom pairs of eyelets must line up while those in between must be off-set. The eyelets can be worked right on the lacing edges of the bodies or they can be set back behind a bone. If worked right on the edge it is advisable to strengthen them by sewing the eyelets over metal rings. The eyelets should be spaced no more than 1¼ inches apart. The lacing cord is knotted at one end, threaded through the eyelets from top to bottom and secured on the outside by passing the cord back through the last hole and tying off.

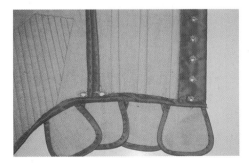

Inside of Dorothea bodies, showing finished seams and bound edges.

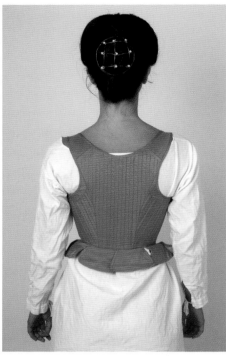

Back view of Elizabeth Vernon bodies, covered in shot taffeta.

Elizabeth effigy bodies

1. Cut all pattern pieces in top fabric and canvas, leaving 12mm (½ in) seam allowances all around. Mark all bone channels on right side of canvas body pieces. Baste canvas pieces to top fabric pieces, wrong sides facing, around sewing lines.
2. Sew bone channels, either by machine or by hand, using double running stitch to make a solid line of stitching. Press.
3. With right sides facing, pin fronts to back panel and sew together, leaving bottom 7.5cm (3in) open to create tab. Press seam allowances open. Trim the canvas seam allowance down to half and then fold the top fabric allowance under and handsew down. With right sides facing, pin shoulder straps to backs and sew. Finish seam as above.
4. Slash between the tabs in front and back panels. Insert boning
5. Bind all edges of the bodies.
6. Work handsewn eyelets.

Elizabeth Vernon bodies

Either pattern can be adapted to create a third style, based on a pair worn by Elizabeth Vernon in her portrait of c. 1595 by an unknown artist. To adapt the Dorothea bodies, the back should be seamed or cut on the fold and the front should be cut as two pieces, with eyelets worked at centre front. The centre front point should be sharpened, as indicated by dashed line on pattern and the eight small tabs exchanged for the eight individually shaped larger ones. To adapt the Elizabeth effigy bodies, cut waistline along dashed line indicated in pattern and sew the eight individually shaped tabs to waist.

Reproduction busks in wood and bone made by Dave Hodgson (www.bodgeramour.co.uk).

Pattern 22: Bodies

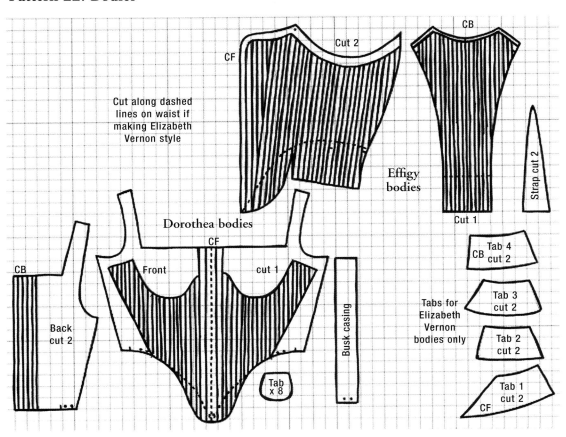

Cut along dashed lines on waist if making Elizabeth Vernon style

Cut 2

CF

Effigy bodies

CB

Cut 1

Strap cut 2

Dorothea bodies

CF

Front

cut 1

CB

Back cut 2

Busk casing

Tab x 8

Tab 4 cut 2 CB

Tabs for Elizabeth Vernon bodies only

Tab 3 cut 2

Tab 2 cut 2

Tab 1 cut 2

CF

Far left: back view of effigy bodies.
Left: Elizabeth Vernon bodies.

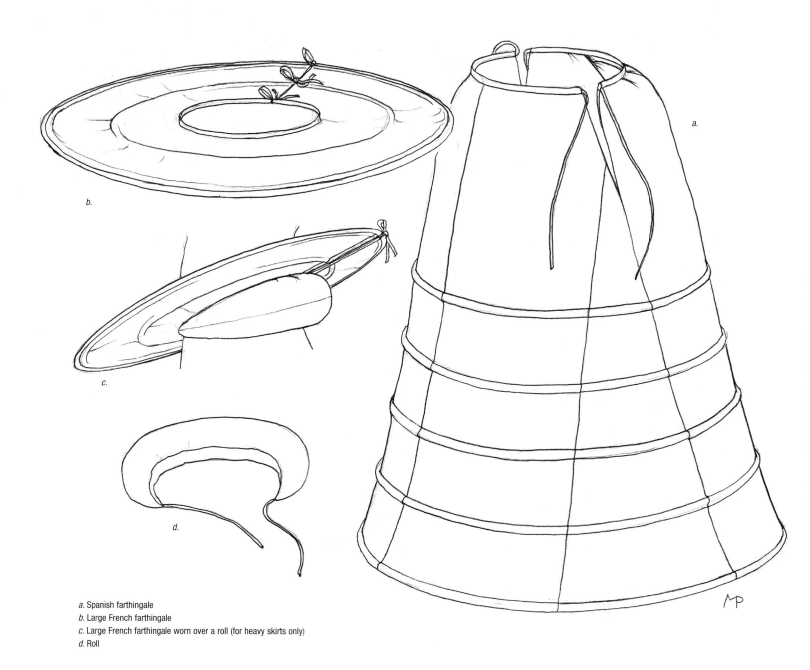

a. Spanish farthingale
b. Large French farthingale
c. Large French farthingale worn over a roll (for heavy skirts only)
d. Roll

Farthingales

For Spanish and large French farthingales, you will need to prepare canes beforehand. For the Spanish farthingale, cut canes to correct finished length plus a 15cm (6in) overlap. For the large French farthingale, cut to the correct finished length without any overlap. Soak overnight in water. This is ideally done in a container of water that is sufficiently large to allow the canes to be tied into hoops for soaking. If this is not possible, a bathtub will do. Once soaked, the ends of each cane should be overlapped and bound. The canes should then be left to dry. Once dry, the canes for the Spanish farthingale should be shaved down at the ends to enable them to be spliced.

Spanish farthingale

This can be made in one layer of canvas or it can be covered with a more decorative fabric. The tapes for the casings can be made from strips of fabric with the edges pressed under.

Pad secured to farthingale waistband with buttonhole-stitched bars.

Materials
- 2.3m (2½ yd) of foundation fabric, 112cm (45in) wide
- 2.3m (2½ yd) of top fabric, 112cm (45in) wide
- 12.5m (13½ yd) of cane or steel boning
- 12.5m (13½ yd) of ribbon or tape, 2.5cm (1in) wide, for casings
- 2.75m (3yd) of ribbon or tape, 4cm (1½ in) wide, for bottom casing/hem binding
- 1.8m (2yd) of tape for ties

1. Cut pieces in foundation fabric, and top fabric if used, allowing 12mm (½ in) seam allowances all around. Mark sewing lines on the wrong side of the fabric and mark channels for hoops on the right side (a wheel and carbon paper is the easiest way of doing this).
2. With right sides facing, sew panels together down all seams except back seam and top 25cm (10in) of side seams, as marked on pattern. Press seams open.
3. If the farthingale is not to be covered, finish the seams by turning the raw edges under and sewing down.
4. If covering, sew panels of top fabric together in the same way as foundation, sewing with wrong sides facing. Press seams open and baste the layers together. Handsew around side openings.
5. Sew casings onto farthingale, leaving the last 7.5cm (3in) at either end of each casing un-stitched. Pin loose ends back out of the way. Use the wider tape for the bottom casing and turn it up under the hem of the farthingale, binding the raw edges.
6. Sew up back seam and press seam to one side. Trim one of the seam allowances down to half and then fold the other one over it, concealing all raw edges, and sew down (flat fell seam).
7. Insert hoops into casings.
8. Make up pad by pinning the two layers together, right sides facing, and sewing all around the edge except for a 7.5cm (3in) gap, as marked on pattern. Snip and notch seam allowance. Turn through. Stuff firmly with wool or cotton fibre. Hand sew opening to close.
9. Arrange the pleats of the farthingale as indicated in the pattern and pin. Tie a tape around the waist of the wearer or a stand, and attach the pad to the back with safety pins. Pin the farthingale onto the tape. Check that pleats are in the right places, adjusting if necessary to get them to sit smoothly. The back

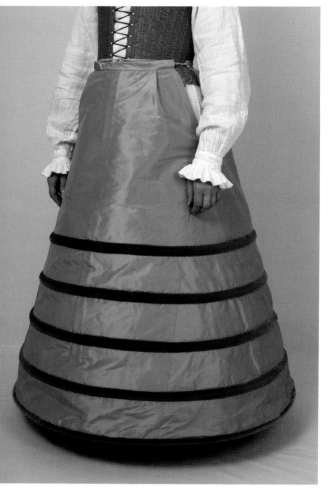

Above: Spanish farthingale made in linen canvas covered with shot taffeta. Cane hoops are covered with orange velvet.
Right: Roll tied over Dorothea bodies covered in satin.

should stick out more than the front. When you are happy with the pleats, remove farthingale from stand/wearer.

10. Finish off hoops by overlapping the ends and binding with strong thread or narrow tape. Sew the ends of the casings down by hand.

11. Sew waistbands to waist of farthingale. Fold band in half along the length and turn the seam allowance under to cover all raw edges; handsew down.
Sew tapes into ends for ties. Work eyelets in waistband if desired for tying to bodies.

12. Remove the safety pins from the pad. Fix pad to farthingale with buttonhole stitch bars (see photograph on page 121).

Large French farthingale

Materials
Canes will need to be used for boning as steels will twist and distort the shape.
- 70cm (¾ yd) of foundation and top fabric, each 112cm (45in) wide
- 5m (5⅜yd) of cane
- Two 17.5cm (7in)-long steel bones.
- 2.1m (2⅓ yd) of ribbon or fabric strip, 4cm (1½ in) wide, for binding edge
- 1.2m (1⅓ yd) of tape for ties

1. Cut pieces in canvas and top fabric, allowing 12mm (½ in) seam allowances all around. Mark sewing lines and channels on right side of top fabric. Cut back opening. With wrong sides facing, pin canvas pieces to top fabric pieces and baste.

2. Sew channels for hoops and bind outside edge with a strip of velvet, being sure not to allow the stitching to encroach on the channel for hoop.

3. With right sides facing, sew waistband to waist of farthingale. Snip into curved seam allowance, fold waistband over to cover all raw edges and handsew down.

4. Stick a piece of zinc oxide tape over ends of canes and feed hoops through channels. Bind off back opening edges with self fabric.

5. Cover the two bones with a strip of self fabric or tape and handsew to underside of farthingale just back from back opening edges.

6. Sew ties to waist band and at end of each hoop. Work eyelets in waistband if desired for tying to bodies.

Rolls

Materials
- 90cm (1yd) of canvas, 112cm (45in)wide
- Woollen fleece/cotton fibre or polyester fibre for filling

Cut pieces in linen canvas or strong calico. Pin together and sew around, leaving a 12.5–15cm (5–6in) gap on the inside line. Snip and notch seam allowance. Turn through. Fill very firmly with wool or cotton fibre. Hand sew opening closed. Sew on ties made from cotton or linen tape using strong thread.

Pattern 23: Spanish farthingale

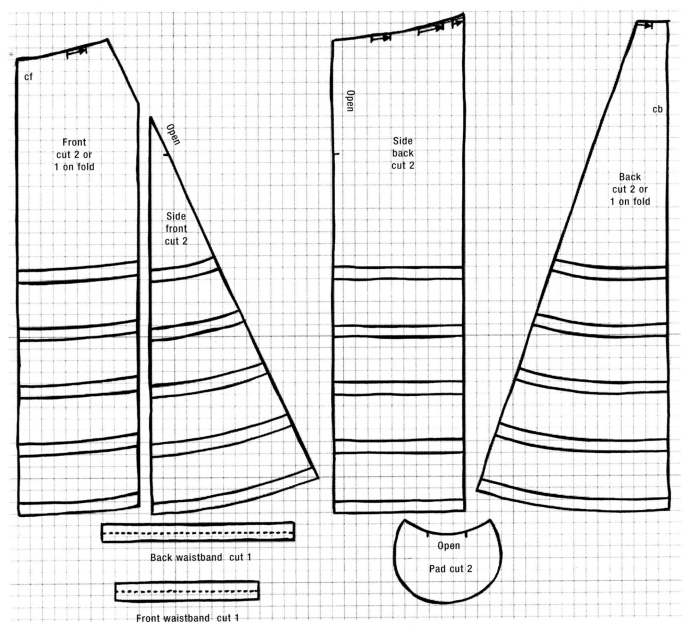

cf

Front
cut 2 or
1 on fold

Open

Side
front
cut 2

Open

Side
back
cut 2

cb

Back
cut 2 or
1 on fold

Back waistband cut 1

Front waistband cut 1

Open

Pad cut 2

Pattern 24: Large French farthingale and rolls

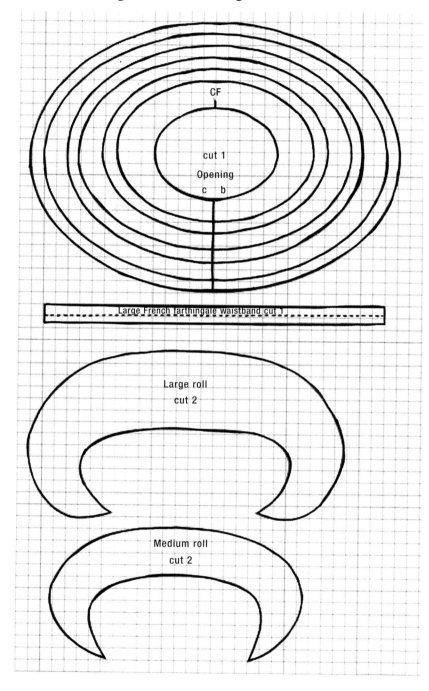

CF

cut 1

Opening

c b

Large French farthingale waistband cut 1

Large roll

cut 2

Medium roll

cut 2

Large French farthingale worn over effigy bodies.

Late Elizabethan lady

The large 'verthingale' sleeves require support in the form of bones or canes. Canes
hold their shape better, but plastic boning is more easily available. If using canes,
cut them to length and soak overnight in water. Once soaked remove from water
and form each cane into a circle, place a pencil over the join and bind it to the
canes with tape. Leave to dry. Drill a small hole in either end to stitch through. If
using bones, add 7.5cm (3in) overlap to each length.

a. Gown with stomacher, tabs
at waist and open-fronted skirt
b. Gown with closed bodice,
hanging sleeves and closed skirt
c. Bodice with revers and stomacher
d. Back view of bodice with
hanging sleeves
e. Gown bodice showing
lacing strips and method of
pinning stomacher over lacing

Gown with closed front and hanging sleeves.

Back view of gown, showing position of hanging sleeves and supportasse/ruff tied to bodice collar.

Late Elizabethan bodies (without revers) and sleeves

Materials

- 5.75m (6¼ yd) of top fabric and lining, each 112cm (45in) wide
- 60cm (⅔ yd) of canvas, 112cm (45in) wide, for interlining bodice
- 65cm (30in) of wadding, 112cm (45in) wide, for interlining sleeves
- 2.5m (3yd) of tape for sleeve bone casings

For optional hanging sleeves:
- 1.4m (1½ yd) of top fabric and lining, each 112cm (45in) wide
- 5.25m (6yd) of bias binding, 12mm (½ in) wide (self or lining fabric is best)

1. Cut all pattern pieces in calico and top fabric (except for sleeve lining), adding 12mm (½ in) seam allowances all around. Add 2.5cm (1in) seam allowance to sleeve head. Cut canvas without seam allowances for bodice fronts and backs. Cut wadding without seam allowance for sleeves. Baste canvas to bodice pieces around outside edges and sew bone channels. Sew tapes to sleeves where marked for bone casings. Baste wadding to sleeves, cutting it back to reveal the ends of the bone casings.

2. Baste the prepared calico pieces, except lacing strips, to wrong side of top fabric pieces. Any applied decoration should be sewn on now.

3. With right sides together, sew bodice back, side and shoulder seams. Sew sleeve seams. Press seams open. Feed prepared bones into channels in bodice. For sleeves, if using boning, overlap the ends and bind with tape; if using canes, sew ends together through drilled holes using strong thread.

4. Turn seam allowances under on sleeve head and cuff, snipping into curves where necessary, and pin and baste down. Turn seam allowance under along curved edge of collar and pin and baste down. Turn seam allowances under along all but the top edges of the skirt pieces and baste down. Press.

5. Cut bodice fronts and backs, skirts, collar, lacing strip and sleeve lining in lining fabric. Make up bodice and sleeve linings and press seams open. Gather up sleeve lining around sleeve head to fit the armhole measurement. Pin the sleeve lining into armhole, matching up SH.P with shoulder seam. Sew around armhole, clipping into seam allowance under arms.

6. Pin linings to collar and skirt pieces, turning raw edges under around prepared edges, and pin and handsew down. Baste layers together along raw edges. Press. Baste calico lacing strip to lacing strip lining. Fold edges of lacing strip in and press down. Press lacing strip in half and handsew layers together around edges. Work eyelets.

7. With right sides together, sew collar and skirts to bodice. Turn seam allowances under all the way around bodice, clipping curves where necessary, pin and baste. Press.

8. Cartridge pleat sleeve head to fit armhole measurement. Pin pleated sleeves to bodice and sew on by hand.

9. Pin lining into bodice, clipping into curves where necessary and handsewing into place. Pin lacing strip inside bodice so that it sits alongside front edge of bone no. 2. Sew in by hand, using strong thread and catching the interlining while taking care not to go through to the top fabric. Back stitches should be worked at either end of lacing strip where the most strain will be. Sew a hook and eye or buttonhole bar at wrist openings. If making up closed front bodice, sew hooks and eyes inside front edges, setting them back by 3mm (⅛ in).

Late Elizabethan bodice with revers

Rever is cut in one with bodice, as indicated by dashed lines.

Follow steps 1–2, above.

3. With right sides together, pin rever facing to rever part of bodice front and sew down outside edge. Press seam open. Grade seam allowances and fold facing to inside (rever facing and rever are now wrong sides together). Baste facing to rever long top and centre front edges. Fold faced rever over to front of bodice, matching balance marks. Baste rever to bodice along shoulder. Sew bodice back, side and shoulder seams, and sleeve seams (all right sides together). Grade seam allowances and press all seams open. Feed prepared bones into channels in bodice.

Continue from step 4, above.

Optional hanging sleeves

1. Cut sleeve in top fabric and lining, adding 12mm (½ in) seam allowances all around.
2. Press seam allowance down on top fabric sleeve heads, clipping into curve, and baste down. With wrong sides together, pin sleeve linings to top fabric, turning raw edge under around sleeve head and clipping into curve. Pin linings to sleeves, wrong sides together, and handsew around sleeve head. Baste around the outside of the rest of the sleeves.
3. Bind off scalloped edges. Press.
4. Cartridge pleat sleeves at sleeve head so that pleated area fits between bodice shoulder seam and mark on bodice armhole. Pin hanging sleeves over bodice sleeves and handsew into place.

Pattern 25: Late Elizabethan lady

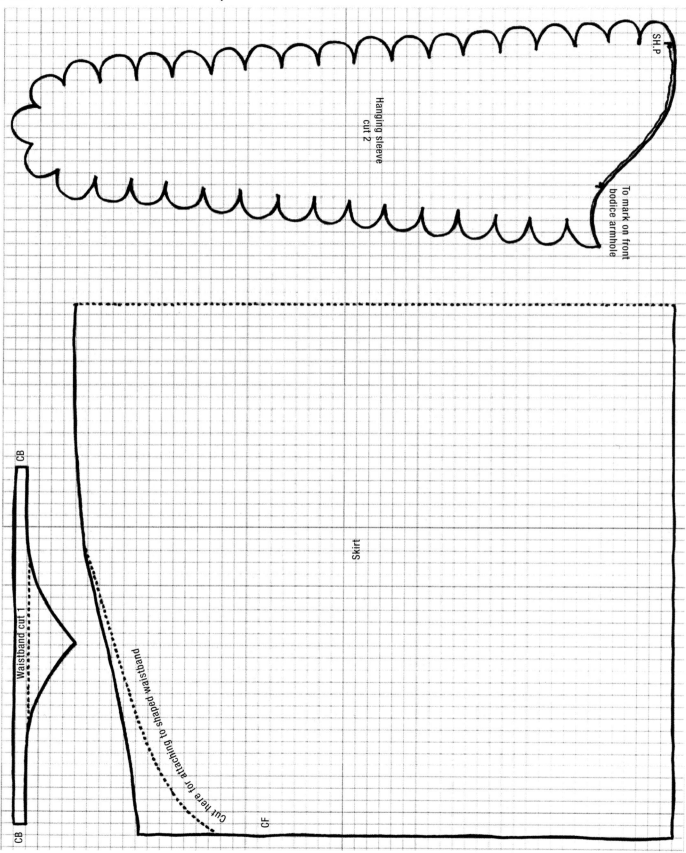

Hanging sleeve
cut 2

SH.P

To mark on front
bodice armhole

CB

CB

Waistband cut 1

Cut here for attaching to shaped waistband

Skirt

CF

Pattern 25: Late Elizabethan lady

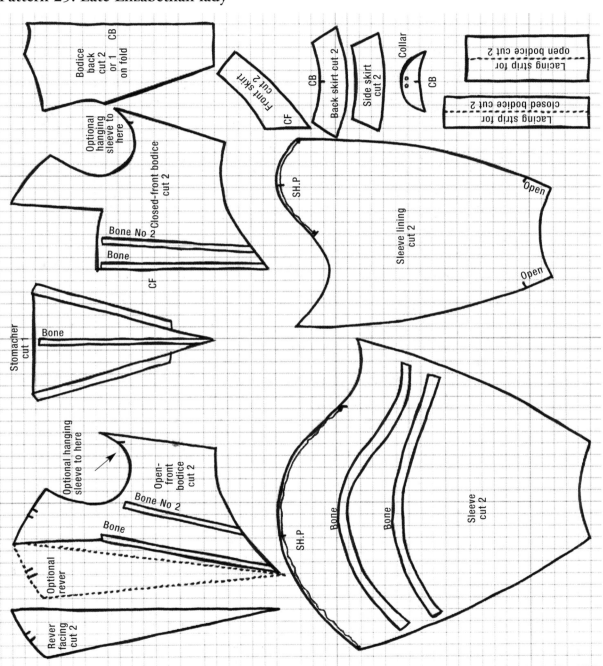

For styles of the 1590s, large neck ruffs may be worn open and pinned to the sides of the bodice.

Late Elizabethan petticoats and skirts

Unlike the Henrician and early Elizabethan styles, these skirts do not need any shaping in the side seams, they are simply made up from straight widths of fabric. Skirts which are to be worn over a large French farthingale or roll will need a total hem circumference of 3.4–3.75m (3¾–4⅛ yd); those worn over a small bumroll, or none at all, will only need 3–3.4m (3⅓–3¾ yd). The length will need to be taken from the side waist and over any farthingale to the hem, which is usually 5–7.5cm (2–3in) off the ground. Add 7.5–10cm (3–4in) for a flounce. The hems are always across the straight grain of the fabric and all shaping is confined to the top edge of the skirt. This shaping is best done over the farthingale, but the pattern gives an idea of the line. Unless there is top fabric to spare, a calico toile should be made up first to get the shape and save on cutting extra seam allowance from the top fabric. Make the under petticoat first and use this as a pattern for the top petticoat/gown skirt. These skirts do not generally need interlining unless heavy surface decoration is to be included, in which case it is best to mount the top fabric onto calico.

Making up late Elizabethan petticoats and skirts

Skirts are often 5 or 7.5cm (2 or 3in) shorter than petticoats. For skirts to go with the late Elizabethan bodices, the pattern should be cut with a shaped 'V' waist, as indicated by the dashed line on pattern. If an open-fronted skirt is desired, place front edge of pattern to the edge of the fabric when cutting out. If a closed skirt is required, place pattern against fold. Skirts can be sewn directly onto the bottom of the bodice, or sewn onto a shaped waistband. If the skirt is going to be sewn onto a waistband, this should be made up first.

Making up waistband

Cut shaped waistband pattern in calico, top fabric and lining, adding 12mm (½in) all around. Cut same in canvas without seam allowance. Baste canvas to calico and baste calico to top fabric. Turn all edges in, clipping into curves, and then baste down and press. Pin lining to waistband, turning raw edges under and clipping into curves. Pin and handsew in place. Press. Sew on hooks and eyes at back opening.

1. Cut out three skirt panels in top and lining fabrics: two should have the dipped shaped waist as shown in pattern (fronts) and one should have a straight edge along the top, marked across from the top of the side back edge. Add 12mm (½in) seam allowances all around except at top edges, where 7.5cm (3in) should be allowed for adjustment.
2. Pin top fabric panels together, right sides facing, and sew together. Press seams open. Make up lining in same way. Cut a slit in centre of back panels from waist down to 25cm (10in) for opening, Press a minimal hem back, grading to nothing at bottom.
3. Putting the lining in by machine: with right sides together and matching seams, pin lining into skirt around hem, and up fronts if they are left open. Sew together. Trim the seam allowance of the lining down by half and turn the skirt the right way around. Put the skirt over an ironing board, top fabric side down, and roll the hem of the skirt between the fingers to get the lining sitting above hem edge by 3mm (⅛in). Press. Pin and baste layers together around top edge. Handsew the layers together around the back opening and strengthen the bottom of the opening with a thread bar worked with buttonhole stitch (see diagram on page 51).

a.

b.

c.

d.

e.

f.

g.

h.

Putting the lining in by hand: press the seam allowance up around the hem, and up fronts of top fabric skirt, if they are left open. With wrong sides together, pin lining into skirt. Turn lining seam allowance under around hem, setting it back from the edge by 3mm (⅛ in), and pin and handsew into place. Pin and baste layers together around top edge. Handsew the layers together around the opening and strengthen the bottom of the opening with a thread bar worked with buttonhole stitch (see diagram on page 51).

4. Level the skirt, following guidelines on page 51.

5. Turn raw edges in on each other around waist, slipstitch, press and cartridge pleat up to fit the measurement along the bottom edge of the bodice or waistband. Pin pleated skirt onto bottom of waistband or bodice and handstitch on.

6. If skirt is to have a flounce, this should be pinned in place on the model/stand over the farthingale. Once pinned, secure with a row of small running stitches. The stitches can be pulled up slightly as they are sewn and secured at intervals with a back stitch. This will create more of a ruffled frill than if sewn with the plain running stitch.

Dressing the late Elizabethan lady

Effigy bodies covered in silk damask are laced on over the smock (a). Large French farthingale covered with satin is tied over bodies (b). The farthingale sits over the bodies' tabs at the back and under the bodies at the front (c). A back-fastening taffeta petticoat is worn over the farthingale (d). This is covered by the gown skirt in shot taffeta, fastening at the back (e). Gown bodice without revers is laced together with a long lace threaded through internal lacing strips (f). The slashed satin stomacher is pinned over the lacing, and the edges of the bodice are pinned to the stomacher (g). A girdle, ruff, gloves, fan and jewels complete the ensemble (h).

Electric or old-fashioned curling tongs make a good substitute for Tudor poking sticks.

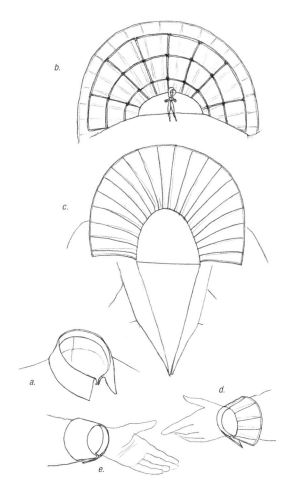

a. Plain man's collar
b. Back view of standing collar with supportasse underneath, tied to bodice collar
c. Darted standing collar pinned to gown bodice
d. Darted cuff
e. Plain cuff

Ruffs, cuffs and collars

Starch

Wheat starch may still be purchased through specialists who supply it for conserving papers and books. Old-fashioned hot starch may also be obtained from some traditional hardware/home stores. Straw stiffener, available from millinery suppliers, works well, but it is noxious and brushes must be cleaned with the equally noxious thinner. The most easily available is spray starch. This can be used, though it may take two or three applications to achieve the desired stiffness in the fabric.

Making up the collars and cuffs

Cut out pattern pieces in linen, adding 12mm (½ in) seam allowances all around. If making up darted version, sew darts in now and press them all to one side. Hem outside edges of collar and cuffs and sew on lace if required. With right sides facing, pin neckbands and wristbands onto collar and cuffs, and sew. Fold bands in half and fold seam allowances under, pin along sewn line to enclose all raw edges. Handsew down, catching ties into each end if including. Starch and press.

Cartridge-pleated ruffs

This method allows the material to be arranged in various ways, which can be altered with each starching. It is the best method to use for very large ruffs where a great deal of material must be reduced down to the neck size. The length of the strip will depend on how deep the ruff is to be, how big the sets are and how long the neckband is. The small ruffs fashionable in the 1560s and 1570s take around 3m (3yd), while the deep ruffs of the 1580s and 1590s take 4–5m (4–5yd). The best method for working out exactly how much will be needed is to prepare a small trial section in scrap fabric of a similar weight. Pleat up 50cm (20in) strip and pin in the sets on the outside edge. Mark a 2.5cm (1in) section on the gathered edge with a pen. Un-pleat and multiply this amount by however many cms (inches) the neckband will be to find out the total length needed.

1. Cut the neck and wristbands first. These should be cut from the same linen used for the ruff itself and interlined with stiffer linen or iron-on interfacing. The bands should measure the same as those on the shirt or smock that the ruff is to be worn with. Press seam allowances under along all edges.
2. Prepare the strip of linen or organza by hemming along one long edge and both short ends with a narrow hem. Embroider or add lace to the outside edge if desired.
3. Cartridge pleat the inside (neck) edge. The size of the pleats will depend on the thickness of the fabric chosen, though the ruff will be most effective if small pleats are worked. Generally pleats which are made using stitches that are 6mm (¼ in) long work well.
4. Pull the ruff up until the pleated edge measures the same as the neckband.
5. Pin one of the long folded edges of the neckband to the top of the pleats. Stitch the tops of the pleats to the folded edge, working 1–2 stitches per pleat. Fold the neckband in half so that all the raw edges are enclosed. Sew the neckband to the other side of the pleats.
6. Starch the ruff using preferred method.
7. Arrange the ruff into figures-of-eight and fasten with pins. Use curling tongs to set the pleats. Remove pins. Neckbands can fasten with ties, either threaded through eyelet holes or sewn in, or with small buttons.
8. Work a pair of eyelets in the centre back of the neckband for tying ruff to gown or doublet collar.

Pattern 26: Cuffs, collars and supportasse

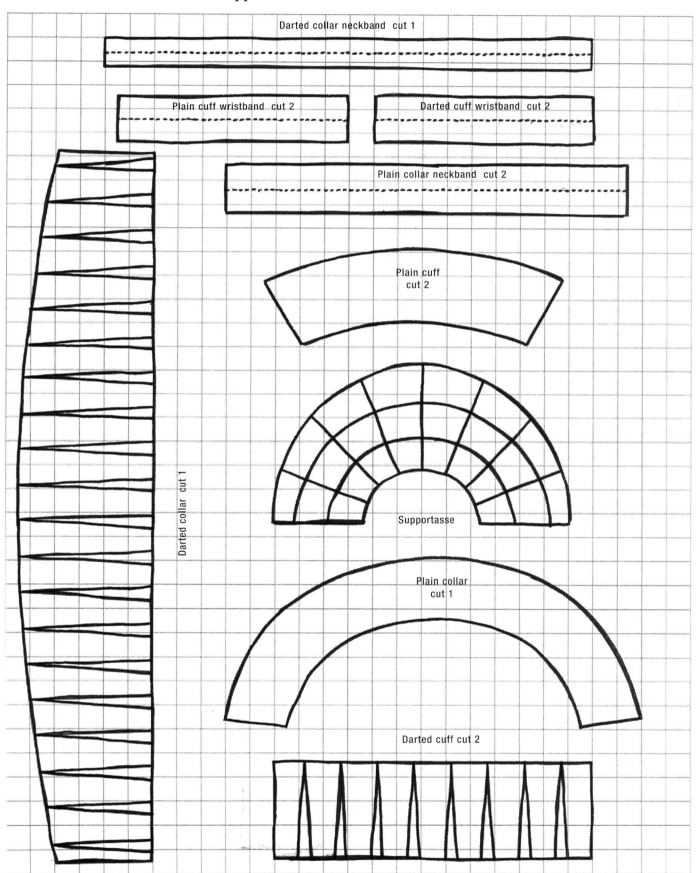

Darted collar neckband cut 1

Plain cuff wristband cut 2

Darted cuff wristband cut 2

Plain collar neckband cut 2

Plain cuff
cut 2

Darted collar cut 1

Supportasse

Plain collar
cut 1

Darted cuff cut 2

Jo Lawler sets a freshly starched ruff using a hot poking stick whilst more dry on the line in the background.

A crisply starched lace-trimmed cuff, temporarily basted to the gown sleeve.

A large lace-trimmed ruff is underpropped by a supportasse and pinned to the front of the bodice.

Stacked box pleats

This method makes arranging the figure-of-eights much easier as the box pleats dictate where they should go. The strip should be six times the length of the band it will be sewn to.

1. Prepare the strip and neckband as before.
2. Pin the strip into box pleats. Press. Repeat the process to create double, or stacked, box pleats. Press.
3. Pin the pleated ruff to the neck/wristband, right sides together, and sew. Press the raw edges down toward the band. Press the seam allowances of the band in, fold band in half and pin over raw edges. Handsew in place
5. Starch ruff using preferred method. Set pleats using curling tongs.

Modern, starch-saving cheat

Sew clear fishing line inside the hem of ruff. Gather up, using either of the methods above. Arrange the pleats, pin and secure with a couple of stitches between the outside edges of each one. A ruff made in this way can be washed and dried without the need for starching as the figures of eight will keep their shape.

Wrist ruffs

Made in the same way as neck ruffs. The strips of linen are usually between 2 and 3cm (¾ and 1¼ in) wide by between 90cm and 1.4m (1 and 1½ yd) long.

Supportasse

Materials and equipment required

- 2.5m (3yd) of heavy gold-plated wire (available from jewellery suppliers)
- Thinner wire to bind the joins
- 90cm (1yd) of ribbon to bind the neck edge
- Small pair of pliers, for shaping corners and flattening ends
- Small pair of round-nosed pliers, for curling the ends of the wire under on themselves.
- More wire will be required if fancy shapes are to be included, as in the extant supportasse (see page 30) and the effigy supportasse (see page 30).

1. Scale up the pattern to use as a template. Cut a piece of wire long enough to go all the way around outside edge, including a 5cm (2in) overlap. Bend the wire into shape, following outside line of pattern, and then overlap the ends and bind off with the thin wire.
2. Cut two pieces of wire to the length of the inner curved lines plus 8mm (⅓ in) for curling under. Shape the wires into the curve using the template as a guide. Flatten the ends with the ordinary pliers. Then use the round-nosed pliers to curl them under to form a hook. Hook the ends over the frame and close the hook by squeezing it between the pliers.
3. Cut the wire for the middle strut, which should measure twice the required length plus 8mm (⅓ in) for curling under. Bend the wire in half over the round-nosed pliers. Still using the round nosed pliers, flatten the ends of the wire with the pliers and curl them under to form a hook. Hook the ends over the frame and close the hooks by squeezing them between the pliers. Wire the other end to the frame with thin wire. Repeat process for remaining struts.
4. Bind neck edge with silk or velvet ribbon, securing at each end with a few stitches. The supportasse is pinned to the underside of the ruff before the ruff is tied to the collar of the gown or doublet.

Hats and headdresses

Elizabethan hat with pleated covering

Materials

- 50cm (24in) of top fabric, 112cm (45in) wide
- 25cm (9in) of lining, 112cm (45in) wide
- 25cm (9in) of buckram and domette, 112cm (45in) wide
- 1.8m (2yd) of millinery wire

The head opening should be cut 6mm (¼ in) larger than the actual head size of the wearer.

1. Cut the brim, side band and tip in buckram. Add 12mm (½ in) seam allowances to centre backs of side band and the inner circle of brim. All the other pieces are cut *without* seam allowances.
2. Sew the centre backs of the side band together by overlapping the buckram and securing with basting stitches down both sides. At this point, check buckram tip fits easily inside top of side band, allowing for wire. Trim down if necessary.
3. Wire the tip, the bottom edge of the side band and the outside edge of the brim. This can be done either by hand, using a wiring stitch, or with a machine zigzag stitch. Overlap the ends by at least 2.5cm (1in) and overstitch securely.
4. Cut the brim, side band and tip in domette, adding 12mm (½ in) seam allowances all around. Cover the wired buckram pieces with the domette, pinning into position and then basting into place. When covering the brim, place the domette on what will be the underside of the brim as this is the part most likely to be seen. The domette should fit smoothly and snugly over the buckram without wrinkles.
5. Pin the tip into the top of the side band to make up the crown. The tip should sit just inside the top edge of the side band and is stitched into place by hand by catching the domette only.
6. Cut out two brims in top fabric, adding 12mm (½ in) seam allowances all around. Do not cut out the middles at this stage.
7. Cover the buckram brim with the top fabric. Start by pinning the first layer of top fabric onto the buckram. Fold the seam allowance over the outside edge of the buckram brim and baste in place. Baste around the head opening, following the pencil line exactly. Now pin the other top fabric brim onto the other side of the brim, turning seam allowances under around the outside edge. Handsew into place. Baste around head opening, following the first row of stitches, and cut out centre.
8. Snip into the seam allowance around head size opening in brim and bend the buckram up against the wire. Sew brim to crown; the snipped seam allowances should sit up inside the bottom edge of crown and the stitches go all the way through all layers.
9. Cut the crown covering in top fabric without seam allowance. If the top fabric frays easily, the edge can be treated with either hot wax or a modern liquid fray check. Alternatively, a lightweight iron on interfacing can be applied to the bottom half, on the inside. Work rows of gathering stitches where marked on crown covering. Position crown covering over crown, securing at the top with a few pins. Pull up gathering stitches, evenly distributing the material around the sides of the crown. Arrange pleats, pin and stitch into place at bottom, taking the stitches through all layers.

a.

b.

c.

a. Elizabethan hat with pleated covering
b. Henrician bonnet
c. Elizabethan bonnet

135

10. Cut side band and tip in lining fabric, adding 12mm (½ in) seam allowances all around. Sew centre backs of side band together and press seam allowances open. Sew tip into side band. Pin lining into hat, turning seam allowance under to hide all raw edges, and handsew into place. Catch lining to top of hat with a couple of small stitches.

11. Add a hatband to cover the raw edge at the bottom of the pleats and jewels and feathers as desired.

Henrician bonnet

Materials
- 50cm (24in) of top fabric and lining, each 112cm (45in) wide
- 25cm (9in) of buckram and domette, each 112cm (45in) wide
- 1.65m (1¾ yd) of millinery wire

1. Cut brim in buckram without seam allowances, except at centre backs where 12mm (½ in) should be added. Join brim at centre back. Wire around both edges.

2. Cut brim in domette, adding 12mm (½ in) seam allowances all around. Lay the domette over the outside of the wired brim and anchor into place with a few pins. Turn edges under and baste all the way around, clipping into curve where necessary.

3. Cut two brims from top fabric, adding 12mm (½ in) seam allowances all around. Join up centre backs and press seams open. Lay one of the top fabric brims over the outside of the wired brim and pin and baste in place as for domette. Sew on any applied decoration. Pin the other top fabric brim inside the wired brim, clipping into seam allowance and turning it under, and handsew in place, setting it back from the edge by 3mm (⅛ in).

4. Cut one crown in top fabric and one in lining, adding 12mm (½ in) seam allowances all around. With wrong sides together, baste lining to top fabric. Gather up outside edge of crown to fit inner edge of brim. Bind the gathered edge of the crown. Pin the crown into the brim and sew in place by hand, setting the bound edge back from the edge of the brim by a scant 2mm (1/16 in).

Elizabethan bonnet

The crown of this hat can be made in two ways: the fullness can either be gathered or darted in. The headband should be cut 12mm (½ in) longer than the head circumference of the wearer; make sure the inner circle of the brim measures the same.

Materials
- 40cm (24in) of top fabric and lining, each 112cm (45in) wide

1. Cut out pattern pieces with 12mm (½ in) seam allowances all around.

2. Sew the ends of the hatband together and press seam allowances open; repeat for hatband lining.

3. With right sides together, pin the two brims on the outside edge and sew around. Grade seams and notch all the way around. Turn through and press. Baste layers together, basting 12mm (½ in) in from inner edge.

4. With wrong sides facing, pin crown lining to crown and baste together. If gathering, sew two rows of gathering stitches around the edge and pull up to

Pattern 27: Henrician bonnet

Crown
cut 1

Brim

CB

CB

cut 1

hatband measurement. If darting, mark out darts on crown lining. Sew every other dart, then one at front, back and sides. Check measurements, working out how much is left to be taken up, and distribute this amount evenly between the remaining darts. This method ensures that the fullness of the crown is taken up evenly all around and that the shape will be symmetrical.

5. With right sides together, pin hatband to crown and sew around. Pin hatband lining to crown (pin and sew from the hatband side so that the first stitch line can be followed exactly). Grade seam allowances.

6. Snip into the brim seam allowance and pin the top fabric hatband to the brim. Sew around *without* catching the hatband lining. If the hatband is to be jewelled, sew jewels in place now.

7. Bring the hatband lining down to cover all raw edges. Pin and sew down by hand. Attach any additional decoration, such as a feather or brooch.

Pattern 28: Elizabethan bonnet

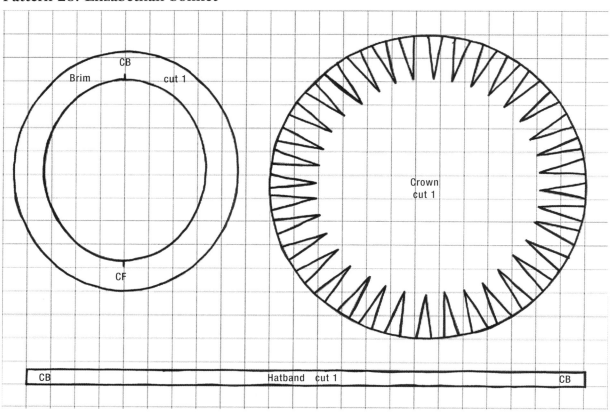

Above: Bonnet crown lined, gathered and bound ready for attaching to the brim.

Left: Above: Henrician bonnet covered with velvet and trimmed with jewels and a large ostrich feather.

Pattern 29: Elizabethan hat with pleated covering

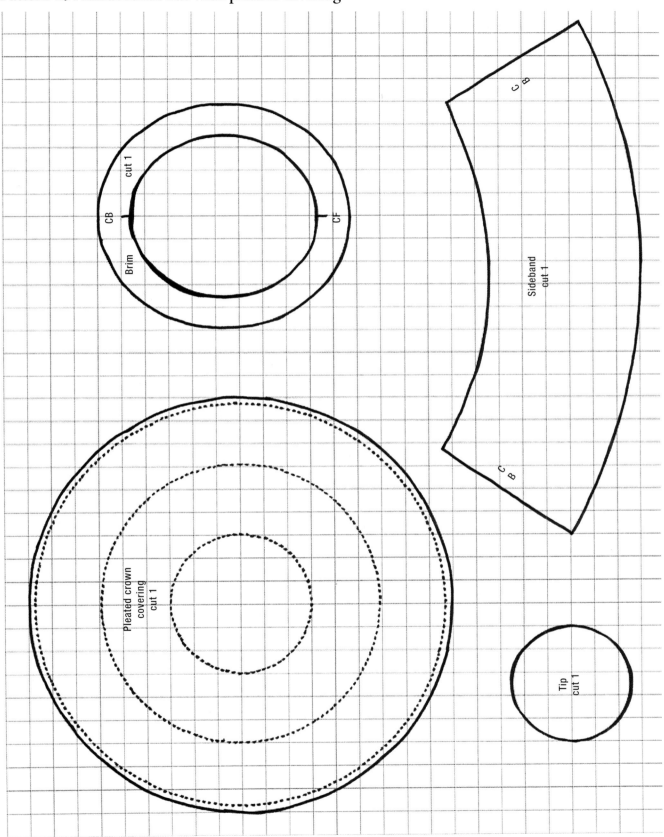

CB

CF

Brim
cut 1

C B

Sideband
cut 1

C
B

Pleated crown
covering
cut 1

Tip
cut 1

Simple coif

These instructions use the bagging out method. The coif can be made in one layer, in which case the seam must be finished by hand and hemmed around the edges.

Materials

- 30cm (12in) of linen, 112cm (45in) wide

Cut four sides and two middle panels, adding 12mm (½in) seam allowances all around. With right sides together, pin two of the side panels to one of the middle panels and sew. Notch around curved seam allowance. Repeat for other pieces. With right sides together, pin the coif together and sew around, leaving a gap of around 5 or 7.5cm (2 or 3in) at the back for turning through. Clip into curved seam allowance, trim corners and turn through. Handsew the gap to close it.

If ties are wanted, they can either be caught in at the corners when bagging out or sewn on afterwards.

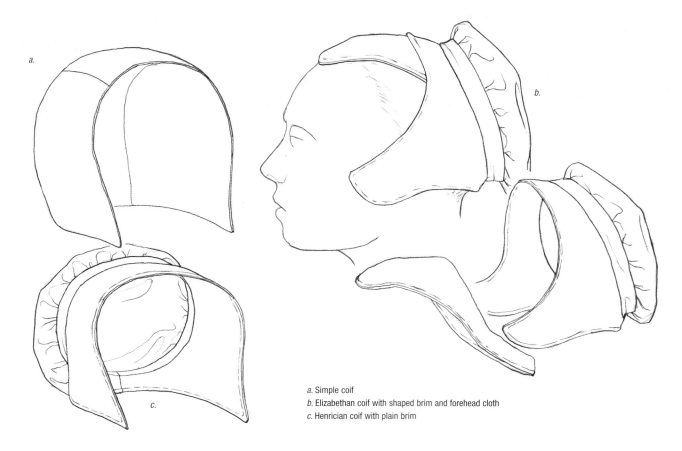

a. Simple coif
b. Elizabethan coif with shaped brim and forehead cloth
c. Henrician coif with plain brim

A man's simple coif worn beneath a soft bonnet and an Elizabethan coif with shaped brim and forehead cloth.

Pattern 30: simple coif

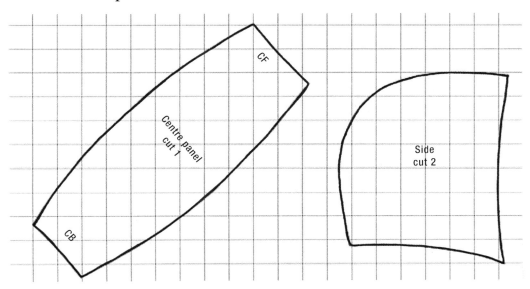

a.

b.

c.

d.

e.

f.

g.

h.

i.

j.

k.

l.

Method of dressing the hair

This method may be used for anyone whose hair is shoulder length or longer. The tapes must be cut long enough to wrap twice around the head. The hair is divided into two hanks with a central parting (a). Each hank is plaited, starting just behind the ear (b), and a ribbon or tape is incorporated into the plait (c). The plaits are bound and tied off, leaving a length of ribbon hanging free (d, e, f). The plaits are laid over the top of the head and secured with a couple of hairpins (g, h). The ends of the ribbon are crossed again at the nape and tied together on top of the head (i, j, k) and loose ends are tucked in and pinned if necessary (l).

Henrician coif with plain brim

Materials
- 50cm (18in) of white linen, 112cm (45in) wide
- 90cm (1yd) of white millinery wire

1. Cut one bag, two headbands and two brims in linen, adding 12mm (½ in) seam allowances all around. Sew up centre backs of headbands and brims. Press seams open.
2. With right sides facing, pin brims together and sew around outside edge. Trim seam allowance down and turn through. Press. Cut a length of wire to measure the same as the outside edge of brim plus a 5cm (2in) overlap. Straighten wire out and then form it into the shape of the brim, using the pattern as a guide. Tape over the ends of the wire with white zinc oxide tape. Place the shaped wire inside the brim and pin into place against the edge. Secure the wire between the brim layers by sewing around the outside edge, using small stitches. Baste the brim layers together around inside edge.
3. Gather the outside edge of the bag to fit the headband. With right sides together, pin one of the headbands to bag and sew around. Pin the other headband to the other side of the bag, pinning and then sewing to follow the first stitchline exactly. Grade the seam allowances. Bring headbands down over raw edges and press.
4. Pin the back of the cap onto the brim through one of the layers of headband. Sew around. Fold the seam allowance of the other headband under and pin over raw edges. Handsew in place.

Pattern 31: Henrician coif with pleated brim

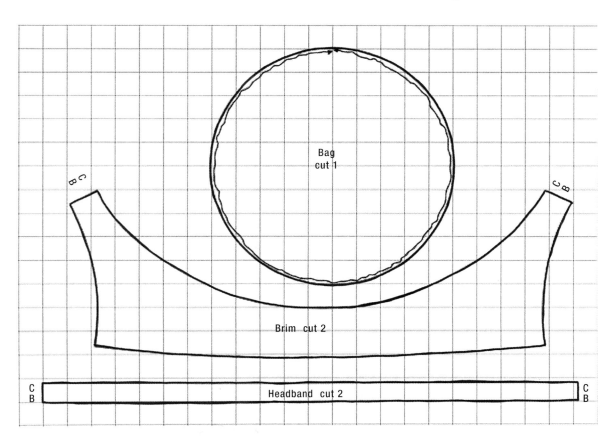

a.

b.

c.

d.

e.

f.

g.

h.

i.

j.

k.

l.

Method of arranging a headrail

This should be arranged over hair which has been plaited as described on page 145. If the hair is short, a linen headband or forehead cloth should be worn to keep the hair off the face and for securing the headrail to. Have two long hairpins ready. A square yard of hemmed linen is folded in half to make a triangle. The folded edge is positioned at the front of the head *(a, b)*. Temporarily pin the headrail to the plaits or headband on top of the head.

The short corners of the triangle are located and folded under *(c, d)*. The long corners are bunched together and crossed at the nape *(e, f)*. The ends are crossed again on top of the head *(g, h)*. The ends are tucked under and secured with the pins *(j)*. The folded edge of the headrail is loosened to form a soft frame around the face *(k, l)*.

Elizabethan coif with shaped forehead cloth

Make up as for Henrician coif. Cut forehead cloth in two layers of linen, adding
12mm (½ in) seam allowances all around. Make up with a wired outside edge as
for brim. To wear, put hair up as illustrated on page 142, put forehead cloth on
first and then place the cap over the top.

Pattern 32: Elizabethan coif with shaped forehead cloth

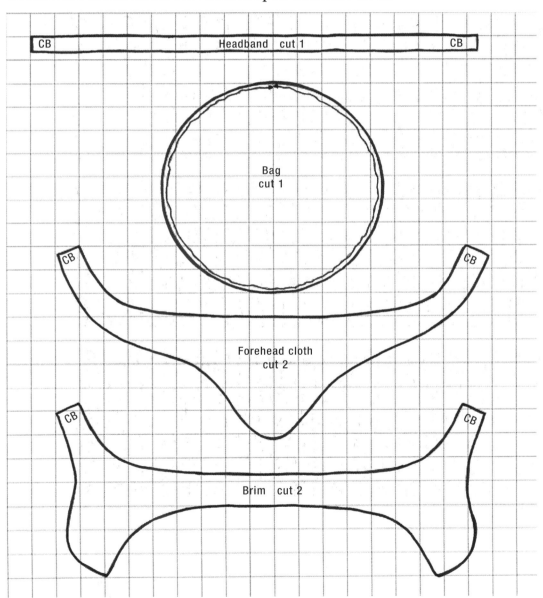

English or gable hood

Materials

- 40cm (18in) of buckram, 112cm (45in) wide
- 70cm (24in) of domette, 112cm (45in) wide, for covering shapes and padding lappets
- 25cm (9in) of white linen or silk, 112cm (45in) wide, for undercap
- 25cm (9in) of white linen or cotton, 112cm (45in) wide, for lining (don't use anything slippery)
- 40cm (18in) of silk, 112cm (45in) wide, for lappets
- 70cm (24in) of black silk or velvet, 112cm (45in) wide, for box and veil
- 3.3m (3¾ yd) of heavy millinery wire
- 1.2m (1½ yd) of lightweight millinery wire

a. Viewed from front
b. Viewed from back showing box and veils sewn under box
c. Viewed from front with one of the veils pinned up

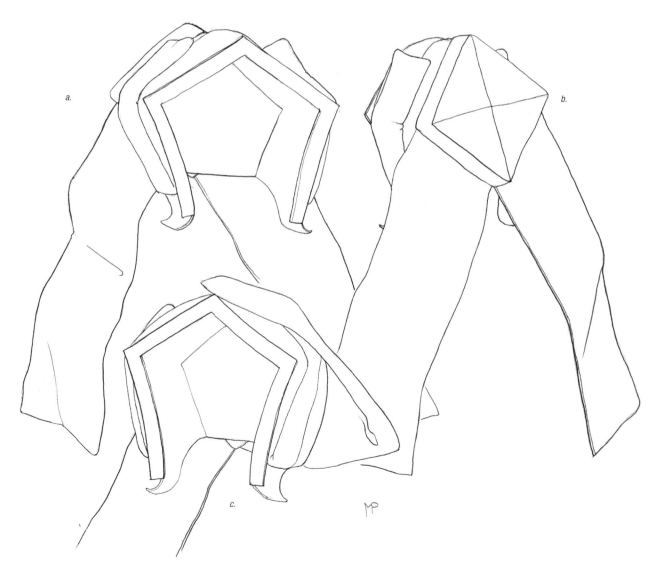

- 25cm (9in) of white linen or cotton, 112cm (45in) wide, for lining (don't use anything slippery)
- Jewels for front of undercap
- 25cm (9in) of striped silk, 112cm (45in) wide, for hair casings (optional)*

*If striped silk is unavailable, stripes can be drawn on a plain silk with a fabric pen.

1. Cut all pieces except lappets and veils in buckram; do not add seam allowance anywhere except for 12mm (½in) at centre backs of box side piece. Join the ends of box side piece by hand, overlapping the seam allowances.
2. Cut a length of (heavy) wire long enough to go all the way around the edge of the undercap with a 5cm (2in) overlap. Cut a piece of (thinner) wire to go all the way around the undercap front, plus an extra 5cm (2in). Sew to the edge of the buckram, either by hand or machine. Make sure the overlapped ends of the wire are securely sewn down at the back in the least visible place. Cut lengths of wire to go around edges for box back and sides, straighten and sew on. Bend the box side piece into a square.
3. Cut the same pattern pieces in domette, adding 12mm (½in) seam allowances all the way around. Lay the domette over the top of wired pieces and use a few pins to anchor into place. Turn edges under and baste all the way around, clipping into curves as necessary.
4. Cut pattern pieces in top fabric, adding 12mm (½in) seam allowances all the way around edges. Pin over wired shapes, clipping curves as before, and baste all around.
5. Attach any jewels to undercap front.
6. Cut lining fabric for all undercap pieces, adding 12mm (½in) seam allowances all way around. Pin into place, clipping edges and turning allowance under; the lining should sit just back from the edge. Handsew into place, using small regular stitches. Remove basting.
7. Bend undercap into shape and pin the back in place. Stitch together with strong thread to secure. Pin undercap front into place and stitch in the same way.
8. Cut the triangles for the box in the black fabric, with 12mm (½in) seam allowances, and make up into a square. Press seams open (if you are making the hood in velvet, use a velvet board or towel when ironing, to avoid squashing the pile). Cut box side in the black fabric, with 12mm (½in) seam allowances. Sew the ends together and press open.
9. Cut two veil strips in the black fabric, cutting on the fold and adding 12mm (½in) seam allowances all the way around. These strips may need interlining if a flimsy fabric is used. Pin veil pieces right sides together and sew down side and across one end, leaving the other end open. Trim seam allowance, turn through and press. Turn raw edges in at veil ends, handsew and press.
10. Cover the wired box shapes in the black fabric, basting into place. Pin box back into box side and stitch in place. Pin veil pieces to bottom edges of black box and stitch in place.
11. Pin completed box to back of white undercap and handstitch into place with strong thread.
12. Cut lappet in top fabric with 12mm (½in) seam allowances and also cut a layer of domette without seam allowances. Baste domette to wrong side of top fabric. Fold lappet in half widthwise and sew down one side. Turn through. Turn raw ends in and sew down by hand. Apply any decoration to lappet. Pin into place over the top of the hood. Catch down with a few stitches at the corners, fold ends back up over hood and secure.

English hood made up without the undercap front, worn over bound hair. Hood made by Caroline Johnson, embroidery on lappets worked by Sylvia Johnson.

Pattern 33: English or gable hood

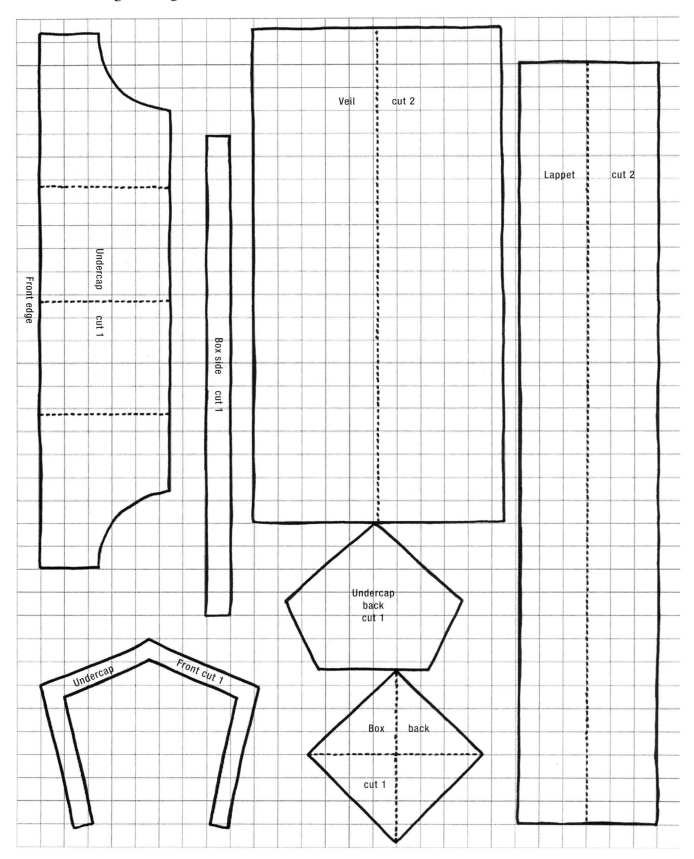

Front edge

Undercap

cut 1

Box side   cut 1

Veil   cut 2

Lappet   cut 2

Undercap
back
cut 1

Undercap Front cut 1

Box   back

cut 1

French hood

A separate undercap can be made up as well as the wired elements (see page 00) by using the same brim patterns and the bag back. This will help keep the hood clean. These hoods can be made with or without the crescent. The billiments can be constructed from beads threaded onto a length of wire or from flat back jewels sewn to a buckram foundation. Strips of metallic braid can also be used.

Materials

- 30cm (12in) of buckram and domette, each 112cm (45in) wide
- 30cm (12in) of white or black silk, 112cm (45in) wide, for undercap
- 30cm (12in) of of white linen or cotton, 112cm (45in) wide, for lining (don't use anything slippery)
- 2.2m (2½ yd) of millinery wire
- 70cm (24in) of black silk, 112cm (45in) wide, for veil
- 8cm (3in) of silk organza/metallic silk organza, 112cm (45in) wide, for pleated frill
- Jewels for billiments

1. Cut the brim and crescent (if included) in buckram; do not add seam allowances anywhere except 12mm (½ in) at centre backs of cap brim. Overlap seam allowances at centre backs of cap brim and sew together by hand.
2. Cut two lengths of wire long enough to go all the way around the edges of both pieces plus a 5cm (2in) overlap. Sew wire to the edge of the buckram, either by hand or machine. Make sure the overlapping ends are caught down securely at the back in the least visible place.

French hood style C covered in shot taffeta, jewelled billiments and satin veil.

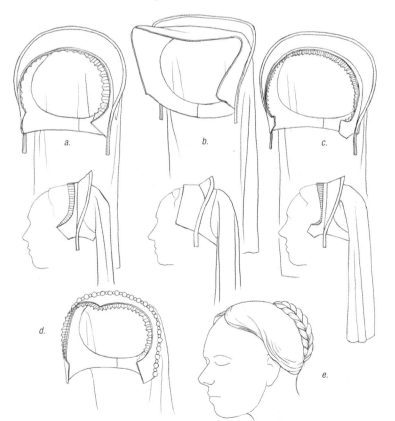

a. Hood viewed from front and side with brim A and crescent A

b. Hood viewed from front and side with brim B and crescent B

c. Hood viewed from front and side with brim C and crescent C

d. Brim A with point at forehead and beaded billiment

e. Hairstyle worn beneath hoods

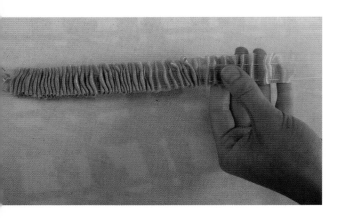

Pleated strip of metallic organza, pinned to ironing board ready for setting with steam.

3. Cut pattern pieces in domette, adding 12mm (½ in) seam allowances all the way around. Lay the domette over the wired pieces and use a few pins to anchor into place. Turn edges under and baste all the way around, clipping into curves where necessary.

4. Cut pattern pieces in top fabric, adding 12mm (½ in) seam allowances all around edges. Pin over wired shapes, clipping curves as before, and baste all around.

5. Cut lining fabric for crescent, adding 12mm (½ in) seam allowances all around. Pin into place, clipping edges and turning allowance under; the lining should sit just back from the edge. Handsew into place with small regular stitches. Remove basting from crescent.

6. Pin crescent into place on cap brim. It should sit approximately 18mm (¾ in) back from the front edge, depending on the decoration you are going to put here. Using strong thread, handstitch bottom edge of crescent through undercap to secure.

7. Lower billament – attach your chosen decoration securely to front edge of cap brim.

8. Cut cap brim lining in linen, adding 12mm (½ in) seam allowances all around. Pin and handsew in place.

9. Cut a strip of the metallic organza measuring 7.5 x 112cm (3 x 45in). Press 12mm (½ in) in around all edges, then fold in half widthwise so that the strip is now 2.5cm (1in) wide. Press. Using strong thread, run two parallel rows of stitches, each stitch 9mm (⅜ in) long, along either side of the strip. Turn on the iron and set it to hot steam setting. Pin one end of the strip firmly to the ironing board and pull up the rest of the strip to form pleats that are tightly packed together. Secure the other end of the strip to the ironing board with a couple of pins. Set the pleats, holding the steam iron just above the fabric. Allow fabric to cool before removing from ironing board.

10. Loosen the pleated strip so that it measures the same as the brim. Pin pleated strip to brim, setting it in just back from the edge on the inside (the thinner folded edge of the pleated strip should be facing outwards). Stitch in place by hand, catching the pleats to the lining only. Remove long pleating threads.

11. Cut veil with seam allowance, seam up centre back and hem by hand. Sew a row of gathering stitches around top edge of veil; this will help to control the shape as it is pinned to hood. Clip curves at edge of veil and pin the seam of the veil to the centre back of the cap brim along the bottom edge. Pin top edge of veil to top edge of crescent and pull up the gathering stitches to ease in excess fullness. No actual gathering is needed here, the gathering stitches are to aid easing in a small quantity of fabric, if any. Make sure veil is pinned smoothly all the way around before stitching securely in place by hand.

12. The method for attaching the upper billiment will depend on the chosen decoration. If the jewels are round beads with a central hole, they can simply be threaded onto a length of wire. The ends can be finished either by bending the very end of the wire round on itself or gluing the last beads on the end. If flat jewels or trims that will not thread onto a wire have been selected, they will need to be attached to the shaped billiment. Cut this from buckram and then either wire it all around with a thinner wire than that used elsewhere or run a single length of the heavy wire down the middle. Cover the billiment in silk that matches the crescent or the veil. Secure the completed billiment to the top edge of the crescent and bottom sides of cap brim, following the line of the veil. Some 4–5cm (1½–2in) should project beyond the edge of the hood and gently curve into the neck.

Pattern 34: French hood

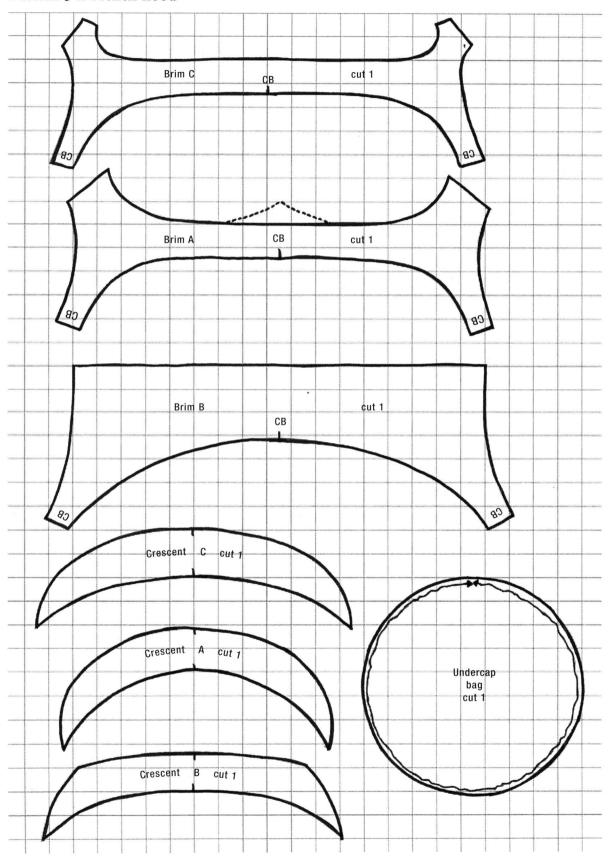

Brim C   CB   cut 1

CB   CB

Brim A   CB   cut 1

CB   CB

Brim B   cut 1
CB

CB   CB

Crescent   C   cut 1

Crescent   A   cut 1

Undercap
bag
cut 1

Crescent   B   cut 1

151

Pattern 34: French hood

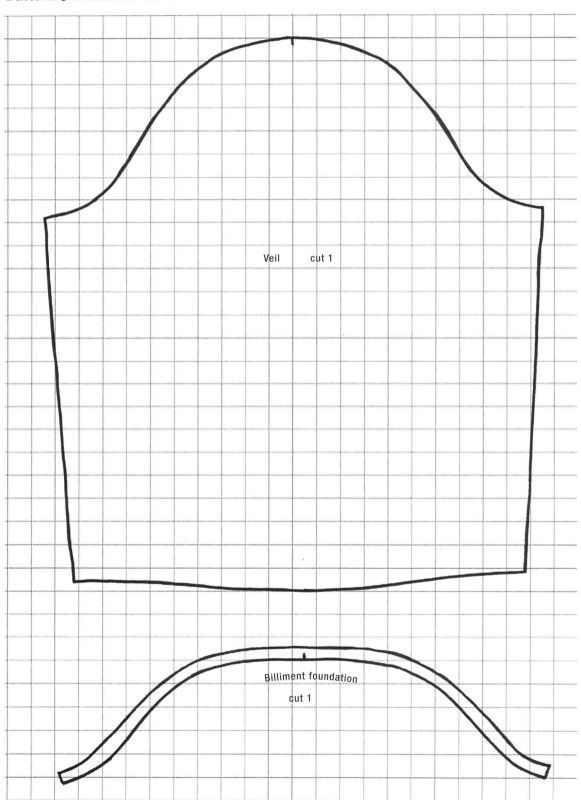

Veil   cut 1

Billiment foundation

cut 1

Bongrace or shadow

The pattern provided is for an all-in-one bag and bongrace. This should be made up in black silk and gathered where indicated. It can replace the bag on the heart-shaped bonnet or Henrician coif and it can also replace the veils of the French hoods.

Simpler, stylized versions are also seen which can be added to the later caps and hoods. They should be pinned or sewn to the back of the cap or hood and flipped over the head, starting either at the bottom near the nape of the neck or at the top near the crown.

Elizabethan hood with bongrace

Materials

- 30cm (12in) of buckram and domette, each 112cm (45in) wide
- 60cm (24in) of lightweight wool or black silk, 112cm (45in) wide
- 30cm (12in) of white linen or cotton, for lining (don't use anything slippery)
- 1.5m (1⅝yd) of millinery wire

1. Cut one brim, using the pattern 'Brim B' from the French hoods (page 151) in buckram and cutting without seam allowances, except at centre back, where 12mm (½in) should be added. Cut brim in domette, adding 12mm (½in) seam allowances all around. Overlap seam allowance at centre backs of brim and sew in place by hand.
2. Wire edges of brim by machine or hand. Lay the domette over the outside of the wired brim, anchoring it in place with a few pins. Turn edges under and baste all the way around, clipping into curve.
3. Cut bongrace pieces in top fabric, adding 12mm (½in) seam allowances all around. With right sides facing, pin together and sew around. Notch curve and turn through. Press. Run two rows of gathering stitches around top half of bag and pull up so that the bongrace measures the same as the back of the brim. Pin bongrace to underside of brim along back edge and handstitch in place.
4. Cut one brim in top fabric, adding 12mm (½in) seam allowances all around. Pin the top fabric brim over the wired brim, and baste around outside edges as for domette. Fold the seam allowance under along the back where it meets the bongrace and hand sew in place, butting the edges together. Sew any decoration or billiments along this edge.
5. Pin brim lining inside brim and handsew in, turning seam allowances under and covering all raw edges. Sew any decorative border or billiment to outside edge of brim.
6. The bongrace can be flipped up over the head and secured with a pin.

a. Heart-shaped bonnet viewed from front and side
b. Elizabethan hood with bongrace

Pattern 35: Bongrace

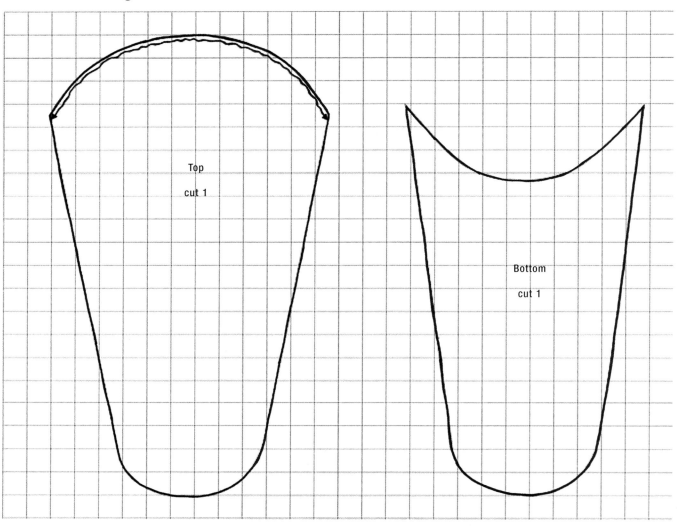

Top

cut 1

Bottom

cut 1

Heart-shaped bonnet

Instructions are given for making this bonnet in black silk with buckram stiffening. It can also be made in white linen or with two layers of white silk organza, either without any stiffening or just wire in the brim. The heart-shaped brim can also be left off and a decorative billiment put in its place to make the neat little Elizabethan version of the French hood, which was worn behind the hair, which was dressed over pads to achieve the heart shape.

The brims of these bonnets are often edged with lace or a decorative border of goldsmith's work. If anything like this is to be added, the brim will need to be made narrower – experiment with a paper or card brim to get the proportions right.

Pattern 36: Heart-shaped bonnet

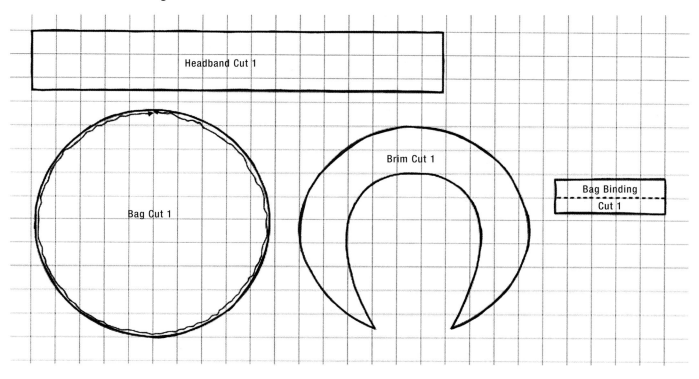

Materials
- 30cm (12in) of buckram and domette, each 112cm (45in) wide
- 60cm (24in) of black silk, 112cm (45in) wide
- 30cm (12in) of white linen or cotton, for lining (don't use anything slippery)
- 2.1m (2¼yd) of millinery wire

1. Cut brim and headband in buckram without seam allowances and in domette with 12mm (½in) seam allowances all around. Wire edges of brim and headband by machine or hand. Lay the domette over the outside of the wired brim, anchoring it into place with a few pins. Turn edges under and baste all around, clipping into the curve.
2. Cut two brims, one headband, one bag and one bag binding in top fabric, adding 12mm (½in) seam allowances all around. Cut one headband and one bag in lining, adding 12mm (½in) seam allowances all around. Lay one of the brim pieces over the wired brim, pin and baste in place as for domette. Pin the other brim to the other side of the wired brim, turning seam allowance under and clipping into curves. Handsew in place, setting this second brim layer back from the edge by 3mm (⅛in).
3. With wrong sides facing, baste the bag lining to the bag. Gather bag up to 54cm (21½in). With right sides facing, sew one long side of the bag binding to the edge of the gathered bag. Fold binding in half and tuck the seam allowance under, covering the raw edges. Handsew into place and press.
4. Bend the wired headband into a horseshoe shape, adjusting shape on head to get it right. Pin gathered bag to underside of headband along one edge, positioning the bound section in the gap of the horseshoe. Sew bag to headband by hand.
5. Pin the top fabric headband over the wired headband, pinning and basting around outside edges as for domette. Fold the seam allowance under along the back where it meets the bag and hand sew in place, butting the edges together. Sew any decoration or billiments in place along this edge.
6. Pin the brim to the front of the headband and whipstitch the edges together from the inside.
7. Pin headband lining inside headband and hand sew in place, turning seam allowances under and covering all raw edges. Sew on any decorative border or billiment to outside edge of brim.

FOOTNOTES

Chapter 1: Making a start

1) Stubbes, P (1583) *The anatomie of abuses*, London
2) St Clare Byrne, M (1981) *The Lisle letters*, London: Chicago University Press, 4 (letter 896) 167–8
3) The Society of Antiquaries administers an annual award for research of this kind in memory of Janet Arnold. Visit http://www.sal.org.uk/grants/janetarnold.php for details
4) Borde, A (1542) *The first boke of the introduction of knowledge*, edited by Furnivall, F (1870) English Text Society, 116.
5) Werner, A (1998) *London bodies: the changing shape of Londoners from prehistoric times to the present day*, London: Museum of London, 108
6) Stirland, A (2005) *The men of the Mary Rose: Raising the dead*, Stroud: Sutton Publishing, 82–84
7) Fagan, B (2000) *The little ice age*, New York: Basic Books, 53, 84 & 94; Lamb, H (1995 – 2nd edition) *Climate history and the modern world*, London: Routledge, 211–213, 228
8) For example, in Pieter Breughel the Younger's *Proverbs* (1559) Staatliche Museen, Berlin
9) See Huggett, J (1998) *The book of children 1480–1680 part 2*, Bristol: Stuart Press, 2–7 for a summary of contemporary guides to good behaviour.
10) Wayland Barber, E (2005) 'How we came to dress the way we do: tales from a scholar's 30-year pursuit of origins' paper presented at Costume Society of America Symposium, Philadelphia, 25–28 May
11) Wright, J (1977) 'I bet you wear blue jeans on the weekend, eh?' in *Ontario Museum Association newsletter* 6, 2, 21–22
12) Radcliffe, P (1987) 'Period dress projects: considerations for administrators' in *Curator* 30, 3, 193–198
13) Malcolm-Davies, J (2004) 'Borrowed robes: the educational value of costumed interpretation at historic sites' in *International journal of heritage studies*, 10, 3, 277–293
14) Kopytoff, I (1986) 'The cultural biography of things: commoditisation as process' in Appadurai, A (ed), *The social life of things*, Cambridge: Cambridge University Press, 64–91
15) Plato (427–347BC) argued that there is a relationship between colour, form, and texture and the 'soul quality' or personality. His followers recommended the expression of personality through clothes; Dives in his purple and Lazarus in his rags are two examples of clothes standing for character (*Luke*, chapter 16, verses 19–20); Erasmus said that 'clothing is in a way the body's body' and from this we may infer the state of a man's character; Shakespeare asserts that 'the apparel oft proclaims the man' in *Hamlet* (act 1, scene 3, line 72)
16) Records commission (1820–1828) '24 Henry VIII c13: "An acte for reformacyon of excesse in apparayle"' in *Statutes of the Realm*; Gurr, A (1992 – 3rd edn) *The Shakespearean stage 1574–1642* Cambridge: Cambridge University Press quoted in Stallybrass, P & Jones, A (2000) *Renaissance clothing and the materials of memory*, Cambridge: Cambridge University Press, 178–179
17) Vincent, S (1999) 'To fashion a self: dressing in 17th century England' in *Fashion theory* 3, 197–218, 212
18) Smith, T (1583) *De Republica Anglorum*, London
19) Miller, H (1986) *Henry VIII and the English nobility*, Oxford: Blackwell, 35; Heal, F & Holmes, C (1994) *The gentry in England and Wales 1500–1700*, Basingstoke: MacMillan, 12

Chapter 2: Clothing the people

1) Guillemeau, J (1612) *The nursing of children*, 21 quoted in Sim, A (1996) *The Tudor housewife*, Stroud: Sutton Publishing, 26

2) Deloney, T (1597) *The gentle craft*, 103 quoted in Buck, A (1996) *Clothes and the child*, Bedford: Ruth Bean, 17
3) Buck (1996) *Ibid.*, 17ff
4) Sackville-West, V (ed) (1923) *The diary of Lady Anne Clifford*, London: Heinemann, 16 quoted in Heller Mendelson, S (1985) 'Stuart women's diaries and occasional memoirs' in Prior, M (ed) *Women in English society 1500–1800*, 181–210, 198
5) TNA: PRO: E101/423/12 f3v
6) Cotgrave, R (1611) *A Dictionary of the French and English Tongues*, quoted in Huggett, J (2002) *Clothes of the Common Man 1580–1660, part 2* Bristol: Stuart Press, 3
7) Thursfield, S (2001) *The Medieval Tailor's Assistant*, Bedford: Ruth Bean, 70. Published in the US by Costume and Fashion Press, an imprint of Quite Specific Media Group, Ltd.
8) Fingerlin, I (1997) 'Seltene Textilien aus Kloster Alpirsbach im Nordschwarzwald' in *Waffen und Kostumkunde*, 39, 1&2, 99–122
9) Anglo, S (1968) *The great tournament roll of Westminster: historical introduction*, Oxford: Oxford University Press, 56
10) Quoted in Huggett, J (2005) *Clothes of the Common Man 1480–1580, part 2*, Bristol: Stuart Press, 5
11) Dunlevy, M (1989) *Dress in Ireland: a history*, Cork: Collins, 77
12) Arnold (1985) *op. cit.*, 92; Emmison, F (1987) *Essex Wills: The Archdeaconry Courts 1577–1584*, 4, Chelmsford: Essex Record Office, item 43
13) de Marly, D (1986) *Working Dress: a history of occupational clothing*, London: Batsford, 8
14) (1859) *Inventory of Henry Fitzroy, Duke of Richmond*, Camden Miscellany, 3
15) Emmison, F (1989) *Essex Wills: The Archdeaconry Courts 1583–1592*, 5, Chelmsford: Essex Record Office, item 386; Emmison, F (1995) *Essex Wills, The Commissary Court 1578–1588*, 10, Chelmsford: Essex Record Office, item 958
16) Arnold, J (1980a) 'Sweet England's jewels' in Somers Cocks, A (ed) *Princely magnificence: court jewels of the renaissance 1500–1630*, London: Debrett's Peerage for the Victoria & Albert Museum, 36
17) Arnold, J (1988) *Queen Elizabeth's Wardrobe Unlock'd*, Leeds: Maney, 68. Published in the US by Costume and Fashion Press, an imprint of Quite Specific Media Group, Ltd.
18) Records commission (1820–1828) *op. cit.*
19) Emmison, F (1994) *Essex Wills, The Commissary Court 1569–1578*, 9, Chelmsford: Essex Record Office, item 582
20) Arnold (1988) *op. cit.*, 68 n70
21) Emmison (1994) *op. cit.*, item 579
22) Arnold, J (1985) *Patterns of fashion: The cut and construction of clothes for men and women c 1560–1620*, London: Macmillan, 109–110. Published in the US by Costume and Fashion Press, an imprint of Quite Specific Media Group, Ltd.
23) Arnold (1988) *op. cit.*, 112–115
24) Carter, A (1984) 'Mary Tudor's Wardrobe' in *Costume* 18, 20; quoted in Marshall, R (1978) '"Hir rob ryall": the costume of Mary of Guise' in *Costume*, 12, 11
25) Arnold (1988) *op. cit.*, 185 & 146
26) Arnold (1988) *op. cit.*, 148; Emmison, F (1990) *Essex Wills, The Archdeaconry Courts 1597–1603*, 7, Chelmsford: Essex Record Office, items 403 & 653
27) Huggett (2005) *op. cit.*, 4–5
28) Pepys Library, Magdalene College, Cambridge
29) Arnold (1988) *op. cit.*, 123–124
30) Levey, S (2000) 'References to dress in the earliest account book of Bess of Hardwick' in *Costume*, 34, 15
31) Arnold (1988) *op. cit.*, 195

32) *Ibid.*, 118
33) Emmison (1987) *op. cit.*, item 263
34) Crowley, R (1550) *One and thirty epigrammes* quoted in Waugh, N (1954) *Corsets and crinolines* London: Batsford, 27; Arnold (1988) *op. cit.*,189
35) Arnold (1988) *op. cit.*, 155
36) Arnold (1985) *op. cit.*, 113
37) Harrison, W (1587) *Description of England*, London
38) Arnold (1988) *op. cit.*, 198
39) TNA: PRO: E315/456 f34r
40) TNA: PRO: E101/427/11 f33; E101/427/18 f20
41) Hunnisett, J (1991) *Period costume for stage and screen: patterns for women's dress 1500–1800* Studio City, CA: Players Press, 49
42) Malcolm-Davies, J, Mikhaila, N and Johnson, C (2003) '"And her black satin gown must be new bodied": the 21st century body in pursuit of the Holbein look', paper presented at The Costume Society's Symposium, University of Leicester, 26 June
43) Mee, S (2004) 'The clothing of the Crayforde girls' in *Costume*, 38, 26–40, 29
44) Broomhall, S (2002) '"Women's little secrets": Defining the boundaries of reproductive knowledge in 16th century France' in *Social history of medicine*, 15, 1, 1–15; *Oxford English Dictionary*
45) Crawford, P (2004) *Blood, Bodies and Families in Early Modern England*, Harlow: Pearson, 26–27
46) *Oxford English Dictionary*
47) Egerton 2806, f.186v, warrant dated 20 April 1583 (British Library) quoted in Arnold (1988) *op. cit.*, 225–226
48) Crawford, P (2004), *Blood, bodies and families in early modern England*, Harlow: Pearson, 25
49) St Clare Byrne, M (1981), *The Lisle letters*, London: Chicago University Press, 4 (letter 861) 83
50) *Ibid.*, 5 (letter 1393) 448
51) Emmison (1994) *op. cit.*, item 173; Emmison, F (1983) *Elizabethan Wills of South-West Essex* Waddesdon: The Kylin Press, item 125; Emmison (1995) *op. cit.*, item 15; Emmison (1989) *op. cit.*, item 98; Emmison, F (1998) *Essex Wills, The Commissary Court 1587–1599*, 11, Chelmsford: Essex Record Office, item 25; Emmison, F (2000) *Essex Wills, The Commissary Court 1596–1603*, 12, Chelmsford: Essex Record Office, item 333
52) Schofield, R (1986) 'Did the mothers really die? Three centuries of maternal mortality in "The world we have lost"' in Bonfield, L, Smith, R & Wrightson, K (eds), *The world we have gained: histories of population and social structure*, Oxford: Blackwell, 231–260
53) Brewer, J, Gairdner, J & Brodie R (eds) (1862–1932) *Calendar of letters and papers, foreign and domestic, of the reign of Henry VIII*, London: HMSO, VI, 556, 243
54) St Clare Byrne (1981) *op. cit.*, 4 (letter 879), 142
55) St Clare Byrne (1981) *op. cit.*, 3 (letter 799) 553
56) Cressy, D (1997) *Birth, marriage and death*, Oxford: Oxford University Press, 76
57) Emmison (1989) *op. cit.*, item 995
58) Litten, J (1991) *The English way of death*, London: Robert Hale

Chapter 3: Looking the part

Quotation from: Churchyard, T (1575) 'The Spider and the Gowte' in *Churchyard Chippes* quoted in Cunnington, P & Lucas, C (1967) *Occupational Costume in England*, London: Adam and Charles Black, 202
1) Corfield, P (1989) 'Dress for deference and dissent: hats and the decline of hat honour' in *Costume*, 23, 64–79; Buckland, K (1979) 'The Monmouth cap' in *Costume*, 13, 23–37
2) Hayward, M (2002) '"The sign of some degree"?: the financial, social and sartorial significance of male headwear at the courts of Henry VIII and Edward VI' in *Costume*, 36, 3–17

3) Werner (1998) *op. cit.*, 76–77

4) Emmison (2000) *op. cit.*, item 404; Emmison, F (1991) *Essex Wills, The Archdeaconry Courts 1591–1597*, 6, Chelmsford, Essex Record Office, item 373; Emmison (1989) *op. cit.*, item 386; Emmison (1998) *op. cit.*, item 1216

5) For example, van Meckenem I (c1500) *The angry wife*, engraving at the National Gallery of Art, Washington DC

6) Anonymous (1586) *Hilleke de Roy and four of her orphans*, Stichting Huize Matthijs-Marijke, Gorinchem, The Netherlands

7) Elyot, T (1542) *Bibliotheca eliotae* quoted in Cunnington, C & P (1970) *Handbook of English Costume in the 16th century*, Boston: Plays Inc, 84

8) Maynard, J (1998) 'Respectability in dress in the novels of Hesba Stretton' in *Costume*, 32, 60

9) Arnold, J (1988) *Queen Elizabeth's Wardrobe Unlock'd*, Leeds: Maney, 11

10) Hulton, M & Shuttleworth, J (1987) *Ten Tudor families*, Coventry: Coventry Branch of the Historical Association, 35

11) Thynne, F (1570) *The debate between pride and lowliness* quoted in Ashelford, J (1988) *Dress in the Age of Elizabeth* London: B T Batsford, 115

12) Stallybrass, P & Jones, A (2000) *Renaissance clothing and the materials of memory*, Cambridge: Cambridge University Press, 68–69

13) Arnold, J (1973) 'Three examples of late 16th and early 17th century neckwear' in *Waffen und Kostumkunde*, 15, 2, 109–124

14) Stubbes, P (1583) *Anatomie of Abuses*, London

15) See Sim (1996) *op. cit.*, 8 for an example in the British Museum

16) Arnold (1980a) *op. cit.*, 8

17) Hulton, M & Shuttleworth, J (1987) *Ten Tudor families*, Coventry: Coventry Branch of the Historical Association, 8–9

18) Arnold (1980a) *op. cit.*, 35-36; Emmison (1998) *op. cit.*, item 492

19) TNA: PRO: E101/417/3 f107

20) Arnold, J (1980) *Lost from her majesties back*, London: The Costume Society Extra Series 7, 37

21) Gaimster, D, Hayward, M, Mitchell, D & Parker, K (2002) 'Tudor silver-gilt dress-hooks: a new class of treasure find in England' in *The Antiquaries Journal*, 82, 157–296

22) TNA: PRO: E101/427/18f1; Buck, A (1990) 'The clothes of Thomasine Petre 1555–1559', *Costume*, 24, 21; Anthony, I (1980) 'Clothing given to a servant of the late 16th century in Wales' in *Costume*, 14, 37; Arnold (1988) *op. cit.*, 208

23) TNA: PRO: E101/417/3, F107

24) Arnold (1985) *op. cit.*, 91–92

25) TNA: PRO: E101/427/11, f33; E101/417/3, f107

26) Essex Record Office, D/DP/A9F quoted in Cunnington (1970) *op. cit.*, 129

27) *Mary Rose* inventory number MR79 A877

28) TNA: PRO: E101/417/3, ff5, 48 and 72

29) Werner (1998) *op. cit.*, 79

30) Cumming, V (1982) *Gloves*, London: Batsford, 21; Emmison (1998) *op. cit.*, item 15

Chapter 4: Choosing the materials

1) Records commission (1820–1828) *op. cit.*; Hunt, A (1996) *Governance of the consuming passions: a history of sumptuary law*, Basingstoke: Macmillan, 295–324

2) Quoted in Youings, J (1984) *Sixteenth century England*, Harmondsworth: Penguin; Harington, J (1779) *Nugae Antiquae*, London, 2, 139–140

3) Emmison (1989) *op. cit.*, item 122; Emmison (1991) *op. cit.*, item 821

4) Burnett, J (1969) *A history of the cost of living*, Harmondsworth: Penguin, 89

5) Crowfoot, E, Pritchard, F & Staniland, K (1992) *Textiles and clothing c. 1150–c1450*, London: HMSO, 152; Arnold (1985) *op. cit.*, 109–110

6) Arnold (1988) *op. cit.*, 146

7) Records commission (1820–1828) *op. cit.*

8) Emmison, F (1993) *Essex Wills, The Commissary Court 1558-1569*, 8, Chelmsford: Essex Record Office, item 275

9) Rangstrom, L (2002), *Lions of fashion*, Stockholm: Atlantis, 35

10) Arnold (1980) *op. cit.*, 79; Emmison (1989) *op. cit.*, item 53

11) Peachey, S (2001) *Textiles and materials of the common man and woman 1580–1660* Bristol: Stuart Press, 21

12) Carter (1984) *op. cit.*, 27

13) Munro, J (1983) 'The medieval scarlet and the economics of sartorial splendour' in Harte, N & Ponting, K (eds) *Cloth and clothing in medieval Europe: Essays in memory of Professor E M Carus-Wilson*, Pasold Studies in Textile History, no 2 London: Heinemann, 53; Emmison (2000) *op. cit.*, item 643

14) Marshall (1978) *op. cit.*, 7

15) Records Commission (1820–1828) *op. cit.*; TNA: PRO: E101/417/3, f107

16) TNA: PRO: E101/424/7 and E101/427/11; E101/427/18 and E101/423/12

17) Hibbert, C (1990) *A personal history of the virgin queen*, London: Penguin, 87; Hollingsworth, M (2004) *The cardinal's hat*, London: Profile, 250

18) Stern, E (1981) 'Peckover and Gallyard, two 16th century Norfolk tailors' in *Costume*, 15, 20–21; TNA: PRO: E101/423/12; TNA: PRO: E315/456 f12v

19) Munro (1983) *op. cit.*, 52–57; TNA: PRO: E101/424/7

20) Arnold (1988) *op. cit.*, 373

21) TNA: PRO: 15/456 f9v

22) Moody, J (1998) *The diary of Lady Margaret Hoby*, Stroud: Sutton, xxxiv

23) Davis, M & Saunders, A (2004) *History of the Merchant Tailor's Company*, Leeds: Maney, 53

24) Alcega, J (1589) *Geometria, pratica, ey traca*, Madrid Trans. Pain, J, & Bainton, C (1999) *The tailor's pattern book*, Bedford: Ruth Bean, 30. Published in the US by Costume and Fashion Press, an imprint of Quite Specific Media Group, Ltd.

25) Levey (2000) *op. cit.*, 20; Mee (2004) *op. cit.*, 26–40

26) Arnold (1988) *op. cit.*, 183

27) Arnold (1988) *op. cit.*, 183; Stern (1981) *op. cit.*, 18

28) *Ibid.*, 23

29) Emmison (1987) *op. cit.*, item 674

30) Arnold (1988) *op. cit.*, 188

31) Arnold (1980b) *op. cit.*, 23

32) Victoria & Albert Museum inv no 348–1905; Museum of London inventory number 77.238; Caley, J (1789) 'Extract from an MS in the Augmentation office' in *Archaeologia* (Society of Antiquaries), 9, 243–252; Arnold, J (1980b) *op. cit.*, items 85, 154, 271 & 377

33) Stern (1981) *op. cit.*, 13–23

34) Arnold (1980a) *op. cit.*, 33

35) Arnold (1988) *op. cit.*, 11

36) Arnold (1980a) *op. cit.*, 66 no57

37) Stallybrass & Jones (2000) *op. cit.*, 25

38) Levey (2000) *op. cit.*, 21

39) Emmison (1987) *op. cit.*, item 501

40) Emmison (1998) *op. cit.*, item 178

41) Spufford, M (1984) *The great reclothing of rural England*, London: Hambledon Press, 122–123

42) Stern (1981) *op. cit.*, 14

43) St Clare Byrne (1981) *op. cit.*

44) Davis & Saunders (2004) *op. cit.*, 52

45) Arnold (1980) *op. cit.*, 34; Emmison, (1987) *op. cit.*, item 137

46) Whetstone, G (1584) *A mirour for magestrates of cyties*, London quoted in Stallybrass & Jones (2000) *op. cit.*, 184, 182, 31 & 29; Stone, L (1965) *The crisis of the aristocracy*, Oxford: Clarendon Press

47) Emmison (1989) *op. cit.*, item 9

48) TNA: PRO: E101/427/18 f21 item 14

49) TNA: PRO: E101/417/3 f21; Arnold (1988) *op. cit.* 234 & 232

50) *Ibid.*, 228

51) Hollingsworth (2004) *op. cit.*, 73

52) Leed, D (2006) '"Ye Shall Have It Cleane": Textile Cleaning Techniques in Renaissance Europe' in *Medieval Clothing and Textiles II*, Netherton, R & Owen Crocker, G, Woodbridge: Boydell & Brewer Press, forthcoming; Sim (1996) *op. cit.*, 44–60

53) Levey (2000) *op. cit.*, 16

54) Stern (1981) *op. cit.*, 20–22 & 17

55) Arnold (1988) *op. cit.*, 174

56) Hovinden, M (ed) (1965) *Household and farm inventories in Oxfordshire, 1550–90*, Historical Manuscripts Commission, JP10

57) Emmison, F (1993) *op. cit.*, item 320

Table 2: Clothing fabrics in the 16th century (pages 36–37)

A) Montgomery, F (1984) *Textiles in America 1650–1870*, New York: W W Norton & Company, 275; Earnshaw, P (1980) *The identification of lace*, Aylesbury: Shire, 10 & 23; TNA: PRO: E315/456, f33v; Stern, E (1981) 'Peckover and Gallyard, two 16th century Norfolk tailors' in *Costume*, 15, 20

B) Montgomery, F (1984) *op. cit.*, 187; TNA: PRO: E101/417/3, f48; Emmison, F (1998) *Essex Wills, The Commissary Court 1587–1599*, 11, Chelmsford: Essex Record Office, item 142

C) TNA: PRO: E101/417/3, f48; Emmison, F (1995) *Essex Wills, The Commissary Court 1578-1588*, 10, Chelmsford: Essex Record Office, item 52; Emmison, F (1989) *Essex Wills: The Archdeaconry Courts 1583–1592*, 5, Chelmsford: Essex Record Office, item 1170

D) Cunnington, C & P (1970) *Handbook of English costume in the 16th century*, Boston: Plays Inc, 221; Huggett, J (1999) 'Rural costume in Elizabethan Essex: a study based on the evidence from wills' in *Costume*, 33, 81; Emmison, F (1989) *op. cit.*, item 278

E) Emmison, F (1993) *Essex Wills, The Commissary Court 1558–1569*, 8, Chelmsford: Essex Record Office, item 847; Emmison, F (1994) *Essex Wills, The Commissary Court 1569–1578*, 9, Chelmsford: Essex Record Office, item 120; Emmison, F (1989) *op. cit.*, item 741

F) TNA: PRO: E101/427/18, f21; Arnold, J (1988) *Queen Elizabeth's Wardrobe Unlock'd*, Leeds: Maney, 196

G) TNA: PRO: E101/417/3, f23; TNA: PRO: E101/423/12, f5r

H) Emmison, F (1994) *Essex Wills, The Commissary Court 1569–1578*, 9, Chelmsford: Essex Record Office, item 550; Emmison, F (1991) *op. cit.*, item 155

I) Cunnington, C & P (1970) *op. cit.*, 225; Emmison, F (1987) *Essex Wills: The Archdeaconry Courts 1577–1584*, 4 Chelmsford: Essex Record Office, item 462; Stern, E (1981) *op. cit.*, 17

J) Buck, A (1990) 'The clothes of Thomasine Petre 1555–1559', *Costume*, 24, 33; Montgomery, F (1984) *op. cit.*, 272; TNA: PRO: E315/456, f44v

K) TNA: PRO: E101/417/3, f8; Essex Co Record Office D/DP A6

L) TNA: PRO: E101/417/3, item 69; Stern, E (1981) *op. cit.*, 17

M) Peachey, S (2001) *Textiles and materials of the common man and woman 1580–1660*, Stuart Press: Bristol, 13; TNA: PRO: E101/417/3, f40; Emmison, F (1983) *Elizabethan Wills of South-West Essex* Waddesdon: The Kylin Press, item 64; Stern, E (1981) *op. cit.*, 23; Emmison, F (1991) *op. cit.*, item 373

N) Montgomery, F (1984) *op. cit.*, 272; TNA: PRO: E315/456, f45v

O) *Ibid.*, 206; TNA: PRO: E101/417/3, f46; Stern, E (1981) *op. cit.*, 17

P) Montgomery, F (1984) *op. cit.*, 238; TNA: PRO: E101/417/3, f59

Q) *Ibid.*, 309; Essex Record Office D/DPA8; Emmison, F (1989) *op. cit.*, item 538

R) Montgomery, F (1984) *op. cit.*, 182 & 250; Stern, E (1981) *op. cit.*, 16; Emmison, F (1990) *Essex Wills, The Archdeaconry Courts 1597–1603*, 7, Chelmsford: Essex Record Office, item 327

S) Montgomery, F (1984) *op. cit.*, 336; TNA: PRO:

E101/423/12, f3r; TNA: PRO: E101/427/18, f1; Essex Record Office D/DP A8
T) Emmison, F (1998) *op. cit.*, item 109
U) Montgomery, F (1984) *op. cit.*, 342 & 376; Essex Record Office D/DP A6; Emmison, F (1987) *op. cit.*, item 777
V) Montgomery, F (1984) *op. cit.*, 159 & 376; Stern, E (1981) *op. cit.*, 16 & 17
W) Records commission (1820–1828) '24 Henry VIII c13: "An acte for reformacyon of excesse in apparayle"' in *Statutes of the Realm*; TNA: PRO: E101/420/1, f13; Hunt, A (1996) *Governance of the consuming passions*, Basingstoke: Macmillan, 314; Emmison, F (1989) *op. cit.*, item 122; Emmison, F (1995) *op. cit.*, item 404; Emmison, F (1989) *op. cit.*, item 857
X) Montgomery, F (1984) *op. cit.*, 340; TNA: PRO: E101/423/12, f4v; Emmison, F (1994) *op. cit.*, item 390; Emmison, F (1983) *op. cit.*, item 47; Emmison, F (1989) *op. cit.*, item 48
Y) Montgomery, F (1984) *op. cit.*, 213; TNA: PRO: E101/417/3, f19; TNA: PRO: E101/423/12, f3r; Emmison, F (1994) *op. cit.*, item 24
Z) TNA: PRO: E101/422/15, f64v; Emmison, F (1993) *op. cit.*, item 345; Emmison, F (1989) *op. cit.*, item 538
a) Montgomery, F (1984) *op. cit.*, 188, 250 & 252; Emmison, F (1989) *op. cit.*, item 340; Stern, E (1981) *op. cit.*, 18
b) TNA: PRO: E101/417/3, f40; TNA: PRO: E101/427/18, f21
c) Records commission (1820–1828) *op. cit.*; TNA: PRO: E101/417/3, f31; TNA: PRO: E101/417/3; E315/456, f33r; TNA: PRO: E101/423/12; Stern, E (1981) *op. cit.*, 19
d) Montgomery, F (1984) *op. cit.*, 188; Records commission (1820–1828) *op. cit.*; PRO E101/420/1, f7; Emmison, F (1987) *op. cit.*, item 839; Stern, E (1981) *op. cit.*, 17; Emmison, F (1991) *op. cit.*, item 832
e) Montgomery, F (1984) *op. cit.*, 211 & 366; TNA: PRO: E315/171, f3r; Stern, E (1981) *op. cit.*, 16; Emmison, F (2000) *Essex Wills, The Commissary Court 1596–1603*, 12, Chelmsford: Essex Record Office, item 388
f) Montgomery, F (1984) *op. cit.*, 295; Buck, A (1990) *op. cit.*, 33; TNA: PRO: E101/427/18, f1; Emmison, F (1987) *Essex Wills: The Archdeaconry Courts 1577–1584*, 4, Chelmsford: Essex Record Office, item 868; Emmison, F (1989) *op. cit.*, item 717; Emmison, F (1998) *op. cit.*, item 311
g) Buck, A (1990), *op. cit.*, 33; Montgomery, F (1984) *op. cit.*, 244 & 271; TNA: PRO: E315/456, f45r ; TNA: PRO: E101/427/18, f21; Emmison, F (1994) *op. cit.*, item 543; Emmison, F (1989) *op. cit.*, item 740; Emmison, F (1989) *ibid.*, item 1254
h) Buck, A (1990), *op. cit.*, 32; Montgomery, F (1984) *op. cit.*, 176; TNA: PRO: E101/423/12; Essex County Record Office D/DP A8
i) Montgomery, F (1984) *op. cit.*, 279; Emmison, F (1987) *op. cit.*, item 324

Ordinary people's clothing (page 12):
A1) Based on a detail in *The Grimani Breviary*, Biblioteca Nazionale Marciana, Venice, c. 1490–1510 published in Zuffi, S (2003) *The Renaissance*, London: Collins, 25–27, c. 1500
A2) *Ibid.*, c. 1500
A3) Based on a monument to Thomas Babington in All Saints' Church, Ashover, Derbyshire, 1511
A4) *Ibid.*, 1511
A5) Based on a figure in *Flodden*, a stained glass window in St Leonard's Church, Middleton, Rochdale, 1513
A6) Based on a 16th-century miner's coat at Snibston Discovery Park, Leicestershire. A study by Cliodna Devit at the Textile Conservation Centre, Hampton Court, suggests that this was once a fashionable medieval garment, later adapted and worn by a miner
A7) Based on a detail from *The Coronation of Edward VI*, Society of Antiquaries, 18th-century copy after a lost

16th-century original at Cowdray House
A8) Based on a detail from *Proverbs* by Pieter Brueghel the Younger, Staatliche Museen, Berlin, 1559
A9) Based on *The Cornharvest* by Pieter Brueghel, Metropolitan Museum of Art, New York, 1565
A10) Based on a *portrait of an unknown lady*, private collection, 1568 and *A Group of English women* by Lucas de Heere, British Museum, 1570
A11) Based on *Twenty-two godly and faithful christians*, a woodcut from John Fox's *Acts and Monuments of the Martyr*, British Museum, 1563
A12) Based on Lucas de Heere, *op. cit.*, 1570
A13) Based on a detail from *The St Bartholomew's day massacre* by Francois Dubois, Lausanne, 1572
A14) Based on a woodcut of William Bullien from Bullein's *Bulwarke of defence againste all sickness*, British Museum, 1562
A15) Based on Francois Dubois, *op. cit.*, 1572
A16) Based on *Tarlton the Clown*, a manuscript illustration (Harley MS 3885, f19), British Museum, before 1588
A17) Based on a woodcut in *Orchesographie* by Thoinot Arbeau, British Library, 1588
A18) Based on a memorial brass representing two wives of John Atte Sea, Herne, Kent in Clayton, M (1968) *Catalogue of rubbings of brasses and incised slabs*, London, HMSO, plate 48, 1604
A19) Based on an embroidered pillow cover (inventory number T.79–1946), Victoria & Albert Museum, c. 1600
A20) Based on Cryes of the City of London, Pepys Library, Cambridge, c. 1600
A21) *Ibid.*, c. 1600
A22) *Ibid.*, c. 1600

Clothing of the elite (page 13):
B1) Based on *Henry VII* by Michael Sittour, National Portrait Gallery, London, 1505; a terracotta bust by Pietro Torrigiano, Victoria & Albert Museum, 1508–9; and a Flemish Books of hours (MS 1093–1975), Fitzwilliam Museum, Cambridge, 1500
B2) Based on a detail from *Charles V's entry into Bruges*, Flemish, Osterreichische Nationalbibliothek, Vienna, 1515
B3) Based on a detail from *The field of the cloth of gold*, by an unknown artist, Royal Collection and Henry VIII by an unknown artist, National Portrait Gallery, London, 1520
B4) Based on an *Unknown man*, Hans Holbein, Royal Collection, c. 1532–34 and Henry VIII and his jester Will Somers by an unknown artist, British Museum, 1538–47
B5) Based on *Edward VI*, National Portrait Gallery, London, c. 1546
B6) Based on *Queen Mary & Philip II of Spain* by an unknown artist, National Maritime Museum, Greenwich, 1558
B7) Based on *Robert Dudley (with dog)* by an unknown artist, private collection, c. 1564 and *Sir Henry Lee* by Antonio Mor, National Portrait Gallery, London, 1568
B8) Based on *Robert Dudley* by an unknown artist, National Portrait Gallery, London, c. 1577 and *James VI* by Robert Lockley, National Portrait Gallery, London, 1574
B9) Based on *Sir Jerome Bowes* by an unknown artist, The Suffolk Collection, Rangers House, London, 1584
B10) Based on *Gilbert Talbot* by the studio of Sir William Segar, Weiss Gallery, 1596
C1) Based on *Elizabeth of York* by an unknown artist, National Portrait Gallery, London, 1500–3; *Henry VII, Elizabeth of York, Henry VIII and Jane Seymour* by Remigius van Leemput, Royal Collection, c. 1667 copy of a lost mural by Hans Holbein; and a brass memorial to Letitia Talyboys, in St Edmund's Church, Assington, Suffolk, 1506.
C2) Based on a monument to two unknown women in St Andrew's Church, Prestwold, Leicestershire, 1520
C3) Based on a monument to Christopher and Elizabeth Matthew in Llandaff Cathedral, Cardiff, 1523; and *Study for a family portrait of Thomas More* by Hans Holbein,

Kunstmuseum Basel, Kupferstichkabinett, c. 1527
C4) Based on Remigius van Leemput, *op. cit.*
C5) Based on *Catherine Parr* attributed to Master John, National Portrait Gallery, London, c. 1545
C6) Based on *Queen Mary & Philip II of Spain*, *op. cit.*, 1558
C7) Based on a *Portrait of a lady*, possibly of the Wentworth family, by Hans Eworth, Tate Gallery, London, c. 1565–8
C8) Based on an unknown woman by an unknown artist (NPG96), National Portrait Gallery, Montacute House, Somerset, c. 1580 and *Elizabeth I, The Pelican Portrait* attributed to Nicholas Hilliard, Walker Art Gallery, Liverpool, c. 1574
C9) Based on *Lettice Knollys, Countess of Leicester* by George Gower, Marquess of Bath, 1585
C10) Based on *Lady Eleanor Herbert* by an unknown artist, Powis Castle, Welshpool, Powys, 1525 and *Lady Elizabeth Southwell* by Marcus Gheeraerts, Viscount Cowdray, 1599

Bibliography

All works quoted in the text are cited with full references in the notes section. Other texts consulted are listed here:

• Ashelford, J (1996) *The art of dress: clothes and society 1500–1914*, New York: Harry N Abrams
• Bradfield, N (1996) *Historical costume of England: from the 11th to the 20th century*, Eric Dobby
• Boucher, F (1996) *A history of costume in the west*, London: Thames & Hudson
• Byrde, P (1979) *The male image: men's fashion in Britain 1300–1970*, London: B T Batsford
• de Marly, D (1989) *Fashion for men: an illustrated history*, London: B T Batsford
• Tarrant, N (1994) *The development of costume*, Edinburgh: National Museum of Scotland/Routledge

Suppliers

United Kingdom suppliers

Many suppliers of specialist materials will only deal with trade orders. Those listed below are happy to deal with the public and most can provide a mail-order service. Alternatively, regular re-enactor's markets are held in the UK where many smaller individual tradespeople sell their goods direct to the public. For further details visit www.livinghistoryfayres.com/ or www.reenactorsmarket.co.uk/

Abimelech Hainsworth
Spring Valley Mills, Stanningley, Pudsey, West Yorkshire LS28 6DW
Tel: 0113 395 5678
www.abimelech.co.uk
Range of high-quality wools including meltons, doeskins and worsteds.

Whaleys (Bradford) Ltd
Harris Court, Great Horton, Bradford, West Yorkshire BD7 4EQ
Tel: 01274 576718. Fax: 01274 521309
www.whaleys-bradford.ltd.uk
Large range of basic materials, including linen, canvas, buckram, wool and silk. Full set of swatches costs £26.00.

Classic Textiles
44 Goldhawk Road, Shepherds Bush, London W12 8DH
Tel: 020 8743 3516
Good selection of cheap wool, linen, velvet and silks, No mail order.

New Rainbow Textiles
98 The Broadway, Southall, Middlesex UB1 1QF.
Tel: 020 8574 1494
Good range of cheap silks and embroidered trims. No mail order.

Historical Management Associates
117 Farleigh Road, Backwell, Bristol BS48 3PG
www.stuart-hmaltd.pwp.blueyonder.co.uk/
Range of fabrics for the common people spun and woven to historical specifications.

Barnett Lawson (Trimmings) Ltd
16–17 Little Portland Street, London W1W 8NE
Tel: 020 7636 8591
www.bltrimmings.com
Trims, ribbons, tassels, feathers etc.

The Cane Store
Washdyke Cottage, 1 Witham Road, Long Bennington, Newark, Nottinghamshire NG23 5DS.
Tel: 01400 282271
www.canestore.co.uk
8mm centre cane suitable for farthingale hoops, 6mm suitable for sleeve hoops, ¼ in chair cane suitable for boning bodies.

Macculloch & Wallis
25–26 Dering Street, London W1R OBH
Tel: 020 7409 0725
www.macculloch-wallis.co.uk
Boning, threads, millinery wire, buckram, domette.

Steve Millingham Pewter Replicas
Church Tower Mint, Hopton Cangeford, Ludlow, Shropshire SY8 2EE
Tel: 01584 823304
www.pewterreplicas.com
Excellent range of Tudor jewellery, buttons and accessories.

Gina Barrett
c/o Accolade, Noseley Hall, Billesdon, Leicestershire LE7 9EH
www.et-tu.com/ginab
High-quality handmade silk wares including laces, tassels, thread buttons and tablet woven girdles.

Plantagenet Shoes
82 Cozens Hardy Road, Sprowston, Norwich, Norfolk NR7 8QG
Tel: 01603 414045 Fax: 01603 491677
www.plantagenetshoes.freeserve.co.uk

KM Garlick, Shoemaker
78 High Street, Ventnor, Isle of Wight PO38 1LU
Tel: 077 545 30422
www.kmgarlick-shoemaker.co.uk

United States suppliers

Burnley & Trowbridge
108 Druid Drive, Williamsburg, VA 23185
Tel: 757-253-1644 Fax: 757-253-9120
www.burnleyandtrowbridge.com
Linens, wools and fustians, pins, needles & other tools, books, steel & spiral boning.

Grannd Garb
295 Main Street, South River, NJ 08882
Tel: 732-390-0506 Fax: 732-390-1694
www.grannd.com
Corset supplies, including boning, hoop steel, steel busks, eyelets, trim, lace, buttons, clasps, patterns, jewels and accessories. Artificial whalebone.

Farthingales
309 Lorne Avenue East R.R. #3, Stratford, Ontario N5A 6S4.
Tel: 519-275-2374 Fax: 519-273-2376
www.farthingales.on.ca/
Large stock of materials geared toward corsetmaking.

Greenberg and Hammer
24 W. 57th St, New York, NY 10019
Tel: 212-246-2835 or 1-800-955-5135
www.greenberg-hammer.com
Theatrical costume supplies including steel and plastic boning.

Greenman Forge
Dan Brown
1143 Bleistein Street, Cody, WY 82414
Tel: 307-272-9368
www.greenmanforge.com
Maker of reproduction pinking tools.

Manny's Millinery
26 W. 38th St. New York, NY 10036
Tel: 212-840-2235
Buckram, wire etc $25 minimum on all orders.

Thai Silks
242 State Street, Los Altos, CA 94022
Tel: 415-948-8611 Fax: 415-948-3426
Free price list; $20 for full range of silk samples, including silk-wool and silk-linen blends.

Fire Mountain Gems
1 Fire Mountain Way, Grants Pass, OR 97526-2373
Tel: 1-800-355-2137
www.firemountaingems.com
Beads, gemstones, pearls.

With thanks to Drea Leed (www.costume.dm.net) for US list